Beginnings of
Freemasonry in America

(1924)

Melvin M. Johnson

ISBN 0-7661-0765-5

THE BEGINNINGS OF FREEMASONRY IN AMERICA

Containing a reference to all that is known of FREEMASONRY in the Western Hemisphere prior to 1750, and short sketches of the lives of some of the Provincial Grand Masters

by

MELVIN M. JOHNSON

GRAND MASTER OF MASONS IN MASSACHUSETTS,
1914, 1915, 1916
33°, ACTIVE S.G.I.G., N.M.J., U.S.A.

ILLUSTRATED

NEW YORK

GEORGE H. DORAN COMPANY

HENRY PRICE

    Founder of Duly Constituted Masonry in America.
    See Chapter V.

PREFACE

The substance of this work was prepared as an address by the then Grand Master to the Grand Lodge of Massachusetts on September 13, 1916. It was an attempt to collate and state all that is known of Freemasonry in the Western Hemisphere prior to A.D. 1750.

After long study and investigation, the manuscript was first put in type in November, 1916. Bound proofsheets were sent to every Grand Secretary in the English speaking world as well as to all those known to the writer to be Masonic students who might be interested— in all about two hundred. A request was made in each case for suggestions, criticisms or additions. Many helpful suggestions were received, but during the four months which elapsed before the Proceedings of the Grand Lodge of Massachusetts for the year 1916 were printed, not a single additional item or incident was called to the writer's attention. A large part of the chronological record and the conclusions herein stated were printed as a part of the Proceedings of the Grand Lodge of Massachusetts for the year 1916, and the address was reprinted in book form by the National Masonic Research Society.

Since publication, Bro. F. de P. Rodriguez, Chairman of the Committee on Foreign Correspondence of the Grand Lodge of Colon (Cuba) has kindly called attention to the organization of a lodge in San Domingo in 1748. This has been verified and inserted herein.

More than seven years having passed without the discovery by any one except myself of another omission or additional incident, the conclusion is justified that the record is as complete as it can be made in the light of the knowledge of the present day. This book is therefore offered as a chronological compilation of all the real known facts concerning Freemasonry in America prior to the middle of the eighteenth century, with references so that the student may verify the original evidence, its sources, and reliability for himself. The writer has personally examined almost all of the original evidence to which reference is herein made.

Some assertions concerning the early history of Freemasonry in the Western Hemisphere, utterly unwarranted and without a shred of justification, have been so publicly made heretofore and copied and recopied by serious Masonic scholars even as late as the current year, as to demand notice herein so that the future student shall not be misled as Gould, Hughan and others have been. Concerning some of them, I shall speak very plainly. Nothing can justify the deliberate concealment of a reliable document or the publication of that which is manifestly fraudulent for the purpose of bolstering up an argument in behalf of some pet theory which the Fraternity is asked to believe.

For instance, if the "dilapidated document" of 1656 or 1658, or the "John Moore letter" or the "Henry Bell letter" had ever existed and had within recent years come to the hands of those to whom they were valuable as proof of claims which were being made, such important documents could be produced or accounted for. No impartial eye has seen any one of them, although the opportunity to view them or to interview any one who has seen them has often and publicly been requested.

Again, as in 1916, I appeal to all, whether members of our Fraternity or not, for the preservation and proper publication of anything which may hereafter be brought to light which will add a real bit of evidence to what we know of these early Masonic days. Such things ought from time to time to be found among the files of historical societies and museums and sometimes in the store rooms of ancient families. When discovered, they ought at once to be submitted to competent students, photographic copies should be taken for preservation apart from the originals, and the widest publicity should be sought in order to bring them to the attention and scrutiny of all interested. I am willing at any time to lend my assistance to this end.

The conclusions of respected historians are freely quoted by those who have not the time, inclination or opportunity to make independent investigation. As a result, an opinion which would have been changed at once if the true facts had been known, nevertheless passes current and is accepted as a matter of course long after the premises upon which it is based prove to be wrong. Because of its importance an example of one conspicuous illustration is worth while.

One Jacob Norton, an Orthodox Jew, once fathered a petition to the Grand Lodge of Massachusetts, which asked a revision of the ritual by the elimination of all reference to the Holy Saints John. The Grand Lodge denied his petition, whereupon he withdrew from his Massachusetts membership and subsequently made bitter attacks upon the history of that jurisdiction.

1851 Mass. 7, 33-34.
1899 Mass. 53.
1906 Mass. 84.

M. W. Joseph Rollins, a Masonic student and Chairman of the Committee on Correspondence of the Grand Lodge of Illinois accepted Norton's conclusions and reargued the case for him. Then certain partisans for their own purposes restated Norton's animadversions and gave them wide circulation. Following this, Bro. Hughan and some other historians, not knowing Norton's bias but assuming the correctness of his statements of fact and following his arguments, based some of their statements and conclusions upon his.

IV Gould, 330.

Certain old newspaper articles, official lists, and manuscripts, unknown in the days of Rollins, Hughan and Gould, have since been discovered which utterly and beyond all cavil or argument prove the falsity of Norton's premises and, therefore, of his and their reasoning and conclusions. Several good Masonic histories were written before these discoveries and before Norton's arguments were unanswerably shown to be wrong. Thus his errors are still perpetuated. Unfortunately and usually innocently, writers occasionally still adopt and repeat Norton's views, quoting as authorities not Norton but those who followed his lead.

Masonic students and historians, therefore, should be careful not to adopt without personal investigation the conclusions arrived at by our best and most revered historians, except they are based upon a knowledge of the whole facts, including the recently discovered evidence, all of which relating to the early history of Freemasonry in America are referred to in the text or citations which follow. Authorities will herein be cited for the author's statements and upon which he has based his conclusions.

In many instances photographic copies of documents

not heretofore reproduced for general circulation and some never heretofore published, have been inserted not only as matters of interest but also to preserve the evidence and subject it to the test and verification of publicity. Those who now or hereafter attempt to write Masonic history, whether as to a single fact or a broad field, must be willing to subject themselves to the same tests applied to all other historians.

The original address has been amplified that it may be suitable for the general Masonic reader whether he reads critically or casually.

MELVIN M. JOHNSON.

Boston, Mass.

P.S. After this book was in type, Wor. Brother William B. Clarke, Past Master of Solomon's Lodge, No. 1, of Savannah, Georgia, very kindly sent me full details of his researches including the recent discovery of an old original record book of his Lodge. The publishers have been good enough to permit a consequent rewriting of the Georgia material at the last minute.

M. M. J.

ABBREVIATIONS

A.B.   Account Book (of the Lodge to which reference is being made).

Anderson. Anderson's Constitutions.

A.Q.C. Ars Quatuor Coronatorum.

B.MS.   Beteilhe Manuscript.

Entick.   Entick's Constitutions (1756).

F.J.   Franklin's Journal.

Gould.   Gould's (larger) History of Freemasonry. Edition of John C. Yorston & Co., 1889.

NOTE: There are four editions of Gould's larger "History of Freemasonry." The first two were published in London and Edinburgh in editions of three and six volumes between the years 1882 and 1887. The first American edition appeared in Philadelphia in 1889, complete in four volumes. This is the edition cited. The last edition was published in 1906 as the principal part of a five-volume set known as "A Library of Freemasonry." References in the following pages to Volume IV of Gould will not be found in the three- or six-volume editions where the page numbers are given below 295; they will be found, however, in Volume IV of the "Library of Freemasonry."

L.B.   "Libre B."

L.H.B.   Lane's Handy Book to the Lists of Lodges.

L.M.R.   Lane's Masonic Records, 1717-1894, 2nd Ed.

Mackey. Mackey's Revised History of Freemasonry, by Robert I. Clegg. (Masonic History Company, 1921.)

1 Mass. Printed Proceedings of the Grand Lodge of Massachusetts, 1733-1792 (containing the Proceedings of the Provincial Grand Lodges at Boston).

Mass.	Printed Proceedings of **Grand Lodge of** Massachusetts for year given.
M.F.M.	The Freemason's Monthly Magazine, by Charles W. Moore, commonly known as Moore's Freemasons' Magazine.
N.E.F.	Nickerson's New England Freemason.
O.L.	Official Engraved Lists of the Lodges, published by authority of the Grand Lodge of England.
O.M.L.P.	Sachse's Old Masonic Lodges of Pennsylvania.
O.R.	Original Record (of the body to which reference is being made).
P.C.	The Pocket Companion and History of Freemasonry by J. Scott, 1754.
Prichard.	Prichard's Tubal-Kain (Dublin, 1760?).
P.L.	The Charles "Pelham List" of the Brethren made and accepted in the First Lodge in Boston, and of those raised and accepted in the Masters Lodge, written in 1751. (Original in archives of Grand Lodge of Massachusetts.)
Preston.	William Preston's Illustrations of Masonry.
Pro. G.M.	Provincial Grand Master.
P-t.	A photo-stat made under the direction of the author is on file in archives of Grand Lodge of Massachusetts.
Q.C.A.	Quatuor Coronatorum Antigrapha.
S.& H.	Stillson & Hughan's History of Freemasonry.
	The abbreviation for a state or country preceded by a year and followed by a page, refers to the printed proceedings of the Grand Lodge for that jurisdiction.

CONTENTS

CONTENTS

ILLUSTRATIONS

THE BEGINNINGS OF FREEMASONRY
IN AMERICA

THE BEGINNINGS OF
FREEMASONRY IN AMERICA

Chapter I

BEGINNINGS

The male secret society is the oldest human institution, older than any other form of religion, older than any other form of education, older indeed than any other form of civil government. And all down through the centuries, the secret society has maintained a powerful hold upon the hearts and minds of men.

Whatever its origin, however its life may be measured, Freemasonry is admittedly the oldest secret society of the civilized world, as well as the largest: Yet, strangely enough, its history is shrouded in mystery. The true facts of its ancient days are a secret, more unknown, more mysterious than its arcana.

Its earliest manuscripts, the "Old Charges" or "Old Constitutions," are Homeric. The scriveners recorded the traditions handed down to them verbally through the centuries and doubtless believed they were really writing history. What they gave us, we now know to be a curious blending of fable and some demonstrable facts. But the facts have so utterly lost their true surroundings as to be as misleading historically as those things which are obviously fable. Euclid, who lived in Alexandria about three hundred years before Christ is, for instance, made a contemporary and pupil of Abraham.

Too many so-called Masonic historians since the days when they should have known better have added fiction to fable and imagination to both, using the manifest errors of their predecessors as gospel, dreams as evidence, and guesses as proof. Moreover, we must confess that there are many speakers and writers on Masonic subjects to-day who do not seem to realize that such methods do our cause more harm than good. Let one instance suffice to illustrate. A very celebrated and respected brother, whose name is a household word in this country, and who is known the world around, once made the statement in a public address that all but two of the signers of the Declaration of Independence were members of the Craft. That declaration from his lips was at once accepted at par and has been repeated thousands of times in addresses throughout the land. For some years the writer tried to verify that statement without success. Among other things, he applied to that brother who had turned the statement loose for his authority. The reply came quickly to the effect that undoubtedly he had in mind authority for what he said at the time he said it, but that he could not remember what it was. Now the fact may be exactly as stated, but many diligent seekers who would like to prove it have utterly failed in their efforts so to do. So many of the Lodges of those days failed to keep or preserve records and so many carefully recorded minutes have been burned or otherwise lost or destroyed that we shall never be able to prove the truth or the falsity of the claim.

Gould was the Thucydides of Masonic history. He first introduced the critical method. He attempted to disentangle the fable from the fact. He fell into many errors. His conclusions are, many of them, wrong. His

work cannot be called authoritative for even he accepted
at par many assertions of others which we now know to
be in error. And, too, later study has disclosed demonstrable facts unknown to him. But he did point the way
to the proper method of studying and of writing Masonic history. Others had written the true facts of their
day and generation as well as those learned from the
lips of their contemporaries. Gould first, however,
taught us that the Masonic historian should be subject
to the same tests of accuracy as all other historians.
Not that we must have a photograph of each event or
the written word of an eye-witness. Legitimate inference and reasonable conclusion have their place here
as well as in all other phases of human affairs. Tradition
even has its just place. But dreamland and the "wish
that is father to the thought" must not be permitted
longer to influence the writing of what purports to be
real history. This does not mean that it should be necessary to present written documents in proof of what we
shall conclude to be Masonic fact. Since the days when
the printing press has come into general use, less weight
is given to tradition and other evidences of fact. Prior
to the days of the printing press but since the evolution
of modern writing the same tests which are applied to
conclusions of the ordinary historian are to be applied to
the conclusions of the Masonic historian, with this exception—that Masonry being a secret society, much less
of its affairs would be committed to writing than otherwise. Back of the days of the development of the writing of documents, the Masonic historian must depend
upon such evidence as is relied upon by any scientific
anthropologist.

How old is Freemasonry? From when does it date its

origin? These and similar questions will never be answered by a date. Before an attempt can be made to find a point at which to start the discussion, a question of definition arises,—When you ask the question, what do you mean by the word "Freemasonry"? If you mean the structural form of the present Grand Lodge system, with particular lodges together with the appendant degrees of the so-called "York" and "Scottish" Rites, then the answer may be made that the stage of stability of this present structure did not come until at least the latter half of the nineteenth century. Indeed, now in the twentieth century that structure is not yet fixed and independent. In important respects such as the "Mark Degree," the English system now differs radically from the American. Definite recognition of the "Scottish Rite" did not become fixed in America until the last quarter of the nineteenth century, and Ireland to-day has not yet reached this stage.

Nomenclature is not now and probably never will be made historically correct. The "Scottish Rite" does not descend from Scotland and the "York Rite" was not founded at York. The "Moderns" were older than the "Ancients." These are but examples.

If by "Freemasonry" is meant the Symbolic system of "blue" degrees as now organized and practised, then the date of crystallization has not yet come. Between 1717 and 1725 (circa) there was a radical recast of ritual. At the end of some nine years of considerable Masonic disturbance and debate, beginning in 1730 with the publications of Prichard's "Masonry Dissected," other radical changes were made by the English Grand Lodge. These were not followed in Scotland or Ireland and, in part, led to the organization of the "Grand

Lodge of the Antients" in 1751. Both the Ancients and the Moderns planted Lodges in America and elsewhere during the long years thereafter until the English reconciliation of 1813. Thus at least these two systems (for they radically differed from each other) were slipped and planted where they took firm root and were in turn slipped and transplanted with the result that even to-day there is much divergence of ritual. And this is true even as to essentials, as to many things which have by students and Grand Lodges been called "Landmarks."

If "Freemasonry" means only what has descended from the Grand Lodge of England, then it dates from the organization of that Grand Lodge in 1717. But that Grand Lodge was organized by lodges theretofore existing and there is abundant evidence of speculative Freemasonry through earlier centuries.

The caterpillar builds its cocoon and changes its shape into a chrysalis, but the life of the chrysalis is the perpetuation of the life of the caterpillar. Even the material elements of its body are those of the caterpillar's body transformed. And so, also, we follow that same life essence and those identical material atoms into the emerging moth, but how different in outward appearance! Just such, the writer believes has been the life-history through countless centuries of what we now call Freemasonry.

Defined as an organization of men, teaching monotheism, morality and immortality, in secret, by symbolism, and inculcating the worship of Deity and friendship for one another, it can have no fixed date of origin. In different forms through the long years of human life upon the earth, its true essence and life may be believed to have been transmitted through the "Men's House" of pre-historic barbarism, the ancient mysteries, the Roman colleges, the cathedral builders, and many other connecting links transmuted and transformed, known by many names, into the Freemasonry which is the highest type of such an organization in this modern world. Recent studies furnish confirmatory evidence of this theory of the descent of Freemasonry which I have been insisting upon in Masonic addresses since 1913.

BEGINNINGS IN AMERICA

It has been argued that Freemasonry began with the Mayas and Quiches in the Western Hemisphere much more than one hundred centuries ago; and that the mysteries migrated to the old world over a land bridge that was broken when Atlantis was destroyed.

> Sacred Mysteries among the Mayas and the Quiches, 11500 years ago, etc., by LePlongeon.

This theory is purely fanciful and pabulum only for the dreamer.

X The Builder (Jan. 1924) 7

When the Western Hemisphere began to be colonized from Europe, our present system of Grand and particular lodges had not come into being. Masonry was then nomadic and lodges were "occasional." It was more operative than speculative. But we still have the Old Charges of a Freemason reduced to manuscript before Colon, the Jew (now generally called Columbus) set his foot upon an island in the West Indies. When first thereafter some of those Freemasons under the Old Constitutions, or Old Charges, came with other colonists to these shores, the fog of time effectually conceals from our historic vision. It is unlikely that the early planting of European civilization in Central America and elsewhere in the Western world brought Freemasonry with it, although the operative Masons certainly came. And there are certain indications in their work to be found in Panama and northwestern South America which indicate that they were speculative as well as operative Masons. Nearly all of their work is marvellously like that of those operative Masons of the Middle Ages from whom we descend. There is less likelihood that either the Pilgrims or the Puritans were of our Craft. As a reasonable inference or at least speculation from known facts, it may be said (though not asserted as definite) that Freemasonry first came to the Western Hemisphere through mariners, merchants and officers, civil and military. This was unmistakably the case in the early eighteenth century.

"Duly constituted" Lodges of Freemasons, as we use the words, never existed prior to June 24, 1717. The unnumbered and mostly unknown Lodges theretofore were but voluntary and indefinite assemblages of those Freemasons who casually or for business reasons found themselves in a given neighbourhood. To this rule there were exceptions becoming more numerous toward the close of the seventeenth century, but it may be said as a generality that there was no such thing as Lodge "membership." All were Freemasons "at large." With certain definite exceptions, no Lodge was a continuing body or had officers with terms which overran each closing or kept records. They were usually occasional bodies having no persevering entity. They were, however, "regular."

The reincarnation or transmutation commonly known

as the "Revival of 1717" changed all this. It provided not only Grand Lodge organization and administrative machinery but included definite provisions for Lodge continuity. It established for all future time the fundamental test of regularity and due constitution as existence under explicit authority lawfully granted by a Grand Master.

In a world which had not harnessed the energies of steam or electricity or gas for the transportation of persons or freight or intelligence, some years passed before these rules of regularity were thoroughly known, much less accepted, by all the Masons familiar with the old haphazard customs. But finally the whole Fraternity wheresoever dispersed recognized and conformed. The Regulations governing regularity (formally adopted June 24, 1721) comparatively soon obtained full sway and have ever since been universally recognized by the Craft. No "duly constituted" Lodge of Symbolic Masonry exists or has ever existed since then—except only the four which together organized the Grand Lodge of 1717 and Mother Kilwinning and her children—without warrant and/or constitution by act of a Grand Master or of his Deputy.

See 1700, *infra.*

The early Lodges and Provincial Grand Lodges were careless about the keeping of records. Even the Mother Grand Lodge itself has no formal record book for more than six years after its organization. And the premier Provincial Grand Lodge of the Western Hemisphere, organized in Boston, Massachusetts, July 30, 1733, has no formal and continuous records written in a book at the time of the recorded events, until 1750.

This has led some argumentative Brethren to assert

that there is naught but tradition of duly constituted Masonry in America prior to 1750. And it has led to this attempt to make a chronological compilation of all the real known facts of Masonry in America prior to the middle of the eighteenth century with references to the original evidence, nearly all of which has been personally and critically examined. Now and then are also included, for convenience of the student, references to certain things which even some of our best historians and their readers have swallowed with much consequent ptomaine poisoning.

No pretension is made that this is complete. It does contain, however, everything for which the investigations of the writer have disclosed credible and authentic evidence. It is hoped that others may be stimulated to publish all possible facts of the period for which they can and do cite authority worthy of and available for examination and test as to historical accuracy.

Chapter II

AUTHORITIES

The principal sources of information are:

1. The official engraved lists published by authority of the Grand Lodge of England.

2. The various editions of the Constitutions.

3. Original record and account books.

4. Manuscripts of the period.

5. Newspapers of the period.

6. The various editions of The Free Mason's Pocket Companion, containing a history of the Fraternity (and in some editions a list of the Lodges) written by J. Scott and first published in 1754.

7. Preston's "Illustrations of Masonry," the first edition of which was issued in 1772.

8. Other manuscripts and publications by those who lived during the period in question, whether written then or shortly thereafter.

1. OFFICIAL LISTS OF LODGES

Valuable sources of information concerning the early Lodges are the official engraved lists which since 1723 were published at least annually by authority of the Grand Lodge of England. Just before 1730 the Lodges were given numbers in these lists, usually in accordance with seniority. When a Provincial Lodge was not reported promptly, as often happened, it was given a position later than that to which it was entitled but corresponding with the date of the receipt of its *report;* and then when a vacancy occurred by the erasure of a Lodge somewhere near the position in which it belonged, the transfer would be made (e.g., the First Lodge at Savannah, Georgia. See 1735, after October 30, *infra*). The early official lists were engraved with artistic representations of the signs of the taverns, etc., in which the Lodges met.

With all of their errors—and they had many—these lists are invaluable to the Masonic student, and in many cases are the sole source of information.

Printed lists were now and then issued, but they were not official and have less probative value. Brothers Hughan and Lane have made exhaustive studies of these lists, the ultimate being reached in Lane's Masonic Records, 1717-1894 (2d Edition, 1895) to which frequent reference is hereafter made.

Of the printed lists the Grand Lodges of Iowa and Massachusetts own a large number, some of which were apparently unknown to Lane.

2. THE CONSTITUTIONS

The first printed edition of the Constitutions and Regulations of the Grand Lodge of England was compiled by Anderson and published at London in 1723.[1] An im-

---

[1] As to its authority and accuracy see "Introduction" by Lionel Vibert to his 1923 facsimile reprint published by Quaritch, London. Bro. Vibert's "Introduction" is a volume in itself. He says, in part, "Anderson's Constitutions of the Freemasons was originally a private venture which gained Grand Lodge sanction by a kind of accident, and it came into general use by a slow evolution. In its own time it almost escaped notice, at least by the general Masonic public. Yet, after a time it came to be to the Craft in general what the Old Charges were to lodges in the Operative period, and continues so to be in spite of

proved edition was issued in 1738. Many editions have since appeared. The first American printing was by Benjamin Franklin, in Philadelphia, in 1734. All contain a history of the Craft. But little weight can be given to the history, as there recorded, prior to the eighteenth century, it being largely an adaptation of the old manuscript Constitutions. A considerable number of these manuscripts still exist written during the years as far back as the fourteenth century, but they are a curious blending of fact and fiction such as usually results when facts are handed down through hundreds of years by tradition.

Even the record of the events from and after 1717 in the printed Constitutions must be scrutinized though they were recorded by participants in the events themselves or by their associates who had first-hand sources of information.

3. RECORDS AND ACCOUNT BOOKS

Few of the Masonic bodies of the early eighteenth century began to keep records in a minute book contem-

---

the fact that since R. F. Gould, Anderson's work and Masonic record have been scrutinized with merciless severity, one of the results being that his attempt at writing a Masonic history has been discounted almost to the vanishing point.

"Yet it would be difficult to estimate its influence on the history of the Craft. Notwithstanding the way in which Grand Lodge received the work after its publication, it took its place as the official manual, so that the fact that it was not official but essentially a private affair was entirely lost sight of. It was taken by the Grand Lodge of Ireland as the model for their Book of Constitutions in 1730. It was reprinted verbatim for use in America by Franklin in 1734. It was pirated in London and later in Dublin by Smith in 1735. And its author's reputation was great enough to carry off the History he wrote for his second edition of 1738, and led the Craft for a century and a half to accept it and reprint it as a serious contribution to the subject. To-day we value the Doctor's labours less highly, but the Constitutions of 1723 is nevertheless one of the most important records of the Craft."

poraneously with the events recorded until several years after organization.

a. The Grand Lodge at London, for instance, was organized in 1717, but its first contemporaneous record book begins June 24, 1723.

b. The Brethren who met in Philadelphia had an *account* book now known as "Libre B" beginning with June 24, 1731, *q.v.*, which came to light in 1884, and is now in the library of the Historical Society of Pennsylvania. This book is in several handwritings. Much of it has been ascribed to Franklin, but in my opinion little, if any, of it is in his handwriting.

In many respects the book is a mystery. On the outside it is inscribed (in very black ink):

"Philadelphia City."

Under this, in brown ink and a different penmanship:

"St. Johns Lodge Libr B."

It is plainly evident that the cover was first marked "Libr A." The "A" was heavily printed. The left side and the cross-line of the "A" remain. The right side of the "A" has been erased and the bulging bells of a capital "B" (as in script) substituted. The marks of erasure were clearly visible when examined by the assistant librarian and the writer on April 12, 1923, yet the overwritten ink seems ancient rather than modern. Brother Sachse neither explains nor mentions this alteration.

The first twenty-three pages are an index to the Masonic accounts which appear in the last third of the book. This index was written in some time after November 5,

1733, for it is evidently written by some one other than the person who made the entries dated on and before that day.

Next are a number of pages which concern the printing in 1791, and later, of Prayer Books, Testaments, and Laws. These pages contain no Masonic references.

From there, the book is blank about two-thirds of the way through. At this place the Masonic entries commence, the first being an account with

"Messrs Shippen & Pratt, Wardens for the year 1736."

The next two pages have the account with "Pratt & Syng," Wardens for 1737. Following this, is the general account of Lodge expenses for 1736 and 1737; two blank pages; and then what is apparently a Lodge account beginning June 24, 1731. (See facsimile, page 64 *infra*.) The purchase of the book itself is charged under date of August 2, 1731.

It is evident, from the accounts with the members which follow, that on the date with which the accounts begin (June 24, 1731) there were *fourteen* members of the Lodge. The entrance or admission fees of all the others were charged at later dates. Entrance was then £3-0-0. Admission was £2-0-0. In June, 1734, the entrance fee was raised to £5-0-0.

The latest entry in the Masonic part of the book is dated June 24, 1738.

This curious book is not a fraud. It is evidently genuine. Why, when and by whom the change from "A" to "B" was made is, to me, a mystery. Signs of the erasure are still plainly visible and yet the ink is apparently as old as some of the internal entries. Neither can I offer any satisfactory explanation for the other peculiarities of the volume.

The earliest published comment concerning this volume, containing a hint of "Franklin's Journal," is to be found in the "Early History" published by the Grand Lodge of Pennsylvania in 1877 (page 4, following page cxix).

1 O.M.L.P., Chapter II.

1899 Mass. 51.

c. The First Lodge in Boston constituted July 30, 1733, began its records at some unknown period. Its earliest record book now known begins with copies of Price's Commission, of the By-Laws of the Lodge, and of Tomlinson's Commission, followed by the record of December 27, 1738, "being the VI meeting of the Quarter." Ebenezer Swan was the Secretary. It closes with the record of July 24, 1754.

Reversed, the volume contains the account book of the Lodge beginning December 27, 1738, the first entry being "To a Ball^{ce} brought from a former Book 34:8:5."

Thomas Oxnard was then Treasurer. This account runs to February 26, 1755.

1 N.E.F. 57 and 279.

1900 Mass. 125.

This volume is in the archives of the Grand Lodge of Massachusetts.

d. The existing records of the Masters Lodge in Boston begin with its constitution, December 22, 1738, Francis Beteilhe, Secretary. This book closes with the meeting of November 6, 1761. Reversed, the volume discloses the account book down to December 21, 1753. A loose sheet is inserted with a rough account from December 1, 1758, to December, 1760. This volume is in the archives of the Grand Lodge of Massachusetts.

e. The known records of Saint John's Lodge of Portsmouth, N. H., begin October 31, 1739, Jonathan Loggin, Secretary.

The volume beginning on this date is now in possession of the Lodge.

f. The minute book of Tun Tavern Lodge of Philadelphia is now in the archives of the Historical Society of Pennsylvania. The entries commence June 28, 1749, and end July 2, 1755.

g. There is in the archives of the American Philosophical Society at Philadelphia a volume entitled "Benjn Franklin^s Journal, began July 4, 1730," and its first entries begin with that day. It is a printer's account book. On the cover are some indistinct letters followed by the inscription

"Leidgers A & B"

Beginning in the summer of 1734, there are scattered entries relating to Franklin's reprint of Anderson's Constitutions, and other entries against the "Lodge of Masons held at B. Hubard's." (Bro. John Hubbard kept the Sun Tavern.) The first entry of Masonic significance follows September 9, 1731. The next entry is after June 13 and before July 7, 1734, and reads:

"Mr. Newinham D^r for a Bind^g of a Mason Book gilt –4–"

The account against the Lodge begins with an undated item; the next item is dated Sept. 1734; then two items are inserted as August items omitted.

Accounts to be continued beyond this book are marked "Transfer'd to Leidger [or Leger] E."

There is no reference to "C" or "D."

Many, but by no means all, of the entries in this book are in Franklin's handwriting.

See 1898 Penn. 85-102; 1899 Mass. 51.

h. The contemporaneous records of the Provincial Grand Lodge at Boston begin April 13, 1750, Peter Pelham, Grand Secretary, exactly seventeen years after the date of Price's Deputation. These records are in the first volume of the official records of the Grand Lodge of Massachusetts and are reprinted in a volume to which I herein refer as 1 Mass. That printed volume covers the Proceedings down to the union of said Provincial Grand Lodge and "The Massachusetts Grand Lodge," (organized December 27, 1769, in pursuance of a commission issued by the Grand Master Mason of Scotland to Most Worshipful Joseph Warren, Esq., to be Grand Master of Masons in Boston, New England, and within one hundred miles of the same, the commission being dated May 30, 1769). Pelham, following the custom of the period, opened his record book with such detail as was then in his possession of previous happenings during those seventeen years.

See 1 Mass. 1-10.

He had his own part in a few of these events but, what is more to the point, he had available information thereof from Henry Price and from the other Brethren who were participants therein and who were his intimate friends and constant associates, as well as from manuscripts now lost.

When Francis Beteilhe was elected Clerk of the Vestry of Christ Church, Boston, he had done exactly the same thing; viz., begun his record book with a brief statement of the preceding history of the Church.

O.R.

4. MANUSCRIPTS OF THE PERIOD

a. The original petition for the constitution of the First Lodge in Boston is still preserved in the archives of the Grand Lodge of Massachusetts.

See 1733, July 30, *infra.*

Facsimile, pg. 81, *infra.*

Investigations have failed to disclose any older similar document in the world.

b. The original petition for the constitution of the First Lodge in New Hampshire is upon the same files:

See 1735/6, February 5, *infra.*

Facsimile, pg. 149, *infra.*

c. The Beteilhe Manuscript.

The Beteilhe Manuscript, so called, of twenty-six pages, is entitled almost to the dignity of a contemporaneous official record. It is in the handwriting of Francis Beteilhe, bound with an original of the Constitutions printed by Franklin in 1734, was purchased some years ago for $375 (1899 Mass. 72, *et seq.*, 1906 Mass. 93, *et seq.*) and is now in the archives of the Grand Lodge of Massachusetts (1916 Mass. 76). The handwriting is abundantly attested by comparison with known specimens of his handwriting in the possession of the Grand Lodge of Massachusetts and referred to in later citations, and also with the record of the Vestry of Christ Church, Boston, of which he was elected Clerk on January 15, 1732/3, serving to and including its meeting for July 30, 1739. There is no clue in the Church records as to why he ceased to serve in the middle of this year except as we may judge from the handwriting itself. His last two entries seem to be written in a larger and feebler hand, certainly in a more straggling style than was his custom. It looks almost as if his style of writing or his control of his muscles was affected by an illness of some sort which might account for his giving up the office. His successor, however, does not seem to have been elected until April 10, 1740. When Beteilhe became Secretary of the First Lodge in Boston and of the Grand Lodge we do not know. He was made in the First Lodge on July 24, 1734, *q.v. infra.* He signs as its Secretary as early as June 23, 1736, *q.v. infra.* He was appointed or reappointed Grand Secretary by Provincial Grand Master Tomlinson on June 24, 1737 (1 Mass. 470). Although not a member of the First Lodge at its constitution he had abundant opportunity to learn the facts which he records not only by his intimate association with the other Brethren in the town of Boston, but also especially because he was the partner of Provincial Grand Master Henry Price from 1736 to 1741.

The records of the Masters Lodge from January 2, 1738/9, to and including August 7, 1739, are in his handwriting. That he gave up this Secretaryship in the same year that he ceased to be Clerk of the Vestry of Christ Church, and that the records of the Masters Lodge for some time after August 7, 1739, *q.v.,* are not in the book give confirmatory evidence of his being afflicted by some indisposition during this year.

The Manuscript starts with a copy of the petition of July 30, 1733, of the Brethren in Boston to be regularly constituted as a Lodge. This covers three pages. Pages four to six inclusive contain an account of the formation of the Grand Lodge by Henry Price, the presentation of the petition of the Boston Brethren, and the constitution of the First Lodge on July 30, 1733, *q.v. infra.* Pages seven to twelve inclusive contain the By-Laws or Regulations of the First Lodge in Boston as adopted October 24, 1733. Pages thirteen and fourteen contain a list of the officers of the Grand Lodge and of the Lodge and also of the Brethren, this list having been written between July 27 and August 23, 1737. Pages fifteen to seventeen inclusive contain votes relative to By-Laws, the first being passed by the Lodge on March 12, 1734/5, and the last on February 9, 1736/7. The eighteenth page is blank. Pages nineteen to twenty-one inclusive contain a copy of the Deputation issued by the Earl of Loudoun, Grand Master of England, to Robert Thomlinson as Provincial Grand Master. Pages twenty-two and twenty-three contain a copy of the letter of Glasgow Kilwinning Lodge, dated February 22, 1736/7, *q.v.* Pages twenty-four to twenty-six inclusive contain a copy of the letter from Edinburgh, dated January 28, 1736/7, *q.v.*

There are twelve names on the Pelham List which do not appear in the Beteilhe Manuscript. These Brethren had probably ceased to be members of the Lodge by July 27, 1737. There is but one name, Captain Roger Willington, on the Beteilhe Manuscript which is not found on the Pelham List and that name is found in the Barons Letter of June 23, 1736, *q.v.* There are but two names on the Beteilhe list prior to the date of the Barons Letter list which are not found on the latter. These slight differences, to my mind, confirm the general accuracy of all of the lists and prove that no one of them is copied from any other but that all were drawn off from some original records which are now lost.

See also 1747, May 27, *infra.*

A facsimile of pages 13 and 14 of the Beteilhe Manuscript is herewith presented.

A List of the Brethren

Henry Price G:M Constituted y Lodge A M 5733

Andrew Belcher D:G:M

James Gordon S: Esqr G:W   Fredk Hamilton J: G:W

Henry Hope M: Wm Gordon S:W:

Andrew Hallyburton J:W:

Francis Beteilhe Secrety

1 John McNeal
2 Edwd Ellis
3 Thos Molony
4 Saml Pemberton
5 Moses Hatteney
6 Thos Phillips
7 Robert Macklean
8 Willm Wesson
9 Robert Kenton
10 John Overing Esqn
11 Saml Curwen
12 Anthony Davis
13 Alexr Gordon

14 Peter Hall
15 John Baker
16 Robert Peasley
17 John Gordon Tyler
18 John Smith
19 Peter Prescott
20 Benjn Pemberton Esqr
21 Hugh Scott
22 John Lisle
23 Rich Pateshall
24 Robert Gardiner
25 Thos Moffatt Doo Phy
26 Char Gordon

Carrd over Leafe

PAGE 13 OF BETEILHE MANUSCRIPT

James Cerke Capt.
Robert Thomlinson
Alexr. Trann
John Osborne
Robt. Boyde Capt.
Benjo. Hallowell
Franc Johonnot
Luke Vardy. Master of the Exchange Tavern
Roger Willington Capt
Hugh McDaniel
Charc. Bladwell Esq
Coll. Jno. Morris
Capt. Jno. Fraizier
Capt. Tho. Reynolds
Capt. James Crawford
Docr Archibold Ramsay
Capt. Peter Tonkin
Capt. Rich Parks.
Shaw Mackintosh Esqr
Natho. Bethune.
Saml. Stone of Salem

Jams. Forbes Capt.
Benjo. Barons
Willm. Hinton Capt.
Thos. Oxnard
Thos. McKnight Capt.
Webber Gorton Capt.
Robert Smith Capt.
Willm Frost Capt.
Robert Oliver
Capt. Jno. Huggett
James Farrell } Mates
Giles Vandellure } of Ships
Capt. Edwd. Clarke of N.York
Albert Denie —
Alexr. French
Thos. Pearson

PAGE 14 OF BETEILHE MANUSCRIPT

For facsimile of pages 4, 5, and 6, see 1733, July 30, *infra.*

d. The Barons Letter.

See 1736, June 23, *infra.*

e. The Pelham List.

See abbreviations, *supra.*

I have compared the Pelham List and the original records of the First Lodge in Boston for the period when they overlap. There are two hundred and twenty-four names on the Pelham List for that period. Eight are given on the List whose names do not appear on the original records as made or accepted on the dates stated. Three names are given on the original records which do not appear on the Pelham List. Of the eight, in at least three instances the List must be correct and the Secretary in these cases omitted from the records of the Lodge some things which actually transpired.

See 1747, May 27, and 1739, July 25, *infra.*

5. NEWSPAPERS OF THE PERIOD

Every newspaper published in Boston prior to March 25, 1750, so far as they are known to exist, has been read.

See IX publications of the Colonial Society of Massachusetts, containing check list of Boston Newspapers, 1740-1780.

Appendix to 1915 Proceedings of American Antiquarian Society.

Extensive but not exhaustive search has been made of the papers published during the period in Charleston, S. C., Philadelphia, New York, and elsewhere. No complete check lists of the existing copies of these papers have been found.

6. THE POCKET COMPANION

7. PRESTON'S ILLUSTRATIONS

Both of these were written by men who copied or paraphrased Anderson. Both were supplemented in succeeding editions. Both occasionally contain lists of the lodges. So far, at least, as they recite facts not recorded by Anderson their statements concerning the events of the eighteenth century have great evidential value.

8. OTHER MANUSCRIPTS AND PUBLICATIONS WILL BE REFERRED TO FROM TIME TO TIME

CALENDAR

Much confusion has arisen over dates from January 1 to March 24 inclusive prior to 1753, because to and including the year 1752 the first day of the new year was March 25 instead of January 1. Consequently old style March 24, 1750, for instance, was the day before March 25, 1751; and January 1, 1750, was the day after December 31, 1750, and not the day after December 31, 1749. In many commentaries on early Masonic matters as well as upon matters of general history this distinction has been overlooked, with resultant confusion. Accuracy of dates has been attempted herein, and for clearness both old and new style have been indicated. For instance, March 24, 1750/1, means the day before March 25, 1751. At the time, that day was officially known as March 24, 1750.

CHAPTER III

EARLIEST TRACES IN THE WESTERN HEMISPHERE

1606,   Nova Scotia.

Dr. Charles T. Jackson, of Boston, while making a survey of Nova Scotia in 1827, discovered upon the shore of Goat Island in Annapolis Basin a flat slab of trap rock with the date 1606 and what some have thought to be the Square and Compass deeply cut though much worn by time and weather. It was at first thought that upon this stone the French had engraved the date of their first cultivation of the soil in memory of their formal possession of the country.

> Historical and Statistical Account of Nova Scotia by Judge Haliburton, published in 1829, Vol. II, p. 155.

Dr. Jackson gave this stone to Judge T. C. Haliburton, and about 1887 his son passed it along to the Canadian Institute of Toronto to be inserted in the wall of its new building. It was duly received and instructions were given to build it in with the inscription exposed but very stupidly the workmen covered it over with plaster and the stone cannot now be traced, although the plaster has been removed at several places to look for it and a reward of one thousand dollars offered for its discovery.

> Early History of Freemasonry in Nova Scotia and Published Lecture by M. W. Bro. Hon. Wm. Ross, delivered in Virgin Lodge June, 1910, pages 3-6.

Brother R. V. Harris's theory concerning this stone seems the most reasonable one presented, namely, that "the stone marked the grave of either a mason or stone-cutter or possibly a carpenter who died November 14, 1606, and not that of a speculative Freemason."

Transactions of Nova Scotia Lodge of Research for Jan. 31, 1916, pages 29 *et seq.*

In 1785, there was a tradition in Nova Scotia that Freemasonry had been known there while the country was in the hands of the French.

See "Charges and Regulations," etc., published by John Howe, Halifax, 1786. The only known copy is in the archives of the Grand Lodge of Massachusetts.

1654,   New England.

Plymouth County Records, Volume X, page 137, contain a reference to a parcel sent from Cooper's Hall, London, March, 1654, to the Apostle John Eliot "for the use of the Indian worke." On the outside are some hieroglyphics which, in part at least, are unintelligible. The first may be intended for "N.E." At its base are some lines which might possibly have been intended for the square and compasses. This, in my judgment, is purely fortuitous. It is a strain on the imagination to find any real Masonic significance in this incident.

1656 or 1658,   Rhode Island.

Brother J. L. Gould of Connecticut published in 1868 at New York a manual entitled "Guide to the Chapter," in which this statement is contained:

"The earliest account of the introduction of Masonry into the United States is the history of a Lodge organ-

THE MASONIC (?) STONE OF 1606
From photograph in possession of the New England
Historic Genealogical Society.

ized in Rhode Island, A.D. 1658, or fifty-nine years before the revival in England, and seventy-five years before the establishment of the first Lodge in Massachusetts." The author states that "The Reverend Edward Peterson, in his 'History of Rhode Island and Newport in the Past,' gives the following account of this early Lodge," etc.

On page 101 of the 1853 edition of Peterson's History the above statement is made in substance and immediately following it in italics are the words: *"Taken from documents now in possession of N. H. Gould, Esq."*

In 1870 M. W. Bro. William S. Gardner, then Grand Master of Massachusetts, wrote to Bro. N. H. Gould requesting a detailed account of the documents referred to. On December 12, 1870, Bro. N. H. Gould replied by a letter quoted in full in 1870 Mass. 358, in which letter he says:

"The document was dual in its nature and as follows: " 'Th^s y^e [day and month obliterated] 1656 or 8 [not certain which, as the place was stained and broken: the first three figures were plain] W^{ee} mett att y House off Mordecai Campunnall and affter Synagog W^{ee} gave Ab^m Moses the degrees of Maconrie.' "

He explains further that the document spoken of was in a very tender state and that after a time it became so broken that he could not have it even daguerreotyped and adds: "But what there is of it was nicely enveloped and tucked away with some of my papers in my house securely but not where I can at present put my hand upon it."

Judge Gardner comments:

"It is almost impossible to treat this story with the attention which the subject demands. It bears upon its face the utter refutation of the assertion made by the Rev. Edward Peterson, and of the claim made by Br. J. L. Gould, of Connecticut. It is unnecessary to argue that, admitting everything in the letter to be true, it affords no proof, not even the probability, of the existence of Masonry in Rhode Island previous to its introduction there by the Provincial Grand Lodge of Massachusetts about 1749. Fragmentary pieces of paper, containing partly illegible writing in the handwriting of no person known, 'nullius filius,' are not sufficient to controvert well-established historical facts. If the Rev. Edward Peterson carefully examined this weatherworn fragment of paper, and made his statement upon the faith and credit of this token, then we need not be surprised to learn that in Rhode Island his History is not recognized as an authority."

The letter of December 12, 1870, was sent to M. W. Bro. Thomas A. Doyle, then Grand Master of Masons in Rhode Island, who replied, among other things:

"I can only say that, from the best information I can obtain in regard to that history, the statement is not to be taken as a fact, unless supported by other reliable testimony. What he has said about Masonry is, I understand, asserted upon the authority of documents in the possession of W. Bro. N. H. Gould. I have made many enquiries about these documents of brethren in Newport, members of the Grand Lodge and others, and do not find that any one has ever seen them; neither do the brethren believe that any proof exists of the truth of Peterson's statement. . . .

"My own opinion is, that the first lawful Lodge of

Masons ever convened in this jurisdiction, was the one which met in Newport, in 1749, under the authority of R. W. Thomas Oxnard, Provincial Grand Master of Massachusetts, which Lodge has existed since that time, and is now known as Saint John's Lodge."

In 1891 M. W. Bro. Sereno D. Nickerson commented:

"It must be confessed that both Grand Masters had good reason for dismissing with contempt the extravagant claim of the historian. The manufacture of documentary evidence to supply missing links in Masonic history is a department of *belles lettres* in which it seems especially dangerous to venture."

Notwithstanding repeated requests and demands, neither the document nor any fragment of it has ever been produced for examination and we are safe in concluding that unless and until the document is produced or accounted for, no credit can be given to it or to any conclusions based upon it.

1697.

Henry Price, founder of duly constituted Masonry in America, was born this year in London. See page 93.

1700,   American Colonies.

It is generally believed, as a warranted deduction from known facts, that Freemasonry was brought into the colonies of North America at a very early period in the eighteenth century and that the immigrating Freemasons soon established Lodges at various places, which they worked without the sanction of warrants.

Mackey 1517.

These occasional Lodges, meeting "according to the Old Customs," were never "duly constituted" but they were, nevertheless, "regular" prior to 1721. They were neither "regular" nor "duly constituted" after June 24, 1721, unless and until lawfully warranted or chartered. On Saint John the Baptist's Day, in 1721, the Grand Lodge at London adopted and promulgated the following regulation:

"VIII. No set or number of Brethren shall withdraw or separate themselves from the Lodge in which they were made Brethren, or were afterwards admitted members, unless the Lodge becomes too numerous; nor even then without a Dispensation from the Grand Master or his Deputy: and when they are thus separated, they must either immediately join themselves to such other Lodge as they shall like best, with the unanimous consent of that other Lodge to which they go (as above regulated) or else they must obtain the Grand Master's Warrant to join in forming a new Lodge.

"If any set or number of Masons shall take upon themselves to form a Lodge without the Grand Master's Warrant, the regular Lodges are not to countenance them, nor own them as fair Brethren and duly formed, nor approve of their acts and deeds; but must treat them as rebels, until they humble themselves, as the Grand Master shall in his prudence direct, and until he approve of them by his Warrant, which must be signified to the other Lodges, as the custom is when a new Lodge is to be registered in the list of Lodges."

As will be seen hereafter the Brethren in Boston were the first in America to be constituted in accordance with this regulation (July 30, 1733). They thus became the first "regular and duly constituted Lodge" in the Western Hemisphere. The Lodge at Montserrat was the second in 1734; the Lodge in Pennsylvania came next in 1734/5; the Brethren in Savannah, Georgia, and Charleston, South Carolina, came next in 1735; and the Lodge in Portsmouth, New Hampshire, followed in 1736.

1705, Boston.

Jonathan Belcher, who was born in Boston in 1681 and was graduated from Harvard in 1699, had all the advantages of education and travel which the opulence of a fond father could give. Among other things he had the opportunity of travel in Europe where he was made a Mason in 1704, according to a letter which he wrote to the first Lodge in Boston on September 25, 1741. His standing was so considerable that on this trip to Europe he was presented to the Princess Sophia and her son, afterwards George II.

His education being finished, he returned to Boston and engaged in business as a merchant. Almost immediately he was chosen a member of the Council and in 1729 again visited England, this time as the agent of the Colony. While he was thus engaged, Governor Burnet of the Colony of Massachusetts Bay died, and Mr. Belcher obtained the appointment of Governor of Massachusetts and New Hampshire, which he held from 1730 to 1741, under which latter date further reference will be made to him.

The point to be noted here is that as in 1705, after being made a Mason in England, he returned to Boston, he may properly be called the Senior Freemason of America.

1914 Mass. 249.
1 N.E.F. 67.

1715.

It has been related within recent years that one Horace W. Smith possessed a letter purporting to have been written in 1715 by one John Moore, Collector of the Port of Philadelphia, in which he spoke of having "spent a few evenings in festivity with my Masonic Brethren."

This letter was for a time exploited as evidence of meetings of the Fraternity in Philadelphia during this year. This letter, however, never existed. Careful inquiry discloses repeated but unsuccessful attempts by the acquaintances of Mr. Smith to see the letter. If he ever had such a letter he could have produced it or accounted for its absence, but he never did so. No one among his contemporaries or among those having had the best opportunity to talk with him and to see the document if it existed can be found who believes there ever was such a letter. No notice would be taken of it here were it not for the fact that such Brothers as Hughan, Stillson and Newton, learned in historical matters, accepted the false statements with regard to this letter at their face value but without making a personal investigation to check up the fact.

Mackey, 1518.

1718/9, January 5,   Boston.

The *Boston News Letter* for this date, page 2, under its news for the Port of Boston chronicles:

"Outward Bound, Jacob William Ship Charles and Free Maſon for Jamaica."

We shall hear of this ship again.
    P–t.

1720,   Boston.

Reverend Brother Montague, formerly settled at Dedham, Mass., in the early part of the nineteenth century, was on a committee to investigate the title of King's Chapel in Boston to certain property rights then in ecclesiastical and civil legal controversy.

Brother Montague was a member of some Army Lodge, the identity of which however is unknown. While abroad on the duties of this committee, Brother Montague discovered evidence that a Lodge of Free Masons had met in King's Chapel in Boston in 1720, although the meetings were shortly discontinued.

In 1826 Brother Montague exhibited the evidence to R. W. Charles W. Moore, then editor of the *Masonic Mirror* (Grand Pursuivant 1833; Recording Grand Secretary from 1834 to 1867; Deputy Grand Master, 1868; Corresponding Grand Secretary, 1869 to 1873; Honorary Past Grand Master, December 10, 1873, Grand Lodge of Massachusetts; Active 33° N.M.J. and Grand Secretary General; Editor of Masonic Magazines, 1825 to 1873).

Brother Moore published a statement of the fact on January 27, 1827, in the *Masonic Mirror and Mechanics Intelligencer*. Unfortunately, critical study of Masonic history was not then in vogue and though Brother Moore subsequently referred to the matter in the third volume of *Moore's Freemasons' Magazine* (1844), page 163, he did not state the nature of the evidence upon which he and Brother Montague relied nor where the original evidence is to be found.

In the concealed pages of some forgotten tome or in some hidden and ancient manuscript, this evidence will probably again be discovered by some delver into the secrets of the past. Until then we shall have to rest content with the knowledge that Brothers Montague and Moore were highly respected by their compeers and were men of unquestioned veracity. The evidence, therefore, of these meetings in King's Chapel as now known neither rises to the grade of unquestioned proof nor falls to the level of tradition. We have the definite knowledge that men of the highest standing in the community actually knew of evidence which satisfied them. Certain known facts lend argumentative support.

Governor Belcher of Massachusetts, to whom we have referred, was a Mason. His son, Andrew, was at some time prior to July 30, 1733, made a Mason upon this side of the Atlantic, as were others referred to hereafter under date of 1733, July 30. Extensive study demonstrates that at least ten of those who on July 30, 1733, applied to Henry Price for the Constitution of the First Lodge were "made here." In their petition they stated in so many words that some of them were "made here," though they omitted to tell who or how many.

See Facsimile, page 81.

Other confirmatory facts will later appear sufficient to warrant the conclusion that the first "regular" Lodge in the Western Hemisphere met probably in King's Chapel, Boston, in 1720.

> 1914 Mass. 249, *et cit.*
> 1888 Mass. 164.
> 1891 Mass. 35.
> S. and H. 447.

1720, August 29,   Boston.

In these days it was customary for members of the Fraternity to speak of Masonic matters by indirection.

For instance, if a cowan or eavesdropper approached while Brethren were talking Masonry one would say, "It rains." This was the cue to turn the conversation. Bearing in mind this habit, it is interesting to read in the *Boston Gazette* for August 29, 1720, the following account:

Charleſtown, *Aug.* 27. On Wedneſday laſt Four Men belonging to this Town went down in a Boat to the Iſlands to kill wild Fowl. On their return home toward Sun-ſet, they eſpied an Heron at ſome ſmall diſtance, which they attempted to ſhoot. And as one of the Company was diſcharging his Piece, Another of the Company, (Seil. Mr. *Benjamin Dowſe*,) unexpectedly ſtarted up before the mouth of the Gun and received the Shot into his own Body, under his right Shoulder, upon which He expired in a minute or two with thoſe words in Acts VII. 59. *Lord Jeſus receive my Spirit*. When the Body was brought on ſhore, it would have melted the moſt Adamantine heart into relentines, to have heard the Weeping and ſeen the Tears, which the whole Town ſhed at the Affecting ſight. He was very much beloved and is univerſally lamented, being a Perſon of Exemplary Piety, and Induſtry, and Good Temper, and *a Widows Only Son*. He was alſo the Town-Clerk and Treaſurer, and One that was very uſeful in teaching the Youth, Writing, Arithmetick, and Singing of Pſalm Tunes. He was decently Buried yeſter day (there being a vaſt concourſe of People at his Funeral) *Ætatis Sua* XXV.
P–t.

Whoever wrote the above article probably was a Mason and intended thereby to inform all Brethren who should read the *Gazette* that Benjamin Dowse was a member of the Craft.

The facts are as he gives them but his choice of italics

does not accord with the custom of the day. Benj. Dowse's father and brother predeceased him. He left a mother and three sisters.

Our learned Brother M. Huxtall thinks that this looks like "the writing of a man who 'took his Masonry seriously,' and (perhaps half unconsciously) introduced the language of the Craft more or less habitually."

1721, June 24.

On this day the Mother Grand Lodge of the Masonic world, that at London, adopted a regulation quoted on page 48, *supra*. This has ever since been the law forbidding the formation of a Lodge without a Grand Master's Warrant.

This Mother Grand Lodge acquired jurisdiction over the new world and every Regular and Duly Constituted Lodge which existed in America during the period with which we are dealing derived its authority directly or mediately therefrom. At least from and after the public promulgation of this rule (1723) every Lodge which met in England or her Colonies without the required authority (and there were doubtless a number of them) was irregular. All such came under the second paragraph of said General Regulation VIII. Clandestine and irregularly made Masons were no more entitled to Masonic recognition in the eighteenth century than they are now in the twentieth century. The so-called Lodges in the Colonies, therefore, meeting without Warrant after 1723 are no part of legitimate Masonic history until they "humbled themselves" as did the Masons of Pennsylvania when they applied for and received recognition from Provincial Grand Master Henry Price, in 1734/5.

Until then, under the law quoted they were "rebels."

And never in any phase of the life of the world have rebels obtained the rights of legitimacy unless the rebellion was successful. In dealing with questions of precedence, primacy is to be accorded to regularity, and obedience to law is to be preferred to violation thereof. The channels of regularity since 1721 are recorded and certain, susceptible of definite historic proof. The story of the irregular Craft is vague, uncertain, and almost wholly traditional. No real historian to-day claims the exercise of warranted Masonic authority in America until the formation of the Provincial Grand Lodge in Boston, July 30, 1733, *q.v. infra*.

1721, July 31, Boston.
The *Boston Gazette* under "Entred Inwards," gives "John Peddie Ship Free-Maſon from New-Caſtle."
     P–t.

1721, Sept. 18, Boston.
Under this date we find in the official records of the Port of Boston and in the *Boston Weekly News Letter* "Outward Bound. . . . John Peddie, Charles & Free-maſon for West Indies."
     P–t.

1722/3, January 17, London.
The Constitutions and Regulations of the Grand Lodge of England were approved for publication, containing General Regulation VIII above quoted, page 48.
     Anderson, (1723).

1723, Boston.
Henry Price removed to Boston.
     See Chapter V.

1727,   Philadelphia.

At one time it was attempted to claim for this year proof of Masonry in Philadelphia because of the finding in 1756 of a manuscript copy of the "Old Charges" dated 1727. The contention is unworthy of serious discussion. The Grand Lodge of Massachusetts owns a similar manuscript dated 1677 but makes no claim by virtue thereof.

1909 Mass. 105-109.

1727, May 25,   Boston.

The *Boston Weekly News Letter* contains an account of a meeting of the Grand Lodge in London on Monday, February 27, 1726/7. This is the earliest known account in any American newspaper of a Masonic meeting. Would the publisher of a Boston newspaper have inserted an account of the Masonic meeting in London if there were not known by him to be a sufficient number of members of the Craft in Boston to whom the item would be interesting reading? Does this not lend force to the argument that there were Lodge meetings in Boston and perhaps elsewhere in the Colonies and that the public generally knew of them? Else why would the readers of the *News Letter* be expected to care for such an item of news as this? The Governor-General was a Mason (page 49). And his son and others were "made here" before 1733 (page 81).

1730, June 5,   London.

The Duke of Norfolk, Grand Master of England, appointed Daniel Coxe, Provincial Grand Master of New York, New Jersey and Pennsylvania for a period of two years. [There has appeared no evidence, however, that he exercised this deputation. He was on this side of the ocean about four months of the year 1730,* but the balance of his two-year term he was in England endeavoring to perfect his title to nearly half of the Continent of North America, which he claimed to own by virtue of a grant to his father, who was physician to Charles I and II. On January 29, 1731, he was present at a meeting of the Grand Lodge of England (X Q.C.A. 139). During that year he registered as a member of Lodge No. 8, meeting at the Devil Tavern within Temple Bar. He does appear in America in 1734 but then his commission had long since expired by limitation. The issuance of the deputation, however, establishes three facts, viz.:

1. That the Grand Lodge of England in 1730 claimed jurisdiction over these Colonies.

2. That the Mother Grand Lodge and its Grand Master held to the doctrine that Regular and Duly Constituted Lodges could exist in British possessions, or at least in the Colonies, only through the authority of the Grand Master of England.

3. That the Mother Grand Lodge and its Grand Master in 1730 having assumed jurisdiction over New York, New Jersey and Pennsylvania, which were then dependents of the British Crown, no one else had authority to establish Lodges in Pennsylvania, New York or New Jersey until at least after June 24, 1732, the end of the term of the deputation, unless it was revoked or superseded.

The establishment of Lodges in Pennsylvania during the term of Coxe's deputation and without his sanction

* See article by David McGregor in *The Builder* for November, 1924, and the author's reply in the December issue.

was, therefore, irregular and in direct contravention of his authority.

IV Gould 362.

1730, July 9,   Philadelphia.

There is an account in the *Pennsylvania Gazette* of the meeting of the Grand Lodge in London, April 21, 1730. From later instances which will be referred to it is *suspected* that this was clipped from some Boston newspaper now lost.

1730, July 27,   Boston.

The *New England Weekly Journal* gives an account of a Lodge held at the Horn Tavern in London on May 12, 1730.

P–t.

1730, August 13,   Philadelphia.

Benjamin Franklin was born in Boston, January 17, 1706. He left Boston in October, 1723, although he was again in Boston the following year. On October 11, 1726, he arrived in Philadelphia after a trip to London.

In 1730 Franklin was not a Mason. He was then twenty-four years old and was publishing the *Pennsylvania Gazette*. In the issue of the *Gazette* August 13, 1730, he reprinted from the *New England Weekly Journal* of July 27, 1730, the account of the Lodge meeting in London, last above referred to. Is it not an irresistible conclusion that there were Masonic Lodge meetings attended by sufficient numbers to make them known to the community at least in Philadelphia and Boston? If in Philadelphia and Boston, why not elsewhere in the Colonies?

The regulations of the Grand Lodge of England, June 24, 1721, adopted in the first instance to apply only within the City of London but almost immediately extended to the British Empire, were not thoroughly known ahd enforced throughout the Empire. It was as late as 1738 before it can be said that they were firmly established everywhere, though prior to 1738, as we shall see later, they had become known to and enforced in those centres of population upon this side of the ocean where Masonry was practised and which were in touch through merchants and mariners with the Mother Country.

1730, August 20, Philadelphia.

Account in *Philadelphia Gazette* of a Lodge meeting in London in June at which "the celebrated Mr. Orator —Henley—was admitted," etc.

1730, Fall of Year. Philadelphia.

The claim once emanated from Philadelphia that a letter was written in 1754 by one Henry Bell to Dr. Thomas Cadwallader in which the writer is alleged to state that at a meeting in Philadelphia in the fall of 1730 application was made to Daniel Coxe for a Charter which was granted by him. It is now admitted by every Masonic student, both within and without Pennsylvania, that there never was such a letter. The story is like that about the Rhode Island document of 1656 or 1658 and the John Moore letter of 1715. No one of them deserves more dignified reference than to call it a "fake" pure and simple.

1888 Mass. 131-137.
1899 Mass. 56.
1909 Mass. 108.
1 O.M.L.P. 10.

1730, December 8.   Philadelphia.

Franklin (not then a Mason) republished in his *Philadelphia Gazette* an alleged exposé of Freemasonry which had been circulated for some time in England. It begins as follows:

"As there are several Lodges of *Free Masons* erected in this Province, and People have lately been much amus'd with Conjectures concerning them; we think the following Account of Free-Masonry from London, will not be unacceptable to our Readers."

The statement that there were "several" Lodges must be taken *cum grano salis*. While there is evidence herein referred to that Brethren did about this time assemble as a Lodge, there is little reason to believe that there was more than one such Lodge.

X Q.C.A. 140, 152.
IV Gould 361.
1883 Mass. 184.
1903 Mass. 52.

1730/1, January 29,   London.

Daniel Coxe was still in England and in attendance upon the Grand Lodge in London. During the year he was registered as a member of Lodge No. 8, at the Devil Tavern within Temple Bar.

X Q.C.A. 140, 152.

1730/1, February,   Philadelphia.

Benjamin Franklin was made a Mason during this month in an assemblage of Brethren in Philadelphia which met "according to the Old Customs" although that method had for ten years been forbidden. Although irregular, they undoubtedly met and worked in Philadelphia as well as in Boston and perhaps elsewhere.

IV Gould, 362.

They became regular in Pennsylvania after February 21, 1734/5, *q.v.*, through the granting by Henry Price of Franklin's petition of November 28, 1734, *q.v.*

1914 Mass. 252, *et cit.*

1730,   London.

Lord Baltimore was made a Mason in England during this year. He was Proprietor of Maryland from 1715 to 1751, and Royal Governor in 1732 and 1733. There is no evidence that he practised or promoted Masonry on these shores, but it is not impossible.

IV Gould 262.

Mackey 1517.

It is recorded in the records of the Grand Lodge of England that Henry Price had returned to London. This year he was a member of Lodge No. 75, meeting at the Rainbow Coffee House in York Buildings (now The Brittanic No. 33).

X Q.C.A. xviii and 183.

1 Mass. 432.

1730,   Georgia.

The third edition (1805) of *Webb's Monitor* (page 299) stated that Masonry in Georgia dated from 1730. This was an error which Webb corrected in subsequent editions. The statement, however, has been copied without correction in several works and has given rise to a curious situation as to which see "1735 after October 30," *infra.*

It is too early to look for Freemasons here. The first

emigrants to Georgia landed on the bluff now occupied by the City of Savannah, on January 31, 1732/3. On this spot there was at the time an Indian village called Yamacraw.

M. W. Brother W. S. Rockwell who wrote the history of the Grand Lodge of Georgia, first published as a part of its Ahiman Rezon in 1859, repeated a statement made in 1856,

15 M.F.M. 354

that "it is not altogether certain that the date A.D. 1730 is erroneous as to the time when the power was conferred upon Roger Lacy; although no formal government existed in the colony of Georgia until 1733, yet the territory now occupied by the State was then under the government of Carolina." But he either forgot or did not know that in 1730 there was not a white settlement anywhere in the province—the whole territory was a wilderness, the hunting ground of savages.

It cannot seriously be contended that the Grand Master of England actually granted the necessary powers for a Provincial Grand Lodge to be erected among the subjects of Chief Tomochichi. Until the landing of Oglethorpe with his emigrants in January, 1732/3, the only white man known to be in what is now Georgia, was a trader by the name of Musgrove, who was married to a half breed named Mary.

2 History of Ga. (Stevens) 89.

As further authority, Brother Rockwell quotes Clavel's "Histoire Pittoresque de la France Maconnerie" (1884) and Ragon's "Orthodoxie Macconnique" (1853). However, it is well known that as a historian no reliance can be placed upon Clavel. Ragon undoubtedly copied the error which Webb made in his first edition and Clavel evidently copied from Ragon.

For Brother Rockwell's views and the conclusive reply of R. W. Charles W. Moore, see

15 M.F.M. 353-362.

The date 1730 published in Webb's *Monitor* was perhaps a typographical error, but in any event Webb recognized the mistake and corrected it at his first possible opportunity. It does seem rather far fetched to try to justify Webb's error without a single fact or authority upon which to base such justification.

See page 138, *infra*.

1731, May 13,   Philadelphia.

"Some Information concerning the Society called Freemasons," quoted from Chambers Universal Dictionary, is published in the *Pennsylvania Gazette*, and in the same issue is a notice of a Masonic meeting in Dublin.

1731, June 24,   Philadelphia.

In January, 1884, the discovery was reported of a book known as "Libr B" containing a statement of the financial affairs of the assemblages of the Brethren in Philadelphia for about seven years. It begins with this date and is the oldest American Lodge account book known. See page 31. From it we are warranted in concluding that on this day and previously the Brethren of Philadelphia assembled as heretofore pointed out. Like all meetings in Philadelphia, Boston, and elsewhere in the Colonies at this period the Lodge was neither "Regular" nor "Duly Constituted." From the entries in "Libr B," we learn that there were fourteen members of the Lodge at this time. Under this date "Libr B" charges the entrance fees of John Hobart (Hubert), Mark Joyce, and Thomas Rodman (Redman), and the remainder of the fees of Benjamin Franklin and Henry Pratt.

"Libr B" and accounts in the *Pennsylvania Gazette* for the next two years refer to a "Grand Master," etc. Brother Gould correctly states, however, that no lingering doubt now remains as to the "Lodge" and the "Grand Lodge" being one and the same body.

IV Gould 234, 361, 363.

Concerning "Libr B" and Brother Sachse's contention concerning early American Freemasonry, see his work called "Old Masonic Lodges in Philadelphia."

A page of "Libr B" is here reproduced.

1731, July 5,   Philadelphia.
   L.B. charges Thomas Whitemarsh's entrance fee.

1731, July 22,   Philadelphia.
   The *Pennsylvania Gazette* publishes an account of a Masonic meeting in London.

1731, August 2,   Philadelphia.
   Entries in L.B. indicate a meeting.

1731, September 6,   Philadelphia.
   Entries in L.B. indicate a meeting.

1731, September 9,   Philadelphia.
   In Franklin's Journal under some date after September 9, 1731, but probably before October 16, is the entry,
      "Blanks for Mason's 100 —5..——"
      F.J.

PAGE OF "LIBR B"

1731, September 27,   Boston.

The *Weekly Rehearsal* publishes an account of the installation at Dublin of the Right Honourable Lord Kingston as Grand Master of Ireland on July 7, 1731.

P–t.

1731, October 4,   Philadelphia.

Entries in L. B. indicate a meeting.

FACSIMILE OF ENTRY IN FRANKLIN'S JOURNAL

1731, November 1,   Philadelphia.

Entries in L. B. indicate a meeting.

1731, December 6,   Philadelphia.

Entries in L. B. indicate a meeting.

1731/2, January 3,   Philadelphia.

Entries in L. B. indicate a meeting.

1731/2, February 7, Philadelphia.

L. B. charges entrance fees of John Hall, Samuel Mc-
Clanan, and Lawrence Reynold.

1731/2, February 17, Boston.

The *Weekly News Letter* relates that "the Society of
Real Masons held their Lodge of St. Michael" at London on September 30, 1731.

        P–t.

1731/2, March 6,   Philadelphia.

L.B. charges entrance fee of David Parry.

1732, April 3,   Philadelphia.

Entries in L. B. indicate a meeting.

1732, May 1,   Philadelphia.

Entries in L. B. indicate a meeting.

1732, May 11,   Philadelphia.

The *Pennsylvania Gazette* has a Masonic notice from
Dublin.

1732, June 5,   Philadelphia.

It is reported that in 1885 there was in the possession
of George T. Ingham, Esq., of Atlantic City, N. J., a
document in Benjamin Franklin's handwriting (except
the signatures) reading as follows:

"Gentlemen of the Lodge
The Committee you have been pleased to appoint to
consider of the present State of the Lodge, and of the
properest Methods to improve it, in obedience to your
commands have met, and, after much and mature Deliberation, have come to the following Resolutions:—

1. That since the excellent Science of Geometry and Architecture is so much recommended in our ancient Constitutions, Masonry being first instituted with this Design, among others, to distinguish the true and skilful Architect from unskilful Pretenders; total Ignorance of this Art is very unbecoming a Man who bears the Worthy Name and Character of MASON; We therefore conclude, that it is the Duty of every Member to make himself, in some Measure, acquainted therewith, as he would honour the Society he belongs to, and conform to the Constitutions.

2. That every Member may have an Opportunity of so doing, the present Cash be laid out in the best Books of Architecture, suitable Mathematical Instruments, etc.

3. That since the present whole Stock is not too large for that purpose, every Member indebted to the Lodge pay what is from him respectively due on Monday night, the nineteenth Instant, that so the whole being ready by the 24th of June, may be sent away by the first Opportunity. And that every one not paying that Night, be suspended till he do pay: For without Care be taken that Rules are punctually observed, no Society can be long upheld in good Order and Regularity.

5. That the use of Balls be established in its full Force and Vigour; and that no new Member be admitted against the will of any present Member; because certainly more Regard ought to be had in this way to a Brother who is already a Mason, than to any Person who is not one, and we should never in such cases disoblige a Brother, to oblige a Stranger.

6. That any Member of this Lodge having a complaint against any other Member, shall first apply himself to the Wardens, who shall bring the Cause before the Lodge, where it shall be consider'd and made up, if possible, before the Complainant be allow'd to make that Complaint publick to the World: the Offender against this Rule to be expell'd.

June 5, 1732.

The Members whose Names are underwritten, being a Majority, agree unanimously to the within Proposals of the Committee (except the fourth, which is cross'd out) and accordingly have hereunto set their hands.

> Will. Pringle
> Thomas Boude
> B. Franklin
> Xtopher Thompson
> Thos. Hartt
> David Parry
> John Emerson
> Law^{ce} Reynolds
> John Hobart
> Henry Pratt
> Sam'l Nicholas.

"Benjamin Franklin as a Freemason," page 21.

1732, June 24,   Philadelphia.

The *Pennsylvania Gazette* for June 26, 1732, recites that a Grand Lodge was held this day at the Sun Tavern in Philadelphia at which W. Allen, Esq. was chosen Grand Master for the Province of Pennsylvania; that Mr. William Pringle was appointed Deputy Grand Master; and that Thomas Boude and Benjamin Franklin were chosen Grand Wardens.

> See 1731, June 24, *supra.*
> 1914 Mass. 252, *et cit.*
> 1883 Mass. 184.

William Allen

William Allen was born in Philadelphia, August 5, 1704, and baptized, August 17, in the First Presbyterian Church. In 1725, he was studying law at the Temple in

London, and returned to Philadelphia prior to September 21, 1726, but appears again to have gone abroad, and did not return until the spring of 1728. During his absence, he was elected a Common Councilman; in 1731 he became a member of the Assembly, serving until 1739; October, 1735, he was chosen Mayor of the City. Allen repeatedly served as Judge of the Orphans' Court and the Court of Common Pleas; in 1741, he was Recorder, succeeding his father-in-law, Andrew Hamilton, and continued in that office until October 2, 1750, when he was appointed Chief Justice of the Province, an office he held until 1774, when he went to England, where he published "The American Crisis," setting forth a plan for restoring the dependence of the American Colonies.

A portrait of Grand Master Allen was painted by Benjamin West before he left Philadelphia, and is described by Brown, in the *Forum*, Vol. 1, pp. 248-249. In this portrait, he has a curled wig and ruffled sleeves, but is otherwise dressed as plainly as possible. The costume is a shade of brown, the face round, with rather straight features, and is distinguished by bonhomie and good sense, rather than by intensity of intellectual action.

Judge Allen was elected a member of the American Philosophical Society, January 19, 1768.

In "Libr B" at the head of his account, commencing June 24, 1731, he is styled "Grandm'r." Brother Allen was afterwards appointed Provincial Grand Master by Lord Byron, the Grand Master of England, in 1750, which office he is supposed to have held for some years. After the Revolution Bro. William Allen returned to Philadelphia, and lived in retirement on his estate at Mount Airy, now the Seminary of the Evangelical Lutheran Church, where he ended his days in comparative obscurity, dying on September 6, 1780. He was buried quietly on the following day. The lane leading from his house to the Wissahickon still bears the name of "Allen's Lane," and has also given the name to a station on the Pennsylvania Railroad branch to Chestnut Hill.

1 O.M.L.P. 29-31.

1732, July 3, Philadelphia.
Entries in L. B. indicate a meeting.

1732, July 24, Boston.
The *Boston Weekly News Letter* contains the following curious statement under its news from London:

"Laſt Monday [April 17] were admitted of the Honourable and Ancient Society of Free and Accepted Maſons, George Skinner of Enfield, Eſq., a blind Gentleman; and the ſame Day the Right Hon. the Earl of Strathmore."

Those who regard the "perfect youth" or "physical perfection" doctrine as a landmark, will have difficulty in reconciling this fact.

1732, August 7, Philadelphia.
Entries in L. B. indicate a meeting.

1732, September 4, Philadelphia.
Entries in L. B. indicate a meeting.

1732, October 19, Philadelphia.
Entries in L. B. indicate a meeting.

WILLIAM ALLEN
From portrait painted by Benjamin West.

1732, October 30,   Boston.

The *Weekly Rehearsal* chronicles a Grand Lodge meeting in Dublin on August 1st.

     P–t.

1732, November 6,   Philadelphia.

L. B. charges the entrance fees of James Brigham and Humphrey Morrey.

1732, December 4,   Philadelphia.

Entries in L. B. indicate a meeting.

1732/3, January 1,   Philadelphia.

Entries in L. B. indicate a meeting.

1732/3, February 5, Philadelphia.

Entries in L. B. indicate a meeting.

1732/3, February 9,   Annapolis, Maryland.

The *Maryland Gazette* contains the following item of interest under its London news, dated September 30, 1732.

On Sunday about Two in the Afternoon, was a Lodge of Free and Accepted Mafons, at the Rofe Tavern in Cheapfide, where in the Prefence of feveral Brethren of Diftinction, as well Jews as Chriftians, Mr. Edward Rofe, was admitted of the Fraternity, by Mr. Daniel Delvalle, an eminent Jew, the Mafter Capt. Wilmot, &c. who were entertained very handfomely; and the Evening was fpent in a Manner not infringing on the Morality of the Chriftian Faith.

     P–t.

Masonic newspaper items had been often published before this in Boston and Philadelphia. Evidently there were by this time enough Masons in Maryland to attract attention. We know that the Royal Governor, Lord Baltimore, was a Mason.

1732/3, February 19,   Boston.

The *Weekly Rehearsal* contains an article relative to the Papal Nuncio under its Parisian news, *viz:*

"On the 5th, the Nuncio having made his Publick Entry in the accustomed Manner, is now bufily employed in the Ceremonious Part of his Functions; that is, in making Vifits to the Princes and Princeffes of the Blood, in paying and receiving Compliments to and fro among the Cardinals, Minifters, and prime Nobility.   On Monday, his Excellency, being a FREE MASON, is to lay the firft Stone towards the building of the great Altar in the Church of S. Sulpice."
P.-t.

1732/3, March 5,   Philadelphia.
L. B. charges the entrance fee of John Crapp.

1732/3, March 22,   Philadelphia.
The *Pennsylvania Gazette* has an account of the initiation of a Jew in London.

1733, April 2,   Philadelphia.
L. B. charges the entrance fee of William Paschal.

1733, April 5,   Boston.
The *Boston Weekly News Letter* has an account of a Grand Lodge meeting in London on January 15, 1732/3.
P.-t.

1733, April 6,   Annapolis, Maryland.

The *Maryland Gazette* contains the following item:

London, Dec. 16.   Yeſterday Seven-night, there was a Grand Committee of Free and Accepted *Maſons*, from ſeveral Lodges, at the Horn Tavern in Palace-yard, Weſtminſter, to conſider of raiſing a Sum of Money, by Subſcription, for the *Relief* of their *poor Brethren*, throughout Britain and Ireland.   If in this, they meet with good *Succeſs*, it will convince the Werld that there is ſome *real Merit* in the *Maſon Word*.

P–t.

Why these Masonic newspaper items in Annapolis unless the Brethren were meeting there also "according to the Old Customs"?

CHAPTER IV

THE FOUNDING OF DULY CONSTITUTED FREEMASONRY IN AMERICA

1733, April 13. London-New England.

On this day, in the Grand Mastership of Lord Viscount Montague, a Deputation issued to Henry Price as "Provincial Grand Master of New England and Dominions and Territories thereunto belonging." This was the second Deputation issued for the western world. That issued to Coxe, however, never having been exercised, the Deputation to Price becomes the first to be transmitted across the seas and being immediately put into operation is the first regular Masonic authority for American Masonry.

The date of Price's Deputation has often been given as April 30th and it is possible the latter date is correct. It was so written by Pelham when he recorded the Commission in the first book of the Provincial Grand Lodge records. It is also so recorded in the earliest volume now extant of the Proceedings of the First Lodge in Boston, in the handwriting of Ebenezer Swan. An inspection, however, of the original record discloses that Swan started to write the word "thirteenth" and after writing the first "e" changed the word to "thirtieth." This indicates that he had something which led him to think the date was the thirteenth but concluded to accept Pelham's authority and therefore changed it to the thirtieth. Probably Pelham was wrong and Swan's first inclination was correct. The fourth page of the Beteilhe Manuscript, written between July 27 and August 23, 1737, expressly gives the date as the thirteenth. (Facsimile, page 85.) The original petition for the First Lodge in Boston, written July 30, 1733, also clearly gives the date as the thirteenth. (Facsimile, page 81.) In the Deputation of the Duke of Beaufort to John Rowe (1768) is found the recitation, "Our Right Worshipful and well beloved Brother Henry Price Esqr of North America, Constituted Provincial Grand Master for North America by Viscount Montague Grand Master April 13th, 1733."

1 Mass. 150.

It is likely that when Charles Pelham wrote his copy, he misunderstood whoever was dictating it to him or misread the original and that his blunder was followed by Ebenezer Swan, though in Swan's mind he had remembered it was the thirteenth. April 13 is confirmed by an entry made by Grand Secretary French in a volume of manuscript records of the Grand Lodge of England which reads as follows:

"N.B. The Deputation of Bro^r H. Price has never come to my hand, but among other loose papers I have found the following memorandum. (Signed) Thos French.

'Viscount Montague, G.M.

Henry Price, Esqr P.G.M. for all North America and the Territories thereunto belonging, Date April 13th, 1733, desire the favour to resign his Provincialship in favour of John Rowe, Esqr to be Provincial G.M. over North America where no other Provincial is appointed.

(Signed)   Beaufort, G.M.

He resigning recommends John Rowe, Esqr. We therefore do hereby con- . . .' "

Henry Price received this Deputation in person (1 Mass. 402) paying the fee of three guineas therefor to Thomas Batson, Esq., then Deputy Grand Master, who with the Grand Wardens signed the Deputation.

1 Mass. 134.

In Civil War days, when paper stock was scarce, the late Right Worshipful Brother Thomas W. Davis, (Mass. Junior Grand Warden, 1883; Grand Secretary, 1908-1914) then a boy, was employed in buying for a dealer all the old papers that could be found in Townsend, Massachusetts, and vicinity. He has told the author that he then bought nearly all the old papers there were in the residences of that town. He distinctly remembered buying of the Wallace (or Wallis) family. What he collected he piled into his wagon and carted to Fitchburg, where it was sold to paper makers. He felt firmly convinced that he had gathered, among others, all the papers of the Wallaces and other heirs of Henry Price and thus had ignorantly and innocently been the instrument of destruction of this very Deputation.

Price's Deputation as copied by Pelham is as follows:

Montague (seal) G:M.

To all and every Our R^t Worsh^l Worshipful and Loving Brethren now Residing or who may hereafter Reside in New England,

The R^t Honble and R^t Worsh^l Anthony Lord Viscount Montague Grand Master of the Free and Accepted Masons of England,

Sendeth Greeting

Whereas Application has been made unto us by our R^t Worsh and well Beloved *Bro^r Mr Henry Price in behalf of himself and several other Brethren now Residing in New England* aforesaid Free and Accepted Masons, that We would be pleas'd to Nominate and Appoint a Provincial Grand Master of Free and Accepted Masons in N: England aforesaid.

Now KNOW YE That we have Nominated, Ordain'd, Constituted and appointed and do by these Presents Nominate, Ordain, Constitute and appoint Our said Worsh¹ and well Beloved Broʳ Mʳ Henry Price, Provincial Grand Master of New England aforesaid and Dominions and Territories thereunto belonging with full power and Authority to Nominate and appoint his Deputy Grand Master and Grand Wardens, and We do also hereby Impower the said Mʳ Henry Price, for us and in Our place and Stead, to Constitute the Brethren (Free and Accepted Masons) now Residing or who shall hereafter reside in those parts, into One or more Regular Lodge or Lodges, as he shall think fit, and as often as Occasion shall require, He the said Mʳ Henry Price, taking special care that all and every Member of any Lodge or Lodges so to be Constituted have been or shall be made Regular Masons, and that they do cause all and every the Regulations Contain'd in the Printed Book of Constitutions (except so far as they have been alter'd by the Grand Lodge at their Quarterly meetings) to be kept and Observ'd and also all such other Rules and Instructions as shall from time to time be Transmitted to him by us or by Thomas Batson Esqʳ Our Deputy Grand Master, or the Grand Master or his Deputy for the time being, and that He the said Mʳ Henry Price or his Deputy do send to us or Our Deputy Grand Master and to the Grand Master of England or his Deputy for the time being annually, an accoᵗ in Writing of the number of Lodges so Constituted with the Names of the several Members of each Particular Lodge, together with such other Matters & things as he or they shall think fit to Communicate for the Prosperity of the Craft.

And Lastly we Will and Require that our said Provincial Grand Master of New England do Annually cause the Brethren to keep the Feast of Sᵗ John the Evangelist, and Dine together on that Day, or (in case any Accident should happen to prevent their Dinning to-gether on that Day) on any other Day near that time as he shall Judge most fit as is done here and that at all Quarterly Communications, he do recommend a General Charity to be Establish'd for the Relief of Poor Brethren in those parts.

Given under Our Hand and Seal of office at London the Thirtieth Day of April 1733 & of Masonry 5733.

By the Grand Master's Command

Thos Batson D.G.M.
G. Rooke S.G.W.
J. Smythe J.G.W.

It has been urged that there is no account of Price's Deputation in the records of the Grand Lodge of England for 1733, and that, therefore, it was not voted by the Grand Lodge. It certainly was not voted by the Grand Lodge, for according to the regulations it was the Warrant of the Grand Master that was a deputation in those days, not a Charter or other instrument from a Grand Lodge. Price's Deputation is by no means the only unrecorded authority to a Provincial Grand Master. It is true that a copy of the Warrant to Coxe appears in the Proceedings of the Grand Lodge of England, but it is also true that there was a recognized Provincial Grand Lodge in Chester before May 10, 1727, yet no record was made of its Warrant, Charter or other authority (X Q.C.A. 73). The same is true of the Provincial Grand Lodge of South Wales, which existed earlier than June 24, 1727 (X Q.C.A. 75); also of the Provincial Grand Lodge of East India, which dates from prior to December 13, 1733 (X Q.C.A. 237).

There is no record of the appointment of a Provincial Grand Master for Ireland, yet a Brother appeared and was recorded as such at the meeting of the Grand Lodge

of England on November 21, 1732 (X Q.C.A. 232).
There are many later instances. As the late Brother
Sadler, Librarian and Curator of the Grand Lodge of
England, wrote in 1910:

"The appointment of Provincial Grand Masters, then
as now, was a prerogative of the Grand Master (and)
consequently never appeared in the Grand Lodge Minutes except in some few instances in the early days of the
Grand Lodge." (Brother Henry Sadler, Librarian and
Curator of the United Grand Lodge of A. F. & A.
Masons of England to Bro. Julius F. Sachse, Dec. 31,
1910, quoted in 1 O.M.L.P. 11, note 16.)

1733, April 26,   Philadelphia.
The *Pennsylvania Gazette* copies from the *Boston
Weekly News Letter* the notice referred to under April 5,
1733, *supra*.

1733, April 30,   London.
The date of Henry Price's Deputation as recorded by
Pelham and Swan.
    1 Mass. 1.
    But see, 1733, April 13, *supra.*

1733, May 7,   Philadelphia.
L. B. charges the entrance fees of Peter Cuff and
Richard Parkhouse.

1733, June 4.   Philadelphia.
Entries in L. B. indicate a meeting.

1733, June 14,   Philadelphia.
Account in the *Pennsylvania Gazette* of a Masonic
meeting in London.

1733, June 25, Philadelphia.

The *Pennsylvania Gazette* for June 28, 1733, recites that a Grand Lodge was held at the Tun Tavern in Philadelphia this day at which Humphrey Murray (Morrey), Esq., was elected Grand Master, and an entertainment was provided attended by distinguished guests.

Humphrey Morrey (Murray).

Humphrey Morrey was a grandson of the first Mayor of Philadelphia. The Morrey family were wealthy Quakers who moved to Philadelphia from New York in 1685. Humphrey, however, renounced Quakerism and was baptized (when an adult) in the First Presbyterian Church in Philadelphia. He was a merchant and distiller. He died between the 6th and 13th day of August, 1735, unmarried and without issue. From his will dated November 7, 1732, it appears that he, William Allen, John Crapp (who served as Franklin's Deputy Grand Master) and Joseph Shippen were cousins.

1 O.M.L.P. 38.

1733, July 2, Philadelphia.

L. B. charges the entrance fee of Owen Owens.

1733, July 30, Boston.

Henry Price formed a Grand Lodge in Boston, appointing Andrew Belcher, Esq., (son of the Governor) his Deputy Grand Master, and Brothers Thomas Kennelly and John Quane, Grand Wardens, *pro tempore.*

1 Mass. 3.

B.MS. 5.

When Charles Pelham (in 1750) wrote the record of this evening in the first existing volume of the Grand

The Humble Petition of the following Subscribers in Behalf of themselves and Worshipfull & antient Brotherhood Belonging to the Society of Free & Accepted Masons now residing Here &c

To the Rt. Worshipfull Bror. Mr. Henry Price Deputed Provinciall, G:M: for these parts By our Rt. Worshipfull & Worshipfull Bros. & Rt. Honble Anto. Lord Visct. Montague G.M. of Great Brittain also His Seal & Sign'd by our Rt. Worshipfull Bros. Tha. Batson &c D.G.M: G. Rooke & Ja. Smyth Esqrs. S. & J. G. Wardens as yr. Deputation Dated in London the 13th. day of April Anno Dni 1733 and of Masonry 5733

Sheweth

That your Petitioners are very Sensible of the Honour done to us here by your sd. Deputation & for as much as We are a sufficient Number of Brothers regularly & duely made we in his Majestys Kingdoms of Great Brittain & Ireland as appeared to you on Examination & are now desirous of Enjoying each other (as well as those made here & their respective Names hereunto annex'd) as Masons in a Regular & Constituted Lodge for our Harmony & Union together as well as our Brethren (may at any time arrive here or such as may be made Bror. hereafter if is to say in due Manner & Form. Therefore We Request as well in our Own Name and Names As well as all other Brethren it may concern if you will Please to give the Necessary orders to all our Brethren within yr Limitts & Power to give their due Attendance on you at a seasonable hour to assist you & the Rest of the Brethren in their Capacitys towards constituting a Regular Lodge at the Sign of the Bunch of Grapes in King Street known by the Name of yr house of Mr. Edw: Lutwych on Monday the 30th Instd. whereby We may be enabled to assist one an other in the true & Lawfull Works of antient Masonry or att any other Place or Places as may seem more Meet & Requisite to our G: M: his Deputys & yr rest of the Bro. may agree upon & then & there to make such Lawfull Laws & Rules not exceeding yr Bollards prescribed to us in our Printed Book of Constitutions or yr Deputation & as will be approved & confirmed of by them According to antient Right & Custom And Lodges to be held on Every Second & Fourth Wednesday in each Month for yr Common Good of us & Brethren Your Compliance herein We doubt not will reflect great on the honour of Masons & Masonry by enlarging it wth many Worthy Gentlemen in this Town & Elsewhere Residing We as are wth Respect Sir Your Affr. Brs. & Servts.

James Gordon
John Waddell
Edmund Ellis
Wm. Gordon
Jno. Blaker
Tho: Antony
Andrw Hallyburton
Robert Pease
Sam. Pemberton
John Gordon

Andw. Belcher.
Henry Hope
Tho: Kennelly
John Leane
Fredk. Hamilton
John McNeall
Peter Hall
Andrew Bowring

FACSIMILE OF PETITION FOR FIRST LODGE IN BOSTON

Lodge record book he either copied from the Beteilhe Manuscript (see pages 86 and 87) or both were taken from an original now lost. For in language so nearly identical that the accounts could not have been written independently, both report that after forming the Grand Lodge, Price ordered his Commission or Deputation to be read, and then ordered to be read a petition of eighteen Brethren addressed to him praying that they might be Constituted into a regular Lodge by virtue of said Deputation. Ten, at least, of the petitioners had been "made here," i.e., had been made Masons in Boston in some of the earlier meetings held, like those in Philadelphia and elsewhere perhaps, without charter or warrant but according to the "Old Customs." Thereupon he granted the prayer thereof and did then and there in the most solemn manner according to ancient custom and form as prescribed by the book of Constitutions, constitute them into a regular Lodge. This original petition, apparently in the handwriting of Henry Hope, who that evening was chosen Master, is still in the archives of the Grand Lodge of Massachusets, bearing the original signatures of the petitioners and a facsimile is here presented.

Copies of both said Deputation and petition are in the Beteilhe Manuscript, the original of which is in the archives of the Grand Lodge of Massachusetts.

Most Worshipful Soreno D. Nickerson and some other historians have thought that the Lodge was not constituted until August 31, 1733, that being the date stated in two letters written by Francis Beteilhe as Secretary of the First Lodge in Boston in September, 1736.

1 Mass. 393.

The date given in the letters, however, was evidently

an error of the scrivener who correctly stated the fact in
the Beteilhe Manuscript.   Both the Beteilhe and Pelham
accounts are definite and detailed.   Moreover, the list
of the Brethren made and accepted in the First Lodge
of Boston with the time when made or admitted, written
by Charles Pelham in 1751 (the accuracy of which is
attested by the list in the Beteilhe Manuscript, the list
enclosed with the Barons letter of June 23, 1736, and the
original records of the First Lodge in Boston from December 27, 1738) not only records the eighteen signers
of the petition as becoming members of the Lodge on
July 30, 1733, but discloses that John Smith was made
on August 3, 1733.   This is improbable if the Lodge
was not constituted until August 31.   Smith's name, in
order as given on the Pelham List, appears also in the
Beteilhe Manuscript and the Barons letter.   It seems certain that the Lodge was organized on July 30 and met
and worked before August 31.

The Lodge, consolidated with two others later, is
now St. John's Lodge of Boston.

The *original Charter* of this Lodge was in the possession of the Grand Lodge as late as December 13, 1826,
when it was voted to return it to St. John's Lodge.   It
had been surrendered February 7, 1783, when Grand
Master John Rowe issued a new Charter upon the union
of the First and Second Lodges.

> O.R. of Mass. Grand Lodge for Sept. 13, and
> Dec. 13, 1826.

This precious document was doubtless destroyed in the
disastrous fire of April 6, 1864, when the Grand Lodge
of Massachusetts lost its Temple and many invaluable
treasures.

"Boston in New England" without date of Constitution or time of meeting is No. 126 on the 1734 English official engraved list of Lodges. Few dates of the constitution of Lodges in distant parts are given in this list. *No other Lodge in America*, however, appears on this list, which closes with No. 128, constituted in 1734.

Hughan's Facsimile.

This is the first time that any Lodge in the Western Hemisphere appears on *any* list of Lodges.

IV *Masonic Magazine*, London (Nov., 1876) 210-215.

This Lodge is the only American Lodge listed in the 1735 list.

L.H.B. 29, 186.

The first appearance of any other American Lodge in an official list is in the engraved list for 1736 where we find No. 139 "Savannah in ye Province of Georgia."

L.H.B. 31.

The first Lodge in Boston advanced in the various enumerations from No. 126 to 110, 65, 54, 42 and 39. It was carried on the English Register until the Union of 1813 although it had passed from that jurisdiction at the time of the Massachusetts Union of March 5, 1792.

L.M.R. 66.

In all lists after 1735 this Lodge is accredited to 1733 and is listed as meeting at the Royal Exchange, in Boston, New England. As a matter of interest a facsimile is here inserted of the 6th page of the official list for 1761, which until now has never been reproduced.

For an illuminating discussion of the official listing of the First Lodge in Boston see:

IV Gould, 247.

Facsimiles of pages 4, 5, and 6 of the Beteilhe Manuscript, containing an account of the first regular constitu-

58	Chelsea	2.^d & 4.th Thursd?	Mar. 3 1732
59	Bath	1.st & 3.^d Tuesday	May 18 1733
60	Henrietta Street Cov.^t Garden	First Tuesday	May 23 1733
61	Bury Lancashire	next Thur. to every Full Moon	Jul. 26 1733
62	Stourbridge Worcestershire	Every Wednsd.	Aug. 1 1733
63	St Pauls Church Y.^d	2.^d & 4.th Wednsd.	Dec. 27 1733
64	Birmingham	Last Monday	1733
65	Boston in New England	2.^d & 4.th Saturd.	1733
66	Valenciennes French Flanders		1733
67	Plymouth	1.st & 3.^d Friday	1734
68	E. Smithfield late the Ship at y. Hermitage	1.st & 3.^d Thursd.	Feb. 17 1734
69	near y. Watch house high Holbourn	2.^d & 4.th Wednesd.	Jun. 11 1735

FACSIMILE OF PAGE 6 OF ENGLISH
OFFICIAL ENGRAVED 1761 LIST

At a Special Chapter

of

Free & Accepted MASONS

Regularly met & Congregated at the house of
Edwᵈ Lutwych at the Sign of the Bunch of grapes
in King's Street BOSTON N. Engᵈ On Munday
July the 30ᵗʰ A D 1733 & of Masonry A: 5733.

The following Brethren being regularly
Met in the Lodge at yᵉ house afores'ᵈ Vnanimously
Agreed to petition, & did then accordingly petition
Our Rᵗ Worspᶠᵘˡ Brᵒ Mʳ Henry Price Provincial
Grand Master of the Free & Accepted Masons
of New England, to Constitute Us in a regular
Lodge, By Virtue of yᵉ power & Authority to him
given by a Deputation from Our Rᵗʰ Worspfull
& Worspfull Brother and Rᵗ Honᵇˡ Anthony
Lord Visco. Montague Grand Masters
of England Dated in London the 13ᵗʰ day
of Aprill A D 1733 And of Masonry A 5733
And sealed with yᵉ Seal of the Grand Lodge
Signed by Our Rᵗ Worspfull Brothers
George Rook Esqᵐ &c Gᵈ W. of England
James Moor Smith Esᵍ

FACSIMILE OF PAGE 4 OF BETEILHE MANUSCIPT

Our said Worshfull G.M. having formed a Grand Lodge, Appointing our R.t W.shfull. Bro. Andrew Belcher Esq. his Deputy G. M.r And our W.shfull Brethren Mess.rs Tho.s Kennelly & John Quane } Grand Wardens pro Tempore Ordered his Commission (or Deputation afores.d to be read, as also our Petition. And granting the prayer thereof, Did then & there in the most solemn manner, according to Ancient Right & Custom, And the Form prescribed in our printed book of Constitutions CONSTITUTE us into a Regular Lodge in Manner & Form, upon which we imediately proceeded (by our S.d R.t Worshfull. G.Master's Order) to Chuse a Master and unanimously Chose our W.shfull Bro. Henry Hope Esq.r Master of this our new Constituted Lodge. Who then Nominated & appointed our Worshfull Brethren M.r Fredemick Gramilton M.r James - Gordon - } his Wardens

3

= vide

FACSIMILE OF PAGE 5 OF BETEILHE MANUSCIPT

which all the Brethren unanimously
Concurred paying the Usuall respect to
our P Worshippull new chosen Master &
Wardens. And presenting them to our R
W full G Master. who Caused them to be
duely examined & being found well qualifye
Approved & Confirm'd them in their Severall
Stations. by Investing them with the Imple=
=ments of their Offices giving each his parti
=cular Charge And admonishing the Bret
=hren of the Lodge to due Obedience &
Submission. according to Our printed
book of Constitutions Charges and
Regulations &c

FACSIMILE OF PAGE 6 OF BETEILHE MANUSCRIPT

tion of a Lodge in America are herewith presented, reading as follows:

At a Special Chapter
of
Free & Accepted Masons

Regularly met & Congregated at the houfe of Edwd Lutwych at the Sign of the Bunch of grapes in King Street Boston, N. Engl^d On Munday July the 30th A.D: 1733 & of Mafonry A: 5733.

The following Brethren being regularly met in the Lodge at ye houfe afores^d unanimously agreed to petition, & did then accordingly petition Our Rt. Worfpl: Bro. Mr Henry Price Provincial Grand Master of the Free & Accepted Mafons of New England, to Constitute Us in a regular Lodge by virtue of ye power & authority to him given by a Deputation from Our Rt. Worfpfull & Worfpfull Brother and Rt. Honble Anthony Lord Visco^t Montague Grand Master of England Dated in London the 13th day of Aprill A.D. 1733 and of Mafonry A.5733 and sealed with ye Seal of the Grand Lodge
Signed by Our Rt. Worfpfull Brothers
George Rook Esqr
James Moor Smith Esqr } G.W. of England

Our said Worfpfull G.M. having formed a Grand Lodge, appointing our Rt. Worfpfull Bro. Andrew Belcher Esqr his Deputy G. M^r and our Worfpfull Brethren Meff^{rs}

Thos Kennelly
     &   } Grand Wardens pro Tempore
John Quane

Ordered his commifsion (or Deputation afores^d) to be read, as also our Petition. And granting the prayer thereof, Did then & there in the most Solemn manner, according to Ancient Right & Custom, and the form prescribed in our printed book of Constitutions

CONSTITUTE us into a Regular Lodge in Manner & form, upon which we imediately proceeded (by our S^d Rt. Worſpfull G. Master's Order) to choose a Master and unanimously choſe our Wſfull Bro. Henry Hope Esqr Master of this our new Constituted Lodge, Who then nominated & appointed our Worſpfull Brethren

Mr Frederick Hamilton $\left.\right\}$ his Wardens
Mr James Gordon

which all the Brethren unanimously concurred paying the usuall respects to our S^d Worshypful new chosen Master & Wardens. And presenting them to our R^t W :full G. Master, who caused them to be duely examined & being found well qualifye^d, approved & confirmed them in their severall stations by Investing them with the Implements of their Offices, giving each his particular Charge and admonishing the Brethren of the Lodge to due Obedience & Submiſsion according to our printed book of Constitutions Charges and Regulations &c.

NOTE. It is evident that preparations had been made in advance for this meeting. Jewels for the officers had been made ready. The occasion was elaborate and formal and followed the English ceremonial which Price had doubtless witnessed while in England. The installation was then, as now, made a part of the ceremony of constitution.

I regard it as demonstrated beyond question or cavil that Henry Price was, as he said himself, the Founder of Duly Constituted Masonry in America and that this First Lodge in Boston was the first regular and duly-constituted Lodge. But this Lodge had theretofore been meeting without any formal authority. No one knows, probably no one ever will know when a Lodge first met in America "according to the Old Customs" but without warrant, charter or lawful constitution. Neither Price

nor any one else has left us any information. What
Price did say was that the First Lodge in Boston was
"the oldest (or first Constituted) Regular Lodge in
America."

See page 332.

From personal association with the Brethren both in
England and America, Price knew whereof he spoke.
And our modern researches confirm his statements.

When Beteilhe says that, even before the petition, the
Brethren were "regularly met in the Lodge," he gives a
clear indication that they had been in the habit of meeting as a Lodge though without any "authority from
home."

1733, August 3,   Boston.
   Meeting of the First Lodge.   John Smith made.
      P.L.

1733, August 6,   Philadelphia.
   Entries in L. B. indicate a meeting.

1733, August 23,   Philadelphia.
   Account in *American Weekly Mercury* that at the Red
Lyon in Canterbury, England, "the celebrated Mr. Tay-
lor" was made a Mason.

1733, August 31,   Boston.
   This is the date of the constitution of the First Lodge
in Boston as given in the Robertson letter of September
1, 1736, and the Barons letter of June 23, 1736, *q.v.
infra.*

   But see, 1733, July 30, *supra.*

1733, September 3,   Philadelphia.
   Entries in L. B. indicate a meeting.

1733, September 12,   Boston.
   Meeting of the First Lodge.   Moses Slaughter and
Thomas Phillips made.
        P. L.

1733, September 29, Philadelphia.
   Entries in L. B. indicate a meeting.

1733, Autumn.
   Benjamin Franklin visited Boston and made the acquaintance of Henry Price.
        IV Gould, 235, *et cit.*
   It may have been that this conference between Price
and Franklin had something to do with that extension
of Price's power over all North America which was
granted to him from London in August of the next year.
(See Chapter VII.)
        1914 Mass. 256, *et cit.*
        1883 Mass. 189.
   Is it not probable that Franklin then obtained from
Price not only much Masonic instruction but also a copy
of the Constitutions which Franklin reprinted in May,
1734?

CHAPTER V,

HENRY PRICE

It is proper here to place on permanent record a brief biography of the life of Henry Price, the "Founder of Duly Constituted Masonry in America." He was born in London about the year 1697. The only information concerning his life prior to 1733 is obtained from his gravestone, except that it is recorded in the minutes of the Grand Lodge of England that in 1730 he was a member of Lodge No. 75, meeting at the Rainbow Coffee House in York Buildings.

X Q.C.A. xviii and 183.

This gravestone until 1888 stood in the old cemetery in Townsend, Massachusetts, a small town situate forty-six miles from Boston upon the border of Massachusetts and New Hampshire. The old burying place is about a mile from the centre of the town, on high land, surrounded by a forest of evergreens and on the northerly side of the County Road.

17 M.F.M. 11.

The stone having become badly cracked and in danger of total destruction, the Grand Lodge of Massachusetts, deeming that the spot where his remains rest should be commemorated by a more suitable monument, obtained in 1888 through the liberality of one of the citizens of Townsend a deed to a plot of land in the new cemetery in the same town, to which the remains of Henry Price were removed. The old gravestone was moved to the

Temple in Boston where it is now preserved. A reproduction of this stone taken where it stood in December, 1871, is herewith presented. In clearly defined letters thereon is the following epitaph:

(Human Face with Wings)
In Memory of
HENRY PRICE, Efq[r].
Was Born in London about the Year of our Lord
1697 he Remov'd to Bofton about the Year 1723 Rec[d]. a
Deputation Appointing him Grand Mafter of Mafons
in New England & in the Year 1733 was Appointed
a Cornet in the Governors Troop of Guards
With the Rank of Major by his Diligence & induftry
in Bufinefs he Acquired the means of a Comfortable Living with which he remov'd to Townfen[d]
in the latter Part of his Life. He quitted Mortality
the 20th of May A D 1780 Leaving a Widow & two Young
Daughters With a Numerous Company of Friends
and Acquaintance to Mourn his Departure Who
have that Ground of hope Concerning his Prefent
Lot Which Refults from his undifsembled Regard
to his Maker & extenfive Benevolence to his
Fellow Creatures Manifefted in Life by
a behaviour Confiftent With his Character
as a Mafon and his Nature as a Man
An honeft Man the Nobleft Work of God.

On June 21, 1888, Henry Endicott, as Grand Master of Masons in Massachusetts, dedicated the monument which now stands over his remains where they lie buried in the new cemetery.

In 1723 he was about twenty-six years of age. How long he remained in Boston after his first residence there is unknown. On April 13, 1733, he was in London for he that day received his deputation as Provincial Grand

Master of New England in person from Thomas Batson, Esquire, then Deputy Grand Master. On January 27, 1768, in a letter written by him to the Grand Lodge of England he says, "I myself paid three guineas therefor to Thomas Batson, Esquire, then Deputy Grand Master who with the Grand Wardens then in being signed my said deputation."

Sometime between April 13 and July 30, 1733, he returned to Boston and remained in this country the rest of his life, although August 6, 1755, he wrote a letter to the Grand Master of England in which he said, "I have some remote thoughts of once more seeing London, with all my Brethren in the Grand Lodge after twenty-two years' absence."

His Masonic career during the period covered by this book will be referred to frequently hereafter and in this chapter we shall for this period deal mainly with other facts of his life.

The first we can learn of him in Boston from any civil official record is to be found on the files of the Court of Common Pleas in Boston at its January term in the year 1733/4 when he brought suit against a debtor and is described in the writ as "Henry Price of Boston," etc., "taylor." At this time it was essential that a litigant's trade or profession should be accurately set forth in the writ; failure in this respect would abate the writ.

During the year 1733 Governor Jonathan Belcher appointed him Cornet in his Troup of Guards with the rank of Major and from that time he was known as Major Price. As late as 1792 his executors refer to him as Major Price and in the inventory of his effects, filed in the Probate Court within a month after his decease, appear a red jacket, red breeches, housing and holsters,

ORIGINAL STONE OVER GRAVE OF HENRY PRICE
From a Photograph taken December 1871.

a pair of horse pistols, spurs, sword, belt and silver-hilted sword. These undoubtedly were his military uniform. The office was that of standard-bearer in the Governor's troop of cavalry. Special privileges were accorded by law to the gentlemen of the Governor's troop and additional favors to its officers. In those days any military commission gave prominence and high respectability to the individual honoured with it; but to hold an official position in the select body-guard of His Majesty's Captain General and Governor of New England was considered an especial favour, and of itself conferred honourable social distinction.

Price carried on his business at the sign of the Brazen Head on Cornhill at a point which is now on Washington Street about half-way between Water Street and State Street and opposite William Court. The great fire of 1760 began in this building, then occupied by Mrs. Mary Jackson and William, her son, as a dwelling house and store.

In 1736 Price formed a partnership with Francis Beteilhe, to whom reference has already been made, and who was closely associated with Price in Masonry as well as in business. Beteilhe was the shopkeeper, while Price carried on the tailoring establishment.

About 1739 they apparently gave up tailoring, for after this time he and his partner are described as shopkeepers until the firm was dissolved in 1741 when Price assumed sole control of the business, after the failure of the health of Beteilhe, and carried it on for some time at the corner of Pond and Newbury Streets, now the corner of Bedford and Washington Streets. Price owned a large lot of land on the southerly side of what is now Bedford Street upon which were a brick store and dwelling house while part of the premises was used as a garden.

In 1740 Price purchased for £1000 a lot of land with buildings thereon situated on the northerly side of King Street, now State Street. When Price purchased this estate there was a wooden building upon it but before November, 1744, he completed the erection upon the lot of a brick dwelling which was begun in the spring; and upon his application the Selectmen gave him permission to erect a sign post in King Street opposite his store. It was the usual custom in those days for a storekeeper to occupy the upper part of the building as a dwelling house with his family. This Price did. He dealt in clothing and dry goods and apparently was very successful, for in 1750 he retired. After this he did not engage in any occupation so far as can be learned but we do know that he possessed a great amount of real estate.

In 1737 Major Price became engaged to Miss Mary Townsend, then seventeen years of age, a daughter of Samuel Townsend of Boston, who died in 1720. She was possessed of some property. In May, 1737, her uncle, James Townsend of Boston, was appointed her guardian. He was bitterly opposed to the marriage, although we do not know the reason. It may have been due to religious differences, for Price was an Episcopalian and Townsend a rigid Puritan. The Puritans of those days were bitter in their opposition to those who followed the religion of the prayer-book. When on July 25, 1737, Henry Price and Mary Townsend were duly published according to the then custom, her Uncle James forbade the banns. His opposition did not prevent the marriage, however, which took place in the fall of 1737, and in October, 1738, a daughter Mary was born to them. Uncle James died in 1738, leaving an estate appraised at £21,000—large for those days. By his will he left public and private bequests but his niece, Mary Price, was not remembered.

In 1739 Price and his partner brought suit against one William Wesson, describing the defendant as a "housewright." Wesson came into court by his attorney and pleaded in abatement that he was a "joyner" and not a "housewright," and the writ was ordered abated. A new action was thereafter brought describing Wesson as "joyner" and the plaintiffs prevailed.

In 1740 Price and his wife Mary sold her interest in a lot of land on Savage's Court in Boston.

In 1742, as a result of an execution levied upon the property of one Thomas Phillips of Boston, in a suit brought by Price, the Major became possessed of the Hartshorn Farm, so-called, and certain other real estate in Townsend, where some years later he made his home.

In 1746 Price purchased a piece of land "with the edifices and buildings thereon situated, at a place called Menotomy Fields, in Cambridge." This is now the town of Arlington and Price made his summer residence on this estate, situated on the great highway from Lexington to Concord, over which years afterward the British troops marched to burn the provincial stores in those towns.

It appears by the records of the Grand Lodge that on April 12, 1751, Brother Price made an offer of the use of his house at Menotomy for the celebration of the Feast of St. John the Baptist, and it was voted that the celebration be held at his house and that the Brethren proceed there in regular procession. When the day came, however, the Brethren went in procession to the house of Mr. Richardson in Cambridge, "Brother Price's house at

Menotomy being encumbered by sickness." The sickness must have been somewhat serious for it is not recorded that Brother Price attended the Feast. Probably it was the illness of his wife Mary, for we have reason to believe that she died about that time.

April 29, 1752, the banns of Henry Price and Mary Tilden, both of Boston, were published and they were married by the rector of Trinity Church on the 25th of May following. Major Price owned half a pew in this church which he held at the time of his decease. In 1750 Price became a member of the Boston Episcopal Charitable Society, instituted in 1724, the second oldest charitable foundation in New England.

During Price's Grand Lodge activity the Episcopal clergymen of Boston and Newburyport frequently officiated and preached sermons before the Grand Lodge upon the Feast Days of St. John the Baptist and St. John the Evangelist, at Trinity and Christ churches in Boston. This was undoubtedly due to the influence of Price, because the general feeling in Boston was hostile to those who adhered to the "religion of the prayer-book."

After Price retired from business in 1750 we find him several times described in writs, deeds and instruments as "gentleman," thus indicating that he no longer followed what was then technically known as the "mystery or degree" of any calling.

Until 1755 he continued to be a resident of Boston, passing the summer season at his country seat in Cambridge.

After his second marriage he either greatly enlarged or entirely rebuilt his house at Menotomy and increased its extent so that his lands stretched out down to the pond, and extended them on both sides of the highway with barns, stables, and everything necessary to the comfortable home of a gentleman and his family. The house was so large that it was generally called the "great house."

In 1755 he took up his permanent residence at Cambridge with his wife and daughter Mary, then about seventeen years of age. He was rich for the times and evidently looked forward to many years of comfort upon this pleasant estate.

In 1759 or 1760 his wife died, followed by the death of his only daughter on October 8, 1760. From then on he lost all interest in his Cambridge home and immediately moved again to Boston. Just thirty-two days after his daughter's death he sold the estate at Menotomy.

After a year or two of residence in Boston he moved to Townsend where he continued to reside until his death. Shortly after moving to Townsend he was chosen to represent that town in the Provincial Legislature in 1764 and 1765. Townsend had not had a representative in the Legislature prior to 1764 for nineteen years. He served upon many committees and evidently became Townsend's leading citizen.

On September 17, 1771, he married again, his third wife being Lydia Randall, a resident of Townsend, who was a widow with a minor son by the name of John Abbott. Their marriage articles—what we now call an ante-nuptial settlement—were made on September 6, 1771. Two children were the offspring of this marriage, Mary and Rebecca, both of whom survived their father.

His estate at Townsend was a large one, embracing several farms, with buildings, mills, mill privileges, mechanical shops, wood lots and hundreds of acres.

He was too old to be a participant in the Revolutionary War but on May 14, 1779, shows his loyalty by adding after the day and year of a conveyance, the words "and third year of the independence of the United States of America."

On May 14, 1780, while splitting rails, his axe glanced and struck him in the abdomen, inflicting a severe and fatal wound. He evidently realized he could not live for his last will and testament was executed on the next day. On the 20th of the same month he died at the age of eighty-three years.

He left what was for those days a large estate. Unfortunately it was afterward greatly impaired by law suits and defective titles and by the devastations consequent upon the War of the Revolution. His will, still on the files of the Registry of the Probate Court for the County of Middlesex in Massachusetts, exhibits clearness of intellect and comprehension as well as his religious character. Indeed at the time of his death he possessed three pews in meeting houses not of his religious faith.

His daughter Mary in 1787 married William Wallis (Wallace) of Pepperell and descendants of the family remained residents of the vicinity until about 1860. His daughter Rebecca was married April 21, 1788, to George Farrar of Townsend. No descendants are known. His widow, Mrs. Lydia Price, married for her third husband Lieutenant Levi Whitney, of Shrewsbury, on November 13, 1780. They lived for many years thereafter upon the Price Homestead.

During his life Major Price had a black servant, probably a slave, called Scipio. He, although lame and infirm from old age, was supported by the estate in suitable comfort for many years.

The records show that during his life Major Price was possessed of real estate in Boston, Hull, Cambridge, Woburn, Concord, Sherburne and Townsend in Massachusetts, as well as in towns in New Hampshire, Rhode Island and Connecticut, fully justifying the inscription on the gravestone that "by his diligence and industry in business, he acquired the means of a comfortable living."

For further details of his life, reference is made to the exhaustive address by the Grand Master of Massachusetts published in the Printed Proceedings of that Grand Lodge for December 27, 1871, from which quotations have been freely made. Also 1883 Mass. 150; 1888 Mass. 90, 107; 1891 Mass. 19; 1899 Mass. 50; 1903 Mass. 44; 1906 Mass. 74; 1909 Mass. 105; 1914 Mass. 253; 1916 Mass. 310.

Price served as Provincial Grand Master not only from his appointment until 1737 but also from July, 1740, to March 6, 1743/4; from July 12, 1754, to October 1, 1755; from October 20, 1767, to November 23, 1768.

During intervening periods he was charter Master of the Masters Lodge and of the Second Lodge in Boston, and Master of the First Lodge. He presided over the Grand Lodge as late as April 30, 1773, in the absence of Grand Master John Rowe, although he then lived over forty miles distant and was seventy-six years of age. His last recorded attendance at Grand Lodge was January 28, 1774.

The portrait of Henry Price, used as the frontispiece

of this book, may be regarded as a real portrait. On
September 29, 1857, M. W. John T. Heard, then Grand
Master of Masons in Massachusetts, visited Townsend,
accompanied by the Grand Wardens and Grand Secretary. They found there William Wallace (Wallis) the
fourth son of Mary who was the daughter of Henry
Price by his third wife. Wallace was then a bachelor
sixty-six years of age, living alone in a small 10' x 12'
single room cottage. M. W. Brother Heard had been in
correspondence with William Wallace in 1856, and had
obtained from him a portrait painted of Henry Price
in 1737, when he was forty years old. This portrait
was in such a shattered state that its restoration was
despaired of. It was, however, placed in the hands of
an eminent artist, Bro. George Howarth, and M. W.
Winslow Lewis informs us that, by the skill of Brother
Howarth, the picture was made as good as new. It
was presented to the Grand Lodge December 30, 1856,
and by order of M. W. Bro. Lewis, was placed in the
west of the Grand Lodgeroom, there remaining until the
fire of April 6, 1864, at which time it was utterly
destroyed.

1888 Mass. 96.
1857 Mass. 53.
17 M.F.M. 11.

Previously, however, a lithographic copy had been
made for use as the frontispiece to the Book of Constitutions in 1857. Fortunately, also, a copy had been
painted for Henry Price Lodge,

1897 Mass. 103

and this copy still hangs in the ante-room to its lodge-
room in Charlestown, Massachusetts. From this copy,
a steel engraving was made which was used by M. W.

Bro. Gardner with his elaborate historical address to which reference has hereinbefore been made.

1871 Mass. 284-393.

Because of the availability of two copies made from the original painting (one of them being in colors) a real portrait of Price was painted in 1914 and now hangs in the West of the Massachusetts Grand Lodge-room. The hand-carved frame bears the pomegranate, lotus and seven-eared wheat which have immemorially been indicia of the Grand Master's office.

1914 Mass. 171.

Chapter VI

BOSTON—PHILADELPHIA—GEORGIA

1733, October 24,   Boston.

The First Lodge adopted its "By-Laws or Regulations."

> O.R.
> B.MS. 7-12.
> 1883 Mass. 159.

These are so quaint and interesting as to be worth quoting. They read as follows:

Ist No Person shall be made a Mason unlefs all the Brethren members Prefent are Unanimous and if but one Member be against him he shall be rejected.

II^{ly} No Brother shall be admitted as Member of this Lodge unlefs all the Members Prefent are unanimous as aforesaid and upon his or their admifsion shall pay twenty shillings, as also their Quarteridge, agreable to a former Vote, so many Lodge nights as is past of that Quarter to be first discounted, and shall consent to the by Laws and regulations of this Lodge by Subscribing their names to the same.

III^{ly} No Brother or Brothers shall shall (*sic*) eat any victuals in the Lodge Room while the Lodge is open, without the leave of the Mafter or Wardens nor call for any Liquor or Tobacco without Leave as aforesaid.

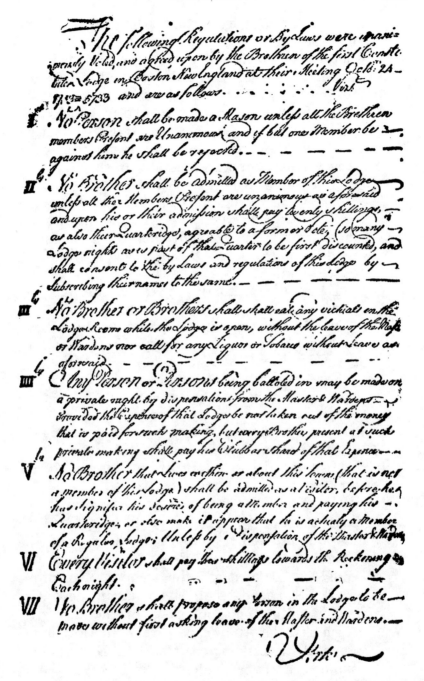

FACSIMILE OF RECORD OF BY-LAWS OF FIRST LODGE IN BOSTON

IIII^ly   Any Person or Persons being balloted in may be made on a private night by dispensation from the Master & Wardens Provided the Expence of that Lodge be not taken out of the money that is paid for such making, but every Brother present at such private making shall pay his Clubb or share of that Expence.

V^ly   No Brother that Lives within or about this Town (that is not a member of this Lodge) shall be admitted as a Visitor, before he has Signified his desire of being a Member and paying his Quarteridge, or else make it appear that he is actualy a Member of a Regular Lodge; Unlefs by a Dispenfation of the Master & Wardens.

VI   Every Visitor shall pay three shillings towards the Reckoning Each night.

VII   No Brother shall propose any Person in the Lodge to be made without first asking leave of the Mafter and Wardens.

VIII^thly   Every Member of this Lodge shall pay eighteen shillings pr Quarter for the Expense of the Lodge, and every member that does not pay his Quarteridge on the first Lodge night of the Quarter, or on the second at farthest (if Prefent) shall be Excluded from being a Member, and all Privilidge of the Lodge.

IX^thly   Every Member shall pay at Least two shillings more pr Qrd. to be applied as Charity Towards the Relief of poor Brethren.

X^thly   Any Member that proposes a Candidate, if Voted or Balloted in; the member that proposed his friend, shall immediately deposite fourty shillings in the hands of the Cashire, which shall be Allow'd as part of the Making, provided the candidate attends at the time he is proposed to be made, but if the candidate does not attend as aforesaid, being duly warned, the said Fourty shillings shall be forfeited and spent and not allowed as part of that making.

XI[thly] The Treasurer or Cashier of this Lodge, upon his quitting his office or when another is chosen in his room, shall render a just and true Accot to the Master & Wardens of the Lodge for the time being of all the money Rec[d], Expended & Remaining in his hands with the Lodge book & Accompts which he is to deliver up to the Master and Wardens in order & fairly stated.

XII[thly] The Master & Wardens of this Lodge shall take care that the Expence of a Lodge night (when there is no making) shall not Exceed three shillings pr Member prefent for the Reconing which sum of three shillings p[r] member or Bro[r] present, the Cashire has Liberty to pay & no more.

XIII[thly] The Master of this Lodge, or in absence, the Grand Master Deputy Grand Master or Wardens, when there is a private Lodge ordered to be held for a Making shall be obliged to give all the Members timely notice of the time and place in writing where such Lodge is held that they may give their attend[ce] and every member being duly warned as aforesaid and neglecting to attend on such Private making shall not be clothed. (The above article Voted Nov: 14th: 1733: 5733).

XIV[thly] No member that is absent from the Lodge of a Lodge night when there is a making, shall have the Benefit of being cloathed for that time.

"Being cloathed" refers to the very ancient custom, now forgotten, of requiring the candidate to furnish each member present with an apron and a pair of white gloves.

1733, November 5, Philadelphia.

L. B. charges the entrance fees of Lambert Emerson, Thomas Hopkinson, and John Newingham.

1733, November 9,   Boston.

Meeting of the First Lodge. Peter Prescott and Benjamin Brenton made.
          P. L.

1733, November 14,   Boston.

Meeting of the First Lodge.
          See 1733, October 24, XIII^thly, *supra*.

1733, November 19,   Boston.

Meeting of the First Lodge. Robert McLean made.
          P. L.
                    Philadelphia.
L. B. charges the entrance fee of Christopher Routh.

1733, December 3,   Philadelphia.

Entries in L. B. indicate a meeting.

1733, December 13, London—Georgia.

The minutes of the Communication of the Grand Lodge of England record:

"Then the Deputy Grand Master opened to the Lodge the affairs of planting the new Colony of Georgia in America, and having sent an account in print of the nature of such plantation to all the Lodges, informed the Grand Lodge that the Trustees had to Nathaniel Blackerby, Esq., and to himself commissions under their Common Seal to collect the charity of this Society towards enabling the Trustees to send distressed brethren to Georgia where they may be comfortably provided for.

Proposed that it be strenuously recommended by the Masters and Wardens of regular Lodges to make a generous collection amounst all their members for that purpose.

White being seconded by Bro. Rogers Holland, Esq. (one of the said Trustees) who opened the nature of the settlement, and by Sir William Keith, Bart, who was many years governor of Pennsylvania, by Dr. Desagulier, Lord Southwell, Bro. Blackerby and many other very worthy Brethren, it was recommended accordingly."

It is known that poor families were sent to Georgia and that the Fraternity contributed toward their relief. The terms of the vote are to *send* poor brethren to Georgia, not to help any one already there.

> X Q.C.A. 235.
> Mackey 1518.

See 1730, *supra*, and 1735, after October 30, *infra*.

1733, December 22, Norfolk, Virginia.

The learned R.W. Brother John Dove, of Virginia, contended that the Royal Exchange Lodge at Norfolk, Va., was established on this date. On several official lists it so appears, being first found upon the list for 1754, near its close, as No. 236. In all lists, however, it is with the 1753 Lodges, following No. 235 accredited to December 20, 1753, and preceding No. 237 accredited to February 9, 1754. It was carried on the lists until the 1813 revision becoming numbers 173, 137, 111, 112, and 102.

> O.L.
> L.M.R. 101.
> L.H.B. 48.

It is evident that 1753 is correct, and that 1733 is an error.

IV Gould, 378.

The information which Brother Dove had led him to suspect at one time that Blandford Lodge at Petersburg, Va., was founded about this time by the Grand Lodge of Scotland. He was misinformed. Blandford Lodge is given in the Scottish list as No. 82, whereas Saint Andrew's Lodge at Boston (1756) is No. 81.

P.C. (1st Edinburgh Ed. 1761) Appendix 112.

Const. G. L. of Scotland (1852 Ed.) 63.

The correct date for Blandford Lodge is probably March 9, 1756. In later editions of his history Brother Dove assigned it to 1757.

1733, December 28,   Boston.

The Feast of Saint John the Evangelist was celebrated in Boston and James Gordon was chosen Master of the First Lodge.

1 Mass. 4.

1733/4, January 7, Philadelphia.

L. B. charges the entrance fee of Richard Howell.

1733/4, January 19, Philadelphia.

L. B. charges the entrance fee of John Waugh.

1733/4, February 4, Philadelphia.

Entries in L. B. indicate a meeting.

1733/4, February 10,   Georgia.

A Lodge met in Georgia, probably, for the first time this day.

See 1735, after October 30, *infra*.

1733/4, February 27,   Boston.
   Meeting of the First Lodge.   William Walker made.
      P.L.

1733/4, March 4,   Philadelphia.
   Entries in L. B. indicate a meeting.

1733/4, March 18, London—Georgia.
   The following was this day adopted by the Grand
Lodge of England:

"Resolved that all the Masters of all regular Lodges
who shall not bring in their contribution of charity, do
at the next quarterly communication give the reasons
why their respective Lodges do not contribute to the
settlement of Georgia."
      O.R.

It is now reasonably certain that, beginning shortly
before this date, a Lodge was doing Masonic work in
Georgia.
      See 1735, after October 30, *infra*.

1734, March 29,   Boston.
   The *Boston Gazette* for April 1, 1734, contains the
following item:

Annapolis Royal, Embark'd from hence for that Place with
Capt. *Peter Blin*.
   On Friday Evening laſt at Mr. *Lutwytche's* long Room in
King-Street, was held a Grand-Lodge of the Ancient and Hon-
ourable Society of Free and Accepted Maſons where His Excel-
lency Governor BELCHER, and a conſiderable Number of the
Fraternity were preſent.
   Capt. *Woodbury* on Friday laſt Arrived here in about 14 Days

ITEM FROM *Boston Gazette* FOR APRIL 1, 1735.

      P–t.

1734, April 1,   Philadelphia.

L. B. charges the entrance fee of Isaac Browne and James Hamilton.

1734, May 6,   Philadelphia.

L. B. charges the entrance fee of Joseph Shippen.

1734, May 16,   Philadelphia.

Benjamin Franklin first advertises in the *Pennsylvania Gazette* his reprint of the Constitutions.

> Benjamin Franklin as a Freemason (Sachse), 3. S. & H. 222.

They were not ready for delivery until August, when he sent seventy copies to Boston. Later in the year he sent still more copies to his brother James in Boston by the hand of his brother Peter.

> F. J.

The few copies of this book known are in the libraries of the Grand Lodges of Pennsylvania, New York, Iowa, and Massachusetts; of the Historical Society of Pennsylvania, of the University of Pennsylvania, and of the Southern Supreme Council, 33°. One perfect copy belonging to Massachusetts is bound with the Beteilhe Manuscript. When they were put together no one knows. They were purchased by the Grand Lodge of Massachusetts in this condition. The Grand Lodge of Massachusetts also owns a copy bearing the autograph upon the title page of William Walker who was made in the First Lodge in Boston, February 27, 1733/4.

1734, May 22,   Boston.

Meeting of the First Lodge in Boston. William Wesson made and Brother Benjamin Pemberton, Esq. admitted.

> P.L.
> B.MS.

1734, June 3, Philadelphia.

L. B. charges the entrance fees of Thomas Bond, William Pyewell, and John Robinson.

1734, June 12, Boston.

Meeting of the First Lodge. Brother Andrew Scott admitted.

P.L.

1734, June 24, Boston.

Celebration of the Feast of Saint John the Baptist and election of Frederick Hamilton as Master of the Lodge.

1 Mass. 4.

The original manuscript of the address delivered upon this occasion is in the archives of the Grand Lodge of Massachusetts. It was printed in full in 8 M.F.M. 289.

There have been those who believed that Benjamin Franklin was present at this meeting (1914 Mass. 256). It would seem, from the event recorded later under this date, that such was not the case. It is the fact, however, that before this time he had visited Boston and become acquainted with Pro. G.M. Henry Price who conferred with him about Masonic matters and laid the foundation for the petition which was sent Price later from Philadelphia.

See pages 91 and 124.

Philadelphia.

The *Pennsylvania Gazette* for June 27, 1734, publishes an account of a Grand Lodge meeting at the Tun Tavern, Philadelphia, this day at which Benjamin Franklin was elected Grand Master. Again distinguished guests honored the entertainment by their presence. The *Gazette* article was copied by the *Saint James Evening Post* for September 3rd, and by *Read's Weekly Journal* for September 7, 1734, both of London.

1734, June 26,   Boston.

Meeting of the First Lodge. Brother Noe Tyler admitted.

    P.L.

1734, July 1,   Philadelphia.

L. B. charges the entrance fees of William Plumsted and Septimus Robinson.

1734, July 24,   Boston.

Meeting of the First Lodge. Francis Beteilhe made.
    P.L.

1734, August 5,   Philadelphia.

L. B. charges the entrance fee of Joseph Breintnall.

1734, August 14,   Boston.

Meeting of the First Lodge. Brothers Hugh Scott and John Young admitted.

    P.L.
    B.MS.
    Barons Letter.

CHAPTER VII

THE FIRST PROVINCIAL GRAND MASTER OF NORTH AMERICA

1734, August,   Boston.

Provincial Grand Master Henry Price's authority was extended over all North America by the Earl of Crawfurd, Grand Master of England.

    1914 Mass. 256-273, *et cit.*, 284.

    1733, April 13, *supra.*

    1734, November 28, *infra.*

    1734/5, February 21, *infra.*

    1871 Mass. 284 *et seq.*

    1883 Mass. 150 *et seq.*

    1888 Mass. 107 *et seq.*

    1891 Mass. 19 *et seq.*

    1899 Mass. 50 *et seq.*

    1903 Mass. 44 *et seq.*

    1906 Mass. 74 *et seq.*

    1909 Mass. 105 *et seq.*

The citations here given refer to many authorities for the statement that Price's jurisdiction was extended over all North America, as reviewed by Gardner, Nickerson, myself and others. Much additional evidence keeps coming to light, among which are the following: An original letter has recently been found in the archives of the Grand Lodge of Massachusetts from Thomas Durant, then Secretary of the Lodge of Portsmouth, N. H., dated April 5, 1755, under the seal of the Lodge and directed to "Henry Price, Esq., Grand

Master of the Lodges of Free and Accepted Masons in North America." On the same files is an original summons sent by John Leverett, then Secretary of the Second Lodge in Boston, dated September 18, 1754, in which he states that he has received orders to summon a Grand Lodge "from our R. W. Brother Mr. Henry Price, Provincial Grand Master of North America which reverts to him by the death of our R. W. Brother Thomas Oxnard, Esq., deceased." The original records of the Lodge at Portsmouth, now in its possession, contain confirmatory references when recording Price's visits to that Lodge on February 12, 1756/7; March 24, June 9, 1768; and October 26, 1769.

In line with the methods of keeping, or rather not keeping records in those days, the Grand Lodge of England had apparently not recorded Price's Commission as extended, with the result that his first successor (Tomlinson) had his deputation for New England only. Oxnard was commissioned in 1743 for the whole of North America, however, and when Oxnard died the Provincial Grand Lodge in Boston on October 11, 1754, voted that a petition be sent to the Grand Master of England for the appointment of his successor, also to be Grand Master of North America. That petition is recorded in full in the Massachusetts records. (1 Mass. 35.) See page 330. Its last paragraph is as follows:

"And Whereas Masonry Originated Here anno 5733, and in the year following Our then G. M. Price received orders from G. M. Craufurd to Establish Masonry in all North America in Pursuance of which the Several Lodges hereafter mentioned have received Constitutions from us. We therefore Crave due Precedency, & that in order thereunto Our GM Elect, may in his Deputa-

tion be stiled GM of all North America, and your Petitioners as in duty Bound shall ever Pray."
See page 369.

This petition set out also the dates of the constitution of Lodges in other colonies subordinate to Price,
including Pennsylvania, as follows:

5734 Philadelphia.
   35 New Hampshire & South Carolina.
   38 Antigua and Annapolis in Nova Scotia.
   46 Newfoundland.
   49 Rhode Island.
   50 Hallifax in Nova Scotia.
   50 Annapolis in Maryland.
   53 New London in Connecticut.
   54 Middletown in Connecticut.
   52 New Haven in Connecticut.

The petition was signed by the following Brethren
as a Committee, viz.:

Hugh McDaniel.
Benjamin Hallowell.
Charles Brockwell.
James Forbes.
Robert Jenkins.
William Coffin.
Henry Leddell.

Is it conceivable that this petition did not truly represent the facts? Henry Price was in the chair and not
one word of suspicion has ever attached to him. Bro.
Benjamin Franklin was present. (1 Mass. 34.) The
Brethren at that meeting and those who formed the
Committee which drafted the petition were well acquainted with the history of Masonry in those times.

Of those who signed it:

McDaniel was made a Mason January 30, 1735 (1 Mass. 398), and rose to D.G.M. in 1737 (1 Mass. 6). He was the accredited representative of Philadelphia to the Grand Lodge in Boston. (1 Mass. 20.)

Hallowell was made a Mason January 23, 1735 (1 Mass. 398), and rose to D. G. M. in 1753. (1 Mass. 27.)

Brockwell was a clergyman, made a Mason January 28, 1746 (1 Mass. 400), and rose to S. G. W. in 1753. (1 Mass. 9, 10, 27, 388.)

Forbes was made a Mason November 20, 1735 (1 Mass. 398), and rose to D. G. M. in 1756. (1 Mass. 44.)

Jenkins was made a Mason July 25, 1739 (1 Mass. 399), and rose to D. G. M. in 1757. (1 Mass. 48.)
            1923 R.I. 64.

Coffin was made a Mason August 8, 1744 (1 Mass. 399), and rose to S. G. W. in 1758. (1 Mass. 53.)

Leddell was made a Mason October 11, 1749 (1 Mass. 400), and rose to M. of the First Lodge in 1752 (1 Mass. 24), and of the Masters Lodge in 1755. (1 Mass. 36.)

They were all close associates of Henry Price and so constant in attendance upon Masonic functions that their names appear literally hundreds of times in the first volume of the printed Proceedings of the Grand Lodge of Massachusetts. Among those voting in favor of the resolution was apparently Benjamin Franklin himself. Of the others voting, Rowe was made a Mason July 23, 1740 (1 Mass. 399), and had been Master of the First Lodge in 1748 (1 Mass. 9); Leverett, passed F. C. October 11, 1749 (1 Mass. 400), having been made abroad, Junior Warden of the same in 1750 (1 Mass. 11); Williams, made May 29, 1746 (1 Mass. 400), Junior Warden of the Masters Lodge in 1750 (1 Mass. 11); Byard, made May 11, 1748 (1 Mass. 400), Senior Warden of the First Lodge in 1750 (1 Mass. 10); Erving, Junior Warden of the same in 1753 (1 Mass. 25); Pelham, made November 8, 1738 (1 Mass. 399), Junior Warden of the Third Lodge in Boston in 1750 (1 Mass. 10); Tyler, made February 11, 1749 (1 Mass. 401), Junior Warden of the First Lodge in Boston in 1752 (1 Mass. 19); Gridley, made January 22, 1745 (1 Mass. 400), was also present at the Grand Lodge, and while at this meeting was elected for nomination as Provincial Grand Master of North America. Ezekiel Price was Junior Warden of the Third Lodge in Boston in 1752 (1 Mass. 20); Stowe had been present at the Grand Lodge as early as 1753 (1 Mass. 26), though I have not his official Masonic record; and Holbrook was Junior Warden of the Second Lodge in Boston in 1752 (1 Mass. 22). Many of them rose to exalted Masonic station. It cannot seriously be contended that these men did not know the facts about which they were talking.

No court in the world would decline to believe the evidence of the men named, who had first-hand knowledge of events of which they were contemporaries and of which indeed they were a part. See further, 1734, November 28, *infra*.

1734, August 19,   Boston.

Franklin's Constitutions are advertised in the *Weekly Rehearsal*.

P–t.

1734, August 15, Philadelphia—Lancaster—Boston—
Carolina.

The following entries are found in Franklin's Journal:

"Omitted 15s For postage 6 by Reynells to
Lancaster
For postage of Commission etc. 11s.4d.&
2s.8d.   14
For Constitutions sent to Boston 70, Caro-
lina 25   11.17.6

                 F.J.   13.11.10"

1734, August 31
"For 3 Constitutions by John Cather-
Wood, Lan^{er} County   7.6
For 1 Do. to Morgan Sexton   2.6"
           F.J.

Another entry, apparently under August, 1734, is as
follows:

FACSIMILE OF TWO PAGES

OF FRANKLIN'S JOURNAL

Brother Sachse says that this refers to Louis Timothee of Charleston, South Carolina, who was sent by Franklin to Charleston to take charge of the printing office established there in 1731 by Bro. Thomas Whitemarsh of St. John's Lodge, who had been equipped with a printer's outfit and sent out by Franklin.

Our curiosity is greatly excited by these entries. We can demonstrate the presence in Boston of only about thirty Brethren. Why *seventy* books? Six more were sent "by Brother Peter" (page 122) and within three months Franklin thought that more might be wanted (page 126). In the improbable event that every brother bought a copy, there must have been more Masons in Boston than we have suspected.

And why were twenty-five or thirty-one books sent to Carolina? I cannot, on known facts, answer. Probably a Lodge "according to the Old Customs."

1734, September.

Above the last two entries from Franklin's Journal appears the following:

"Lodge of Mason's at Br. Hubards Dr.
For tickets	5
For tickets	4.3.4
Sept. 1734 For a finely gilded constitution to the Proprietor	5
For one Do. for the Lodge	5 "

It is a puzzle which I have not been able to solve to account for the entries upon the page in question. The page starts out with a charge to Isaac Brown for a Mason Book on June 11, 1736, and continues with Brown's account down to September of the following year. Thus the charges against the Lodge of Masons, which are apparently in 1734, follow entries two years later, while on the same page below the date supposed to be August 15, 1734, are items against one John Fruin dated 1731.

On the opposite page of the Journal are found entries against the Lodge in 1736-7. Upon some date of which I am not certain but which is apparently about this time, there is an entry for 100 catechisms and 6 Mason books, "sent to Broth. James by Brother Peter." This probably refers to books sent to Boston.

1734, September 4,   Boston.

Meeting of the First Lodge. Robert Kenton made and Brother John Lyle admitted.

    P.L.
    B.MS.
    Barons Letter.

1734, September,   Montserrat.

The *American Weekly Mercury* for December 24, 1734, recites under date of "London, October 1," that "the Earl of Craufurd, Grand Maſter of the Siciety (*sic*) of Free-Maſons, hath ſign'd an Inſtrument for eſtablishing a Lodge of Maſons in the Iſland of Montſerat."

    P–t.

1734, October 7,   Philadelphia.

Entries in L. B. indicate a meeting.

1734, October 8,   Philadelphia.

On this date Franklin charges Philip Syng for binding a Mason book 1.6.

    F.J.

1734, October 9,   Georgia.

Lodge meeting at which Sir Patrick Houstoun was made.

See page 143, *infra*.

1734, October 23,   Boston.

The Provincial Grand Lodge at Boston wrote a letter to Benjamin Franklin. Unfortunately we have no indication whatever of its contents except that it referred to Price's recovery from an illness.

1914 Mass. 283.

1734, November,   Philadelphia.

Franklin's Journal contains the following entries:

"Mr. Thomas Penn, Proprietor.
 For a book of Constitution   6.0
 James Bingham for Binding a Mason book 1.6
 Mr. Newingham for binding a Mason book gilt 4.0
 Edward Evans for a Mason book 2.6"
  F.J.

1734, November 7,   Philadelphia.

L. B. charges the entrance fees of Josiah Rolfe and Philip Syng.

1734, November 13,   Boston.

Meeting of the First Lodge. Richard Patteshall and Samuel Curwen made.

  P.L.
  B.MS.
  Barons Letter.

CHAPTER VIII

FRANKLIN'S APPOINTMENT AS PROVINCIAL GRAND MASTER FOR THE PROVINCE OF PENNSYLVANIA

1734, November 28, Philadelphia.

On this day Benjamin Franklin as the head of what he calls the "Grand Lodge" for the Province of Pennsylvania, wrote two letters to Price—one official and one personal. They read as follows:

Right Worshipful Grand Master and Most Worthy and Dear Brethren:

We acknowledge your favor of the 23d of October past, and rejoice that the Grand Master (whom God bless) hath so happily recovered from his late indisposition: and we now, glass in hand, drink to the establishment of his health, and the prosperity of your whole Lodge.

We have seen in the Boston prints an article of news from London, importing that at a Grand Lodge held there in August last, Mr. Price's deputation and power was extended over all America, which advice we hope is true, and we heartily congratulate him thereupon and though this has not been as yet regularly signified to us by you, yet, giving credit thereto, we think it our duty to lay before your Lodge what we apprehend needful to be done for us, in order to promote and strengthen the interest of Masonry in this Province (which seems to want the sanction of some authority derived from home, to give the proceedings and determina-

124

tions of our Lodge their due weight) to wit, a Deputation or Charter granted by the Right Worshipful Mr. Price, by virtue of his Commission from Britain, confirming the Brethren of Pennsylvania in the privileges they at present enjoy of holding annually their Grand Lodge, choosing their Grand Master, Wardens and other officers, who may manage all affairs relating to the Brethren here with full power and authority, according to the customs and usages of Masons, the said Grand Master of Pennsylvania only yielding his chair, when the Grand Master of all America shall be in place. This, if it seems good and reasonable to you to grant, will not only be extremely agreeable to us, but will also, we are confident, conduce much to the welfare, establishment, and reputation of Masonry in these parts. We therefore submit it for your consideration, and, as we hope our request will be complied with, we desire that it may be done as soon as possible, and also accompanied with a copy of the R. W. Grand Master's first Deputation, and of the instrument by which it appears to be enlarged as above-mentioned, witnessed by your Wardens, and signed by the Secretary; for which favours this Lodge doubt not of being able to behave as not to be thought ungrateful.

We are, Right Worshipful Grand Master and Most Worthy Brethren,

Your Affectionate Brethren and obliged humble Servts, Signed at the request of the Lodge,

B. FRANKLIN, G. M.

Philadelphia, Nov. 28, 1734.

DEAR BROTHER PRICE:—I am glad to hear of your recovery. I hoped to have seen you here this Fall, agreeable to the expectation you were so good as to give me; but since sickness has prevented your coming while the weather was moderate, I have no room to flatter myself with a visit from you before the Spring, when a deputation of the Brethren here will have an opportunity of showing how much they esteem you. I beg leave to recommend their request to you, and to inform you, that some false and rebel Brethren, who are foreigners, being about to set up a distinct Lodge in opposition to the old and true Brethren here, pretending to make Masons for a bowl of punch, and the Craft is like to come into disesteem among us unless the true Brethren are countenanced and distinguished by some special authority as herein desired. I entreat, therefore, that whatever you shall think proper to do therein may be sent by the next post, if possible, or the next following.

I am, Your Affectionate Brother & humb Servt

B. FRANKLIN, G. M.

Pennsylvania.

Philadelphia, Nov. 28, 1734.

P.S.—If more of the Constitutions are wanted among you, please hint it to me.

(Address upon said letters:)

"To Mr. Henry Price

"At the Brazen Head

"Boston,

"N.E."

These original letters were destroyed at the burning of the Masonic Temple in Boston on April 5/6, 1864, prior to which time the official letter hung in a frame in the Temple observed by all men. As to their authenticity see statements and affidavits in 1871 Mass. 306, 356-361. They were, for instance, exhibited to the Committee of the Grand Lodge of Pennsylvania on March 22, 1855, as related in 14 M.F.M. 188; see also 1888 Mass. 118.

In the official letter, Franklin, acting as he himself says at the request of his Lodge, acknowledges its want of lawful authority and prays that Price by virtue of his Commission from Britain, which had been extended over the whole of North America, would confirm the Brethren

BENJAMIN FRANKLIN
Reproduced from an original sent by Franklin from
Paris to his niece and inscribed on the back, in his own
handwriting, "For Mrs. Dorcas Stickney in Newbury"

of Pennsylvania in privileges which they then enjoyed of holding their Lodge although without "the sanction of some authority derived from home." He further admits that the Grand Master of Pennsylvania would thereafter yield his chair whenever the Grand Master of North America, to wit, Henry Price, should be present. This letter is a flat and explicit admission made officially that the Brethren of Pennsylvania had no authority, and that they were irregular without it; and they prayed for the grant thereof.

Benjamin Franklin when he signed the letter of November 28, 1734, as Grand Master and "at the request of the Lodge," knew what he was writing *ex cathedra.* It is also submitted that the Brethren who officially requested their Grand Master to send the petition to Price, knew more about the facts of that day and generation than some partisan historians one hundred and fifty years later who have struggled to convince the Masonic world that Franklin, Price, and their associates were all wrong as to these facts.

Should all other evidence and argument be disregarded, these letters are definite and final. They establish that Pennsylvania Masonry was wanting in authority, i.e., was not duly constituted; that Henry Price was the "Founder of Duly Constituted Masonry in America."

1914 Mass. 257, *et cit.*, 283.

1871 Mass. 356-359.

The Deputation or Warrant granted Franklin and the Brethren of Pennsylvania has disappeared as have all of Franklin's American Masonic documents. (There are no Pennsylvania Grand Lodge records prior to July 29, 1779, and no Lodge minute book for that jurisdiction earlier than that beginning June 28, 1749, *q.v.*)

Franklin's letter states as his source of information that Price's authority had been extended over all North America; "We have seen in the Boston prints an article of news from London, importing that at a Grand Lodge held there in August last, Mr. Price's deputation and power was extended over all America."   Because of the delays in transportation of the mails in those days, this means that the article which Brother Franklin saw must have been published some time between the first of September and the middle of November, 1734.   At that time there were five Boston newspapers.   The oldest was *The Boston News Letter*.   Complete files of that paper for the period in question have been examined and no such article is found therein.

The *Boston Gazette* was at that period frequently publishing Masonic items.   Only three copies of the *Boston Gazette* after August 19, and before December, 1734, are known to exist.   September 16th is in the library of the Massachusetts Historical Society; October 21st and November 25th are in the library of the Bostonian Society.   They have been examined and no such item has been found.   The paper was issued, however, on August 26th, September 2nd, 9th, 23rd; October 7th, 14th and 28th, and November 4th, 11th and 18th, but no copies of these issues are now known to exist.   Probably the item Franklin saw was in one of these issues.   He frequently quoted from the *Gazette* and the missing copies are those which would have come to him immediately preceding the writing of these letters.

The *Boston Post Boy* began with the issue of October 7, 1734.   No copies of this paper, however, are known to exist prior to April 21, 1735.

A copy of each issue of the *New England Weekly*

Journal for the period has been searched but no such article has been found. This statement applies also to the *Weekly Rehearsal*, except that no copy of this for September 16, 1734, is known.

We may safely assume that Franklin told the truth and therefore must possess our souls in patience until, if ever, the print to which he referred is found. There is much other evidence than Franklin's letter or the missing print that Price's commission was extended as stated, all of which has been quoted or referred to in citations. The reporter who wrote the newspaper article, however, was in error in thinking that the commission was extended at a *meeting* of the Grand Lodge, for in those days the Grand Lodge neither issued nor endorsed Provincial Grand Masters' commissions. That was a prerogative of the Grand Master. We, in this day and generation, can well understand from familiarity with our newspapers how a reporter can get the essential fact as a basis of his article and yet mistake many of the details. He would not have written the report unless he had information of the fact that the Commission had been extended. Unless he were a well informed member of the Craft, however, he would easily fall into the error of stating that the act was of the Grand Lodge instead of the Grand Master.

On this subject, see the important recent discovery cited under 1734/5, February 21, *infra*.

1734, December 2, Philadelphia.
  Entries in L. B. indicate a meeting.

1734, December 11,   Boston.
  Meeting of the First Lodge. Anthony Davis made,

Brothers Robert Gardiner, and William Grice admitted.
P.L.
B.MS.
Barons Letter.

Montserrat—Philadelphia.
The *American Weekly Mercury* of Philadelphia publishes the item quoted under 1734, September, *supra*.

1734, December 27,   Boston.
Celebration of the Festival of Saint John the Evangelist.
1 Mass. 4.

1734/5, February 21, Boston-Philadelphia.
Meeting of the Provincial Grand Lodge in Boston.
Appointment of Benjamin Franklin as Provincial Grand Master for Pennsylvania by "HENRY PRICE GRAND MASTER OF HIS MAJESTY'S DOMINIONS IN NORTH AMERICA."

In 1916 the author discovered an item of news, dated Boston, February 24, 1734/5, published by the *American Weekly Mercury* (Philadelphia), No. 795, "March 20 to 27, 1735," as follows:

"BOSTON, Feb. 24.

"On Friday laſt was held a Grand Lodge of that Ancient and Honourable Society of *Free and Accepted Maſons*, at the Bunch of Grapes Tavern in King Street, where Mr. *Henry Price*, Grand Maſter of His Majeſty's Dominions in North America, Nominated and Appointed his Grand Officers for the Year enſuing, viz: *Andrew Belcher*, Eſq., Deputy Grand Maſter; Mr. *James Gordon*

ry Sufferers by laft Wednefday's Storm. we had another very hard Gale of Wind laft Night at S. S. E. and South, which ftill continues, and has done great Damage. The Friends Adventurer, Capt. Manby, for Maryland, that was afhore at Gilkicker, is overfet, and fuppofed to be broke in pieces, there being nothing of her to be feen. The Princefs of Orange, Capt. Dent, the Warden, Capt. Wigram, and the Mary, Capt. Lithered, are alfo broke to pieces. The Coddrington, Capt. Borafton, for Antigua, loft all her Mafts, but rode out the Storm at Spithead, and came Yefterday into the Harbour, as did the Wisbech, Capt. Norris, having rode the Storm, but loft her Foremaft and Bowfprit. Came in the Princefs of Afturias, Holman, in Ballaft from Cadiz; the Amelia, Spillman, from London for Malaga; the Succefs, Snelling, from ditto for New-England, fhe had been afhore on the Horfe; the Richard and Anne, Carter, from Harwich for Cadiz; the Sarah, Chapman, from London, bore for the Flat; the three Sifters, Grindal, ditto for Maryland. Such quick repeated violent Storms and Loffes as this Winter has produced, far exceeds any in the Memory of Man.

The Swallow Brig. Leonard Bizer, Mafter, bound from Peterfburgh to Briftol, who was forced on Shore at Portfmouth in the Storm on Wednefday laft, got off on Thurfday, and went into the Harbour to refit, as did the Anne, Higginfon, for Jamaica

The Auguftus Cefar, Capt. Hampton, bound to Leghorn, and the Britannia, Kelfey, for Cadiz, are put into Sheernefs, to repair the Damage they had receiv'd in the late Storm at the Nore; the former's Sheet Anchor broke, which obliged them to cut away her Main Maft, and that carried away her Mizzen Maft.

[N. B. *The farther Particulars of this Storm we fhall prefent in our next.*]

BOSTON, Feb. 24.

Laft Week, at the Court of Affize and general Goal Delivery held here for the County of Suffolk. Two Negro Fellows were tried, one for Burglary and Felony, in breaking into the Houfe of Capt. Greenwood, and ftealing fundry Bills of Credit, and the other for felonioufly fetting Fire to his Mafter's Hay, by which his Barn, Dwelling Houfe, Shop, and other Buildings were deftroyed, near Barton's Point in this Town, fome Months fince; but for want of legal Evidence they were both acquitted, tho' 'tis thought by all they were guilty of the Facts.

Yefterday arrived here Capt. Smith from the Bay of Honduras, who came out in Company with Capt. Durfey and others; he fays they left 9 Sail in the Bay, one of which was Capt. Way of this Town, and that two others went in as they came out. 'Tis faid Provifions are very fcarce and dear in the Bay.

On Friday laft was held a Grand Lodge of that Ancient and Honourable Society of *Free and Accepted Mafons*, at the Bunch of Grapes Tavern in King Street, where Mr. *Henry Price* Grand Mafter of His Majefty's Dominions in North America, Nominated and Appointed his Grand Officers for the Year enfuing, viz.

Andrew Belcher Efq; Deputy GrandMafter; Mr. *James Gordon* and M. *Frederick Hamilton* Grand Wardens for this Province; And Mr. *Benjamin Franklin* Provincial Grand Mafter for the Province of *Pennfylvania*.

Extract of a Letter from Charleftown, in South Carolina, dated January 18. 1734.

'Our Affembly met here according to Adjournment on Tuefday the 14th Inftant, but the Governor not being fully Recovered of his Illnefs, no Bufinefs is done yet. Our Planters here find themfelves very miftaken in their Eftimation of the laft Crop of Rice, fince fome of them, who after having their Rice in the Barn, thought to have 300 Barrels, found when beaten out but 100. In fome Plantations the Buggs come into it and deftroy it, fo that Rice ftill will keep up its Price.

We hear from *Rh. Ifland*, That the beginning of laft Week Capt. *Durfey* and another Veffel belonging to that Place, arrived there from the Bay of *Honduras*, and that the other Veffels which came out with him were daily expected. 'Tis faid Capt. *Durfey* brought the *Spanifh* Sloop which he took in the Bay as far as the Mouth of the Gulf, and then civilly difmifs'd her; but the *Spaniard* was fo uncivil as to follow the Fleet for a confiderable Time, in hopes no doubt of taking fome of them, till Capt. *Durfey* fired at him and obliged him to leave off the Chafe

March 3. Laft Week arrived Capt. *Cary* from Cadiz, who left London the latter end of November. and that Place the begining of January with Advice, That by Letters from London in the begining of December a Peace was likely to be accommodated. The following is a Paragraph of a Letter to a Gentleman in this Town, Dated *Cadiz, Dec.* 30th 1734. " I faw " a Letter this Day from *Alicant*, giving an " Account that Capt. *Ellis Bennett* in the Six " Brothers, and 5 or 6 fail more of Englifh " Ships were Caft away in that Bay, but all " the Men faved.

We hear Mr. Alderman *Vining* of *Portfmouth*, (Brother to *Benjamin Vining* Efq; Colector of *Salem*) has the Honour of Knightwood conferred on him.

We are told, a certain Perfon in this Town has beat his Apprentice fo unmercifully that his Life is difpared of, which may ferve as a Caution to prevent the like abominable inhumane Cruelty.

On Tuefday laft his Excellency our Governor, with the Advice of his Majefty's Council, iffued a Proclamation, appointing Thurfday

and Mr. *Frederick Hamilton*, Grand Wardens for this Province; and Mr. *Benjamin Franklin*, Provincial Grand Mafter for the Province of *Pennfylvania*."

P–t.

A reproduction of the last column of page 2 and the first column of page 3 of this number of the *American Weekly Mercury* is herewith presented.

We are now, for the first time, in possession of the date of Franklin's appointment, for which he had petitioned less than three months before.

1734, November 28, *supra*.

And we have also from Pennsylvania's own press unequivocal evidence of the extension of Price's authority over all North America, and Pennsylvania's recognition thereof.

See also 1734, August, *supra*.

Vain search for a reference to this item has been made in the Printed Proceedings or in the elaborate official and quasi-official publications of the Grand Lodge of Pennsylvania, including the works of Brother Julius F. Sachse, its librarian and historical spokesman for many years. Frequent and extensive use is made therein of quotations from newspapers both before and after the date of this one. This most important and vital bit of history having escaped notice in these works, it is evident that no weight can be given to conclusions which this item negatives. No argument is worth consideration unless based upon the truth and the whole truth.

As Brother Sachse omitted to publish this fact, one can hardly help wondering if there does not still remain in the great libraries of Pennsylvania other information which remains unpublished.

The life of Franklin is so well known that a sketch is omitted.

See "Benj. Franklin as a Freemason," by Sachse.

1734/5, March 12,   Boston.

Meeting of the First Lodge which amended the 8th Article of its By-Laws by providing:

"That no Person Shall be a Member of this Lodge, that has not on a Lodge Night, been publickly balloted in accord^g to Our Constitutions, and Consents to our by-Laws, and pays the Lodge for his Making, unlefs by a Dispensation from the Master & Wardens of the Lodge."

B.MS. 15.

CHAPTER IX

1735

1735, March 26,   Boston.

Meeting of the First Lodge at which the following vote was passed:

"That any Member of this Lodge that goes abroad, or beyond Seas, Shall Still continue a Member & be entitled to all the priviledges of the Lodge, if he Constantly attends when here in Boston and pay his quarteridge or Clubb as the other Members doe

That no Member ſhall offer to paſs his Word for a Brother for his Quarteridge, or Clubb, but Shall pay Money down."

B.MS. 15.

1735, March 28,   Philadelphia.

The *American Weekly Mercury* of Philadelphia, publishes the item quoted under

1734/5, February 21, *supra.*

1735, April 17, London—South America.

In the Grand Lodge of England a motion was agreed to for Randolph Took, Esqʳ to be Provincial Grand Master for South America.

X Q.C.A. 254.

This vote was inadvertent or the scrivener was in error for since the institution of the office of Provincial Grand

Master (1727) the appointment thereto has always been a prerogative of the Grand Master.

> Preston (Portsmouth, 1804) 306.
> 1914 Mass. *255*.

The Deputation was issued by Lord Weymouth.

> Anderson (1738 Ed.) 195.

1735, After April 17, Charles Town, South Carolina.

The first Lodge at "Charles Town," South Carolina, appears for the first time upon the Official English Lists in that for 1760, as No. 251. Later it took the place vacated by Bristol Lodge as No. 74. The Lists accredit the Lodge to 1735, and it was Warranted under Lord Weymouth, installed G. M. April 17, 1735.

> P.C. (3rd Eng. Ed. 1764) 382.

Hammerton's deputation as Pro. G. M. for South Carolina did not issue until after April 15, 1736 (*q.v.*), and he appears as the Master of the Lodge when it met "for the first time" on October 28, 1736, (*q.v.*). There accordingly is some ground for the arguments, which have been heard, that this Lodge was constituted by Hammerton under his commission and not by Lord Weymouth, direct, or that authority for the 1735 Lodge came from Boston.

> See 1735, Dec. 27, *infra*.
>
> See also a discriminating and careful study of the situation in the first chapter of Mackey's History of Freemasonry in South Carolina.

The date of the Constitution of this Lodge is given in the 6th Edition of Jachin and Boaz (London 1765) as November 12, 1735. No reliance can be placed upon that month and day, however. Bristol Lodge, Gloucestershire, Constituted November 12, 1735, was No. 74 in the 1755 listing. It was erased in 1757, but the date of Constitution was retained in the lists against the number, although no Lodge was given. This is the case in the Official List for 1761 (original in archives of Grand Lodge of Massachusetts), where "Solomon's Lodge in Charles Town, South Carolina," meeting the 1st and 3rd Thursdays, is given as No. 251, with 1735 as the date of Constitution. It is inserted between Lodges Constituted in 1756 and 1759, thus indicating about when the information officially reached the Grand Officers. Later Solomon's Lodge was put in No. 74, vacated by Bristol Lodge. This brought it with the 1735 Lodges, where it should be, but the *date of the Constitution of Bristol Lodge was left*. Thus the date (other than the year) clearly does not belong to the South Carolina Lodge. Furthermore, its placement ahead of the Lodge at Savannah does not indicate priority of Constitution, but merely the convenience of the engraver.[1]

1735, May 13.
Franklin charges F. Hopkinson for binding a Mason book 1.6.

F.J.

1735, June 2,   Philadelphia.
Entries in L. B. indicate a meeting.

1735, June 12,   Philadelphia.
The *Pennsylvania Gazette* publishes the following, referring to the English Grand Lodge meeting of March 31,

[1] Bro. W. J. Songhurst, the learned secretary of Quatuor Coronati Lodge, says, "Early printed lists were mostly unofficial. So also were some of the engraved lists. And even with the official lists the engravers frequently rubbed out the particulars of a Lodge and engraved particulars of a new one under the old date."

1735 (X Q.C.A. 247), among items of London news, viz.:

"On Monday Night was held a Quarterly Communication of the most Ancient and Honourable Society of Free and Accepted Masons, at the Devil Tavern, Temple Bar; most of the Grand Officers and upwards of Three Hundreds Masters and Wardens of Lodges, properly cloathed were present; particularly the Right Hon. the Earl of Crawford, Grand Master; Sir Cecil Wray, Bart. Deputy Grand Master; Sir Edward Mancell, Bart. and John Ward, Esq.; Grand Wardens. His Grace, the Duke of Richmond, his Grace the Duke of Buccleugh, the Right Hon. the Lord Balcarras, Dr. Desaguliers, and several other Persons of the first quality and Distinction. A handsome Sum was disposed of towards the Relief of several poor Brethren. They unanimously chose the Right Hon. the Lord Viscount Weymouth, Grand Master, for the Year ensuing; Sir Cecil Wray, Bart. and Sir Edward Mancell, Bart., Grand Wardens; After which a most elegant Oration in Praise of Masonry, was pronounced by ———— Bowman, Esq. which received the universal Approbation of that Antient and Honourable Fraternity."

1735, June 24,   Boston.

Celebration of the Festival of Saint John the Baptist.

About this time the First Lodge moved from Edward Lutwyche's Bunch of Grapes Tavern to Luke Vardy's Royal Exchange Tavern.

    1 Mass. 4.

Philadelphia.

The *Pennsylvania Gazette* for July 3, 1735, gives an account of a Grand Lodge held at the Indian King Tavern, Philadelphia, on this day at which James Hamilton was chosen Grand Master as Franklin's successor.

James Hamilton.

James Hamilton, son of Andrew Hamilton, Provincial Councillor and champion of the liberty of the press, was born at Bushhill in Philadelphia about 1710. He was Senior Grand Warden in 1734 and Grand Master in 1735, during which years he lived in Lancaster. He was elected to various offices in the Province: was Mayor of the City of Philadelphia in 1745; qualified in the Provincial Council January 17, 1745/6, after which he went to England and in 1748 returned with a commission as Lieutenant Governor, the first native to be appointed to that office. He died in New York, August 14, 1783, aged 73.

    1 O.M.L.P. 35.

1735, June 30,   Boston.

  The *Weekly Rehearsal* contains the following item:

"London, April 18. Yefterday about two o'Clock in the Afternoon, the Proceffion of the Antient and Honourable Society of Free and Accepted Mafons paffed from Grofvenor fquare to Mercers-Hall, where a grand Dinner was provided for them. The Proceffion began in the following Manner, viz. one Kettle-Drum; four Trumpets, two and two, two French Horns; with two Hautboys; and two Baffoons, all on white Horfes, with Leather Aprons and white Gloves.

"After thefe, fix Coaches, with the twelve Stewards with their white Wands, follow'd by an infinite Number of Gentlemen's Coaches, the Officers of each Lodge being diftinguifhed by the proper Badges of their Office pendent to red Ribbons, or Squares, Levels, Plumets, &c. fome Silver, others Gold, the Grand Mafter and Grand Wardens clofing the Proceffion."

    P–t.

1735, July 14, Boston.

The *Boston Post Boy* copies from the *Pennsylvania Gazette* its account of the Grand Lodge meeting in Philadelphia, June 24, 1735, *q.v.*

P–t.

1735, October 2, Philadelphia.

Entries in L. B. indicate a meeting.

1735, October 9, Philadelphia.

The *Pennsylvania Gazette* has a notice of a meeting of the Grand Lodge of Ireland.

1735, After October 30, Savannah, Georgia.

Webb's Monitor in its third edition holds the following statement: "The Grand Lodge of Georgia is holden by virtue and in pursuance of the right of succession legally derived from the most noble and most worshipful Thomas Thynne, Lord Viscount Weymouth, Grand Master of England, A.D. 1730, by his warrant directed to the right worshipful Roger Lacey," etc.

See 1730, Georgia, page 61, *supra.*

The statement, of course, was entirely in error and Webb made a correction in subsequent editions. Weymouth was not Grand Master in 1730 and the warrant issued by him to Mr. Roger Lacey, merchant, for constituting a Lodge at Savannah, Georgia, was issued some time during that part of 1735 when Weymouth was Grand Master; viz.—after April 17.

Anderson (1738 Ed.) 195.

P.C. (2nd Eng. Ed. 1759) 380.

Entick 336.

Roger Lacey was one of the Stewards at the Grand

JAMES HAMILTON

Lodge held in London, March 17, 1730/1. No one knows just when he went to Georgia. Some years after the founding of Savannah he was the agent to the Cherokee Tribe of Indians, and founder of the trading post where Augusta now stands.

As fixing the date with a trifle more accuracy, I find that in the Official English List for 1737 "Savannah in ye Province of Georgia" is given as No. 139. No. 138 is reported as Constituted October 30, 1735. No. 140 was Constituted March 1, 1735/6. It is evident, therefore, that the date of the Constitution of this Lodge is probably after October 30, 1735, and certainly before March 1, 1735/6.

The Lodge at Savannah first appears on the Official List for 1736 as No. 139 and is the second Lodge in America enrolled on the Official English Lists; although in the later English Lists the Lodge at Charleston, South Carolina, took one number's precedence over the Lodge at Savannah, Georgia. That this does not, in this case, indicate earlier Constitution, see "1735, after April 17," *supra*. For further evidence that 1735 is the correct date, see also

Preston (Portsmouth, 1804) 185.

L.M.R. 70.

L.H.B. 31.

The Grand Lodge of Georgia, in the preamble to its Constitutions adopted about 1856, made the following remarkable statement: "The Grand Lodge of Free and Accepted Masons of the State of Georgia, existing by virtue of a Warrant issued by Thomas Thynne, Lord Weymouth, Grand Master of England, dated A.D. 1733, and renewed by Sholto Charles Douglas, Lord Aberdour, Grand Master of England, A.D. 1755," *etc.*

R. W. Charles W. Moore in July, 1856, pointed out that this preamble was incorrect in the following particulars: "1. The Grand Lodge of Georgia does not exist by virtue of a Warrant from Lord Weymouth. 2. Lord Weymouth was not Grand Master of England in 1733. 3. Lord Aberdour was not Grand Master of England in 1755. 4. The Grand Lodge of Georgia had no existence in 1733."

He proceeded conclusively to prove these negations and pointed out that the Warrant which was issued by Lord Weymouth in 1735 was for a particular Lodge, not a Provincial Grand Lodge, in Georgia.

15 M.F.M. 263, 353-362.

The first appointment of any Provincial Grand Master for the Province of Georgia was made by Lord Aberdour sometime between May 18, 1757, and May 3, 1762.

Preston (Portsmouth, 1804) 202.

The Grand Lodge of Georgia has amended its preamble so that the corresponding part of it now reads as follows: "The Grand Lodge of Free and Accepted Masons, according to the Old Institution, of the State of Georgia, existing since 1733, and by virtue of, and in pursuance of the right and succession legally derived from the Most Noble, and Right Worshipful Thomas Thynne, Lord Viscount Weymouth, Grand Master of England, for the year of Masonry Five Thousand Seven Hundred and Thirty-Five, by his warrant directed to the Right Worshipful Roger Lacey, and by the renewal of the said power by Sholto Charles Douglass, Lord Aberdour, Grand Master of Scotland, and for the year Five Thousand Seven Hundred and Fifty-Five and Five Thousand Seven Hundred and Fifty-Six, the Grand Master of England for the years Five Thousand Seven Hundred and Fifty-Eight, by his warrant directed to the Right Worshipful Gray Eliot," *etc.*

It is not clear how an existence in 1733 can be "by virtue of, and in pursuance of" the act of a Grand Master in 1735. The author must confess that he does not understand quite what this means, although Brother Rockwell's arguments have been carefully considered.

15 M.F.M. 353-359.

The only known document upon which such statements can be predicated is the second charter of Solomon's Lodge, issued in 1786. That charter was the first granted by the Grand Lodge of Georgia upon its organization. Its preamble states that Roger Lacey obtained his warrant in 1735, and that Gray Elliott was appointed Provincial Grand Master in 1756. The *Savannah Gazette* for December 19, 1786, gives an account of a meeting of the Grand Lodge held on December 16, 1786, and states that Major General Samuel Elbert resigned as the third Provincial Grand Master of Georgia, and was succeeded by the election of William Stevens as Grand Master.

Brother Sidney Hayden in his "Washington and his Masonic Compeers" (page 342) speaks of "King Solomon's Lodge at Savannah which had commenced its work under an old oak tree in 1733 when the first settlement of Georgia began."

Brother Hayden gives us no suggestion of his authority, if he had any, for this remark made one hundred and thirty-three years after the event.

In February, 1733, Oglethorpe arrived at Port Royal with a charter, "in trust for the poor," dated June 9, 1732, to establish a colony south of the Savannah River to be called Georgia. He proceeded to the Savannah

River and began to fortify his new settlement to protect the immigrants from the Indians, who then inhabited the locality, and the Spanish, who claimed to own it. The record tells us that for "almost a year, the Governor dwelt under a tent." It doesn't seem likely that either a Lodge or Grand Lodge was organized under such circumstances.

W. Brother William B. Clarke of Solomon's Lodge, No. 1, of Savannah, Georgia, has recently made a searching investigation and has collated much material which he has put fully at our disposal.

Benjamin Sheftall came to Georgia in the early days of the Colony. His granddaughter in 1859 gave Solomon's Lodge a gavel made from a piece of the oak tree under which her uncle, Sheftall Sheftall, often told her that his father (Mordecai, son of Benjamin) told him that Oglethorpe had opened a Masonic Lodge in 1733. The tree was located a few miles from Savannah, at what is now known as Sunbury. Benjamin was Master of Solomon's Lodge in 1758, and Mordecai and Sheftall Sheftall both were members in later years.

The minutes of Solomon's Lodge for December 21, 1858, record the tradition that a Lodge, later known as Solomon's Lodge, was opened by Oglethorpe, February 10, 1733. This would mean February 10, 1733/4.

Remarkable confirmation of this tradition has just been discovered by Brother Clarke in what is evidently the original record book of this Lodge for a part of the years 1756 and 1757. One page thereof, herewith reproduced, contains a list of members in 1757, to wit:— 17 "E. P."; 9 "F. C."; 10 "M. M."

This list seems to prove a renewal of activity in 1756 and would suggest dormancy for the twenty preceding

FACSIMILE OF 1757 ROSTER OF SOLOMON'S
LODGE, SAVANNAH, GEORGIA

years. It warrants us in concluding, however, that N. Jones, Daniel Nunes, and Moses Hunes were made Masons in Georgia in 1733/4 (*i.e.* in 1734, prior to March 25); also that Sir Patrick Houstoun was made in Georgia, October 9, 1734, and raised sometime in 1735. Add to all this the action of the Grand Lodge of England, December 13, 1733, and March 18, 1733/4 (*q.v.*), and proof of Freemasonry in Georgia in 1733/4 is convincing.

Solomon's Lodge asserts that it now owns a Bible presented to the Lodge by Oglethorpe. It certainly has an old Bible and an affidavit that prior to 1881 it contained a "fly-leaf upon which was written in the hand of General Oglethorpe the date of presentation as 1733, and signed with his name"; also that "the fly-leaf was stolen while the book was being exhibited at Atlanta in 1881."

Noble Jones, whose name is first on the list, was Master during the period covered by these records, and, part of the time, was Colonel commanding the British troops in Savannah.

Daniel Nunes was a physician. On this account, General Oglethorpe urged the Trustees of Georgia in England to disregard some objections which were there voiced to a Jew becoming a member of the Colony.

Charles Pryce was a judge.

Sir Patrick Houstoun was a member of the King's Council and Register of Grants, and the father of Sir George Houstoun who later became Master of Solomon's Lodge and Grand Master of Georgia.

Gray Elliott is named in the present charter of Solomon's Lodge (dated 1786) as the second Provincial Grand Master of Georgia.

James Habersham became Master and later Secretary of Solomon's Lodge and in 1786 was the first Grand Treasurer of the Grand Lodge of Georgia.

John Morel was a prominent merchant.

John Graham was, when the list was made, Lieutenant Governor of Georgia and owned the largest plantation in the Colony.

A consideration of these names attests the high standing of the fathers of Freemasonry in Georgia, and seems to tie these newly discovered records to the present Solomon's Lodge, No. 1.

It is the writer's opinion that a Lodge met in or near Savannah "according to the Old Customs" in 1733/4 and that it became "duly constituted" after October 30, 1735, but before March 1, 1735/6. This was about the time that Oglethorpe (having returned to England in 1734) returned to Georgia with some three hundred emigrants of the better class, among them being the celebrated Methodist divine, John Wesley.

Further evidence of the early existence of Freemasonry in Georgia was discovered some five years ago when Brother W. H. Mitchell of Solomon's Lodge was asked to repair the brick work of the foundations of a church which was erected by the Salzburger Colony, founded at Ebenezer twenty-five miles from Savannah. The colony was founded in 1734 and the church built soon thereafter. On the western gable of this church and just under the eaves of the roof there is a handmade brass square and compass. On several of the bricks, handmade by the original builders, he found the square and compass indented. These were not outside bricks which could be easily reached, but were those concealed behind the face brick, so that the marks could have been placed there by none but the original workmen.

Roger Lacey died in 1738 and for twenty years there-after there was no Pro. G. M. for Georgia. During this period the colony dwindled to less than five hundred in-habitants and came near going to the wall. When things began to revive, Elliott evidently rebuilt the Lodge in 1756 and was rewarded by appointment as Pro. G. M. in 1758.

1735, October 31,   Boston.
Meeting of the First Lodge. Alexander and Charles Gordon made. Brothers Capt. James Cerke and Dr. Thomas Moffat admitted.
> P.L.
> B.MS.
> Barons Letter.

1735, November 12,   Boston.
Meeting of the First Lodge at which a vote was passed relative to the construction of the 8th Article of the By-Laws.
> B.MS. 16.

1735, November 20,   Boston.
Meeting of the First Lodge. Capt. James Forbes made.
> P.L.
> B.MS.
> Barons Letter.

1735, December 1,   Philadelphia.
Entries in L. B. indicate a meeting.

1735, December 27,   Boston.

Celebration of the Festival of Saint John the Evangelist. Captain McLean chosen Master of the First Lodge.
    1 Mass. 4.

South Carolina.

Charles Pelham, in 1750, when, as Grand Secretary of the Provincial Grand Lodge at Boston, he began his book of records by recording the principal events theretofore, wrote under date of December 27, 1735, that "about this time sundry Brethren going to South Carolina met with some Masons in Charlestown who thereupon went to work, from which sprung Masonry in those parts."

This may be the Lodge referred to under 1735, after April 17, *supra*.

See also page 189.

Undoubtedly, Pelham knew whereof he spoke; but we are hardly warranted in assigning December 27, 1735, as a definite date or in making too explicit assertions about it. If it be not Lodge 251, then it is doubtless the Lodge referred to under January 26, 1737/8, *infra*. There is, it seems to me, hardly original evidence enough to warrant any definite conclusion. Too much weight, however, cannot be given to Pelham's assertion that from this movement sprung Masonry in South Carolina. He may not have known the exact facts about the authority obtained from England above referred to. (See 1735, after April 17, *supra*.) Moreover, he does not recite the issuance of any warrant or deputation. On his bare statement, the Lodge would be irregular although meeting "according to the Old Customs."

At the same time, there is no evidence that No. 251 did not spring from Massachusetts for there is nothing to show the exercise of any authority direct from England prior to October 28, 1736, *q.v.* Pelham had sources of information in 1750 of which we are not to-day aware. He was intimately associated with those who had participated in the events from 1733 onward, and could have gained much information at first hand and from them.

1735/6, January 4,   **Boston.**
Meeting of the First Lodge at which it was voted:

"That the Charge of making a Single Brother Shall be Eight pounds this Currency."
    B.MS.

1735/6, January 13,   Boston.
Meeting of the First Lodge. Robert Tomlinson, John Overing, Esq., Benjamin Barrons (Barons), and Alexander Tran made.
    P.L.
    B.MS.
    Barons Letter.

1735/6, January 14,   Boston.
Meeting of the First Lodge. Capt. William Hinton and John Osborne made.
    P.L.
    B.MS.
    Barons Letter.

1735/6, January 21,   Boston.

Meeting of the First Lodge. Thomas Oxnard, and Capts. Robert Boyd and Thomas McKnight made.

> P.L.
> B.MS.
> Barons Letter.

1735/6, January 23,   Boston.

Meeting of the First Lodge. Capt. Benjamin Hallowell and Capt. Webber Gofton made.

> P.L.
> B.MS.
> Barons Letter.

1735/6, January 30,   Boston.

Meeting of the First Lodge. Francis Johonnot, Capt. Robert Smith, Hugh McDaniel, and Luke Vardy (Master of the Exchange Tavern) made.

> P.L.
> B.MS.
> Barons Letter.

1735/6, February 5,   Boston.

Meeting of the First Lodge. Robert Oliver and Capt. William Frost made.

> P.L.
> B.MS.
> Barons Letter.

Portsmouth, New Hampshire.

On this day six Brethren of Portsmouth, N. H., executed a petition to Henry Price for the Constitution of a Lodge at Portsmouth. The original petition is in the

To the Right worshipfull & Worshipfull — Henery Price Grand master of the Society of free and Excepted Mason's held in Boston, and to ye rest of the Brothers Greeting —

Wee the under named persons of the holy and Exquisite Lodge of Ste John do request a deputation and power to hold a Lodge According to order as is and has been granted to faithfull Brothers in all parts of the World; wee have our Constitutions both in print and manuscript as good and as ancient as any that England can afford —

Worthy Sir — wee request ye above as a favour hearing that there is A Superiour Lodge held in Boston, and if Granted, it will encourage us to keep a Constant corraspondance, by comunicating our brotherly affections, one to another once a Quarter, which Concludes us as wee ought Sir yor Obedient Servants —

Portsmouth February ye 5 Day 1735

Robt Brough
Tho: Cabman
John f mills
Jonathan Wailer
Wm Canterbury
Willm Grogan

FACSIMILE OF PETITION FOR FIRST LODGE IN NEW HAMPSHIRE

archives of the Grand Lodge of Massachusetts. A fac-simile is herewith presented. We do not know the exact date of the Constitution of this Lodge except that it was some time in 1736. Its earliest existing record book begins October 31, 1739, *q.v.*, with the adoption of a set of Regulations or By-Laws.

Note, from the language of the petition, that the Lodge was already organized.

1735/6, March 20,   Philadelphia.
Franklin charges John Hubbard 2.6 for a Mason Book.
F.J.

1735/6, March 24,   Boston.
Meeting of the First Lodge. Charles Bladwell, Esq., made.
P.L.
B.MS.
Barons Letter.

1735,   Philadelphia.
There is a tradition without any evidence to support it that Franklin laid the Corner-stone of the State House (Independence Hall) in Philadelphia, during this year.
Benjamin Franklin as a Freemason (Sachse), 27-30.

In the *Pocket Companion* (Dublin, 1735 Ed.) a Lodge is given as No. 116 at The Hoop, in Water Street, in Philadelphia. Such a Lodge was never on the English Register.
L.M.R. 56, 480.

By fanciful and strained reasoning some Brethren have sought to say that it belongs as No. 79 on the English Register which happens this year to be blank. But that it does not belong there is evident from the fact that on the earlier and later English lists, No. 79 is duly accounted for. Moreover this Lodge is not to be found in the later published Irish lists.

If a Lodge at The Hoop existed before 1733, it could not have had the place of No. 79 which belonged until that year to the Lodge at Castle, Highgate, when it united with No. 4. No. 79, thus vacated, was officially filled by the Lodge at the Two Angels and Crown, Little Saint Martin's Lane.

X Q.C.A. 241, 246.

L.M.R. 57.

CHAPTER X

1736

1736, April 6,   Philadelphia.
  Entries in L. B. indicate a meeting.

1736, After April 15, London—South Carolina.
  The Earl of Loudoun issued a Deputation to John
Hammerton, Esq., as Pro. G. M. for South Carolina.
        Preston (Portsmouth, 1804), 186.
        Anderson (1738 Ed.) 195.
        Entick (1756 Ed.) 333.
        P.C. (London, 1759) 115.

John Hammerton.

Of John Hammerton, Mackey tells us in his History
of Freemasonry in South Carolina:

"He was a man of talent and of considerable civil distinction in the Colony.   In 1732 he was the Receiver
General of his Majesty's Quit Rents, and in 1734, the
Secretary of the Colony.   In 1738, he is recorded as having received the appointment of Register and Secretary
of South Carolina for life.   These were all offices of
great honour and trust, and his appointment to them is
an evidence of the high esteem in which he was held by
the parent government."

He did not exercise this deputation until October 28,
1736, when he was content to serve also as the Master of
Solomon's Lodge.

1736, April 26, Boston.

The *Boston Evening Post* contains the following item:

"Some private Societies of Gentlemen who call themselves Free Masons, having been set up in Holland, the Mob began to shew their Dislike to such Meetings, by threatening to pull the Lodge or House where they assembled, about their Ears; but soon after the States of Holland thought fit, it seems, to pass a Resolution against such private Assemblies; whereupon the City of Amsterdam published a Placart against them, in Substance as follows, viz.:

Forasmuch as the Magistrates in the City of Amsterdam have heard, that there are Persons in it, who, under Pretence of being Members of a certain Society called Free Masons, have had the Assurance to form and frequent Conventicles and unlawful Assemblies upon that Account, and that some have made use of their Houses and Lodgings for holding the said prohibited Assemblies; The Magistrates having it at Heart to take Care of the Tranquility and Welfare of the City and its Citizens, have thought it proper and necessary, to forbid and prohibit all Persons in the said City and its Jurisdiction, as they are by these Presents forbidden and prohibited, to hold and frequent such unlawful Conventicles, whether with the Names of Free Masons, or any other specious Title which they may affect; as also to hire, lett, and make use of their Houses, Chambers, Barns, Cellars, Coach-houses, or other Places, for the holding of such Assemblies, under Pain of being severely punished, as Disturbers of the publick Peace, &c.

Such another Placart has been published against them at the Hague, and 'tis said their Lodges or Assemblies are to be suppressed throughout the whole Province of Holland; for the Dutch, it seems, look upon them as Accademies not only of Libertinism and Debauchery, but of Faction and Rebellion, and therefore those, who keep

or frequent ſuch Aſſemblies, are to be puniſhed as Diſ-
turbers of the publick Tranquility."
P–t.

1736, May 12,   Boston.
Meeting of the First Lodge. Patrick Robertson made.
P.L.

1736, May 31,   Boston.
Meeting of the First Lodge. Capt. John Frazier and
Col. John Morris made.
P.L.
B.MS.
Barons Letter.

1736, June 7,   Philadelphia.
Entries in L. B. indicate a meeting.

1736, June 9,   Boston.
Meeting of the First Lodge. Brother Capt. John Hug-
get admitted. Mate John (James) Farrell and Mate
(Capt.) Giles Vandelure made.
P.L.
B.MS.
Barons Letter.

1736, June 14,   Boston.
The *Boston Evening Post* contains an account of a society erected at Rome under the name of *La Cuchiara*,
after the model of the Free Masons, and its immediately
meeting with persecution by some of the Priests.
P–t.

1736, June 23, Boston.

Meeting of the First Lodge at which the following votes were passed:

"That all New made Brothers, Shall Signify upon the Same Night of their Making for the next Lodge night follow^g Wheither they will be Members or Not, And if they defire to be Members, Then they Shall be Admitted In, without a vote, paying twenty Shillings Entrance For their Quarteridge."

"That Every foreign Brother Admitted in, Member of this Lodge Shall pay two Shillings & Six pence to the Tyler."

"That our prefent Secretary be Excufed & free from all Charges & Expenfes of this Lodge."

B.MS. 16.

Bro. Capt. James Crawford admitted.

P.L.

B.MS.

In the archives of the Grand Lodge of Massachusetts is the original draft of a letter dated this day:

"From the Holy Lodge of St. John held in Boston New England" to "the Rt. Hbl. and Rt. Worshipful Grand Master or Deputy G. M. or G. W. of the Grand Lodge of the Free and Accepted Masons In England" of good wishes and of recommendation "of our Rt. Worshipful Bro. Mr Benj^a Barons (our present S. G. W.)"

This letter with an accompanying list of names of the Free and Accepted Masons who were then members of the Lodge are also in Beteilhe's handwriting. The letter has the original signatures attached of Henry Price, G. M., James Gordon, D. G. M., and Francis Beteilhe, G. Sec'y., although they are all crossed out in ink. The letter and list either were retained as copies, or else for some reason were not issued. They are clearly genuine. The watermarks and texture of the paper are those of the period. The handwriting is unquestionably the same and even the ink is obviously the same that was used upon other documents by Beteilhe. Every name on the list is to be found on the Pelham List of 1751 except those of Captain Roger Willington and Saml. Wethered. The former is on the Beteilhe List of 1737 and both are upon the original records of the First Lodge in Boston. The list, so far as I know, has never been published. They read as follows:

> "From the Holy Lodge of St John's Held in Bofton New England the 23^d Day of June A.M. 5736.

Most Worthy and Dear Brethren,

Our great Affection for the whole Fraternity will not permit Us, to Slip this favourable Opportunity, to Give you Sincere Afsurance of our due Regards, for all our Most Worthy Brethren, regularly Met in the R^t Worshipful Holy Lodge of St John, under the Protection of the Heavenly Canopy And in Particular, That of England.

Our hearty good Wishes, We forward to You under the Recommendation of our Rt Worfpf. Brother Mr Benj^a Barons (our present S.G.W.) Who's great Meritts has Contributed very much to the flourishing State of Masonry in this great Town.

Our Lodge was Constituted by Our Right Worfhipfull Grand Master Mr Menry Price (Provincial Grand Master) on the 31st day of August A:D: 1733 & is held at the Royall Exchange Tavern in King Street Boston. And Meet the 2d & 4th Wednesday in every Month; It is Adorned with the most Eminent Gentlemen of this Place, And kept in it's Primitive Beauty & Purity.

We Should think our Selves thoroughly Happy, if any favourable Opportunity, would offer to Convince all Our Worthy Brethren, of our true Affection for their Person; and for their Interests in thefe Parts: But in a particular Manner for thofe of your Rt Worfhipfull Lodge; to whome

We Remain with due Respect
Most Worthy & Dear Brethren
Yo^e Affectionate Bro^s and very
humble Servents.

Francis Beteilhe, G.Sec'y.   Henry Price, G.M.
James Gordon, D.G.M.

See 1883 Mass. 157.

A List of the Names of the Free & Accepted Masons who are Members of the Holy Lodge of St John. Held in Bofton In New England.

Mr Henry Price. G.M

His Excell^y Jon^a Belcher, Esqr

Andrew Belcher Esqr

Benj^a Pemberton Esqr

Henry Hope Esqr

Capⁿ James Cerke

Capⁿ Roger Willington

Mr John McNeal

Brethren made In Bofton

Mr James Gordon D.G.M

Mr Benj^a Barons S.G.W.

Mr Robert Tomlinfon J G W

Capⁿ Robert Mackeleen M.

Mr Hugh McDaniel S.W.

Mr John Ofborne jun. J.W.

Francis Beteilhe Secty

Charles Bladwell Esqr

Doc^r Thos Moffatt

John Overing Esqr

Mr Thos Phillips

Mr Andrew Hallyburton

Mr Thos Oxnard

Capⁿ Willm Hinton

Capⁿ Robt McKnight

Capⁿ Webber Gofton

Capⁿ Robert Smith

Capⁿ Willm Frost

Capⁿ Robert Boydd

Capⁿ James Forbes

Capⁿ Benj^a Hallowell

Doc^r Robert Gardiner

Mr Moses Slaittewey

Mr Alex^a Gordon

Mr Char^s Gordon

Mr Alex^a Trann

Mr Sam. Pemberton

Mr Willm Wefson

Mr Robt Kenton

A List of the Names of the Free & Accepted Masons
who are Members of the Holy Lodge
of St. John. Held In Boston
In New England.

Mr. Henry Price. G. M.
His Excell.y Jon. Belcher Esq.
Andrew Belcher Esqr.
Benj.a Pemberton, Esq.
Henry Hope Esqr.
Capt. James Corke
Capt. Roger Willington
Mr. John McNeal

Brethren made In Boston
Mr. James Gordon D. G. M.
Mr. Benj.a Barons S. G. W.
Mr. Robert Thomlinson J. G. W.
Capt. Robert Mackeleer M.
Mr. Hugh McDaniel S. W.
Mr. John Osborne jun.r J. W.
Francis Beteilho Secty.
Charles Bladwell Esqr.
Doc.r Thos. Moffatt
John Overing Esqr.
Mr. Thos. Phillips
Mr. Andrew Hallyburton
Mr. Thos. Oxnard
Capt. Willm. Hinton
Capt. Robt. McKnight
Capt. Webber Coston
Capt. Robert Smith
Capt. Willm. Frost
Capt. Robert Boyd
Capt. James Forbes
Capt. Benj.a Hallowell
Doct. Robert Gardiner
Mr. Moses Sleutterey
Mr. Alex.r Gordon

Mr. Char.s Gordon
Mr. Alex.r Trann
Mr. Sam.l Pemberton
Mr. Willm. Wilson.
Mr. Robt. Kenton.
Mr. Robt. Peasley.
Mr. Peter Prescott
Mr. John Baker
Mr. Sam: Curwin
Mr. Ant.o Davis
Mr. John Smith
Mr. Sam: Wetherd
Mr. Hugh Scott
Mr. John Gordon.
Mr. Rich.d Patshall
Mr. Fran.s Johonot
Coll. Jn. Morris
Capt. John Fraizier
Capt. Jas. Farrell
Capt. Giles Vandelluse
Capt. John Huggott
Mr. Fred.k Hamilton
Mr. Thos. Molony
Mr. Edm.d Ellis.
Mr. Luke Nardy (Master of the Royall
Exchange Tavern

FACSIMILE OF LIST ACCOMPANYING LETTER OF FIRST LODGE IN
BOSTON RECOMMENDING MR. BENJ. BARONS, JUNE 23, 1736

Mr Robt Peaſeley

Mr Peter Preſcott

Mr John Baker

Mr Sam: Curwin

Mr Ant^o Davis

Mr John Smith

Mr Sam: Wethered

Mr Hugh Scott

Mr John Gordon

Mr Richd Pateſhall

Mr Fran Johonot

Coll^o Jno Morris

Capⁿ John Fraizier

Capⁿ Ja^s Farrell

Capⁿ Giles Vandellure

Capⁿ John Huggott

Mr Fred^k Hamilton

Mr Thos Molony

Mr Edm^d Ellis

Mr Luke Vardy (Master of the Royall Exchange Tavern

1736, June 24,   Boston.

The *Boston Evening Post* for June 28, 1736, has the following account of the celebration of the Festival of Saint John the Baptist on this day:

"Thursday laſt, being the Feſtival of St. John the Baptiſt, the Annual Meeting of the Free and Accepted Maſons, they accordingly met at the Royal Exchange in King-Street, Boſton: The Grand Maſter Nominated and Appointed Meſſieurs Hugh Mac Daniel and John Osborne Wardens for the Year enſuing; after which they had an elegant Entertainment, his Excellency the Governour, the Rev. Mr. Commiſſary Price, and ſeveral other Gentlemen of Diſtinction being preſent."

     P–t.

     1 Mass. 5.

Philadelphia.

The *Pennsylvania Gazette* for July 8, 1736, reports that Thomas Hopkinson, Gent., was chosen Grand Master of the Province of Pennsylvania at a Grand Lodge held in Philadelphia this day.

1736, June 28,   Boston.

A petition was forwarded for the appointment of

Robert Thomlinson (or Tomlinson) to succeed Henry Price as Pro. G. M.

> 1871 Mass. 309.
> 1883 Mass. 159.

1736, July 5,   Philadelphia.
   Entries in L. B. indicate a meeting.

1736, July 15,   Philadelphia.
   The *Pennsylvania Gazette* has an account of the election of Thomas Hopkinson as Grand Master of the Province of Pennsylvania.

Thomas Hopkinson.

Thomas Hopkinson was born in London, April 6, 1709. He studied law, and about 1731, emigrated to Pennsylvania. He was elected Junior Grand Warden June 24, 1734; Deputy Grand Master in 1735; and Grand Master in 1736. He was appointed Master of the Rolls, June 20, 1736; chosen Common Councilman, 1741; and became a member of the Provincial Council, May 13, 1747. He was one of the incorporators of the Philadelphia Library Company, one of the original trustees of the College (now the University of Pennsylvania), and the first president of the American Philosophical Society. In 1751, he is mentioned among the "Departed Saints of the Law." He married a niece of the Bishop of Worcester, was the father of Francis Hopkinson, a signer of the Declaration of Independence, and the grandfather of Joseph Hopkinson, the author of our patriotic song, "Hail Columbia." Bro. Hopkinson died in Philadelphia, November 5, 1751.
   1 O.M.L.P. 37.

THOMAS HOPKINSON

1736, July 22, Philadelphia.

The Pennsylvania Gazette gives an account of a Masonic parade in London.

1736, July 27, Boston.

The *New England Weekly Journal* of this date had the following item:

"London, March 20,

On the 15th of next Month an extraordinary Feaſt is to be held at Fiſhmongers Hall by a ſelect Number of Free Maſons, in Honour of his Highneſs the Duke of Lorrain's Narriage (*sic*), who is one of the Brethren.

N.B. Every Brother is to introduce two Siſters to this grand Feaſt, to convince the Publick that they are no Enemies to the fair sex."

P–t.

1736, August 2, Philadelphia.

Entries in L. B. indicate a meeting.

1736, August 11, Boston.

Meeting of the First Lodge. Shaw Mackintosh, Esq. and James Stevenson made.

P.L.

B.MS.

1736, September 1, Boston.

Henry Price, G. M., James Gordon, D. G. M., Robert Tomlinson, M., Hugh McDaniel, Sr. W., John Osborne, Jr. W., and Francis Beteilhe, Sec'y, wrote a letter of recommendation for Brother Patherick (Patrick) Robertson.

1 Mass. 393.

See 1736, May 12, *supra,*

and 1736, November 2, *infra.*

1736, September 6,   Philadelphia.

    Entries in L. B. indicate a meeting.

1736, September 8,   Boston.

    Meeting of the First Lodge.   Brother Nicholas Davis admitted.

         P.L.

1736, October 4,   Philadelphia.

    Entries in L. B. indicate a meeting.

1736, October 28,   Charleston, S. C.

    The *South Carolina Gazette* for October 29, 1736, has the following item:

"Last night a Lodge of the Ancient and Honourable Society of Free and Accepted Maſons, was held, for the first time, at Mr. Charles Shepheard's, in Broad Street, when John Hammerton, Eſq., Secretary and Receiver General for this Province, was unanimouſly choſen Maſter, who was pleaſed to appoint Mr. Thomas Denne, Senior Warden, Mr. Tho. Harbin, Junior Warden, and Mr. James Gordon, Secretary."

    R. W. William G. Mazyck, Grand Historian of the Grand Lodge of South Carolina, says that this item is "absolutely unimpeachable evidence that Solomon's Lodge No. 1 of Charleston is the oldest Masonic body in the western hemisphere, the record of whose establishment is absolutely unassailable." Though this claim is shown by the preceding pages to be untenable, it is only fair to state his contention.

Philadelphia.

Franklin, in his Journal, charges the Lodge at Bro. Hubbards

"Oct. 1736	For 1100 Tickets	4.11.8
	For Advertisements	10.0 "
	F.J.	

1736, November 2, Boston.

Brother Robertson presents his letter of recommendation (see 1736, September 1, *supra*) to the Lodge Glasgow Kilwinning and it is recorded in full upon the minute book of that Lodge.

> 1 Mass. 393.
> See also 1736/7, January 28 and
> February 22, *infra.*

1736, November 8, Philadelphia.

Entries in L. B. indicate a meeting.

1736, November 10, Boston.

Meeting of the First Lodge. Capt. Thomas Renolds (Reynolds) made.

> P.L.
> B.MS.

1736, November 19, Boston.

Meeting of the First Lodge. Capts. Peter Tomkins (Tonkin) and Richard Parks made.

> P.L.
> B.MS.

1736, November 24,   Boston.

Meeting of the First Lodge. Dr. Archibald Ramsay made.

> P.L.
> B.MS.

1736, December 6, Philadelphia.

Entries in L. B. indicate a meeting.

1736, December 7, London—Boston.

On this date the Earl of Loudoun, Grand Master of England, issued his Deputation to Robert Thomlinson as Provincial Grand Master of New England.

> B.MS. 19.
> 1 Mass. 5.
> 1871 Mass. 309, 349.
> 1900 Mass. 126.
> Anderson (1756 Ed.) 333.
> P.C. (2nd London Ed.) 115.

1736, December 20, Philadelphia.

Entries in L. B. indicate a meeting.

1736, December 22,   Boston.

Meeting of the First Lodge at which the following vote was passed:

"That when ever any Town-dweller Shall be propofed to be Made, the 5th Article in the General Regulations in the printed-book of Constitutions, Shall be Strickly Observed."

> B.MS.

The 5th Article referred to provides that no man can be made or admitted without one month's notice to the Lodge (unless by Dispensation) and due enquiry.

1736, December 27,   Boston.

The *Boston Gazette* for January 17, 1736/7, contains the following item:

"It being St. John's Day the 27th of December laſt, a Grand Lodge was held at the Royal Exchange Tavern in King ſtreet Boſton by the ancient and honourable Society of Free and Accepted Maſons there, Mr. Henry Price Grand Maſter appointed his Deputy Grand Maſter and Grand Wardens for the Year enſuing, viz. Mr. Robert Thomlinſon Deputy Grand Maſter, Mr. Hugh McDaniel Sen. and Mr. John Osborne Jun. Grand Wardens."

> P–t.
> 1 Mass. 5.

South Carolina.

Gould says that James Graeme was elected Pro. G. M. for South Carolina.

> IV Gould 394.
> But see, 1737, July 21, and August 18, *infra.*

1736/7, January 3,   Philadelphia.

Entries in L. B. indicate a meeting.

1736/7, January 12,   Boston.

Meeting of the First Lodge. Nathaniel Bethune made.

> P.L.
> B.MS.

1736/7, January 28,   Boston.

The Lodge of Glasgow Kilwinning addresses a letter to Thomlinson, Provincial Grand Master, in answer to that presented by Brother Robertson (1736, November 2, *supra*).

> 1 Mass. 394.
> B.MS. 24.

It would be interesting to know how this Lodge knew of Thomlinson's appointment. It had been petitioned for and the Commission had been issued (December 7, 1736), but the Commission was not received in Boston until April 20, 1737, *q.v.*

Is it not a fair guess that Brother Robertson delivered the petition and received the Commission for transmission to Thomlinson, before he visited Glasgow? And, also, that perhaps he brought the Commission with him on returning to Boston?

1736/7, February 7, Philadelphia.
Entries in L. B. indicate a meeting.

1736/7, February 9,   Boston.
Meeting of the First Lodge at which the following vote was passed:

"That if at any time hereafter any foreign Brother Should Come to the Lodge and after due Examination found to be but an Enter'd Apprentice, Shall be defired to withdraw in proper Time: Unlefs he defires to be made a Fellow Craft. Which Shall be granted, he paying forty Shillings, for Such Admittance."

> B.MS.

1736/7, February 22,   Boston.
Glasgow Kilwinning Lodge addresses to the First Lodge in Boston a letter of recommendation of Capt. Robert Paisly.

> 1 Mass. 394.
> B.MS.

1736/7, March 7,   Philadelphia.
Entries in L. B. indicate a meeting.

1736/7, March 21,   Boston.

The *Boston Evening Post* quotes the *South Carolina Gazette* of February 19, 1736/7, as announcing that the "Free Mafon, Capt. Phoenix from Jamaica," had been "taken and condemn'd by a Spanifh Man of War near the Havannah."

P.-t.

Chapter XI

1737

1737, April 4,   Philadelphia.
Entries in L. B. indicate a meeting.

1737, April 13,   Boston.
Meeting of the First Lodge. Samuel Stone of Salem made.

> P.L.
> B.MS.

1737, April 20,   Boston.
The Commission of Provincial Grand Master Thomlinson arrives in Boston.

> 1 Mass. *5.*
> 1914 Mass. 262.
> 1736, December 7, *supra.*

Robert Tomlinson (alias Thomlinson).
Provincial Grand Master for New England from April 20, 1737 to July 16, 1740.

Of Tomlinson's birth and early life we know nothing. His religious activities, his business career, and his wife's family name would indicate that he came from Antigua. The first we know of him is that he was married March 2, 1730, to Elizabeth Gerot (or Gerret) by the Rev. Timothy Cutler, D.D., Rector of Christ Church, Boston. Neither the birth nor baptismal records show children having come to their home, and there is nothing in the scanty records of the probate of his estate to indicate that either a widow or child survived him. October 29, 1734 (Suffolk Registry of Deeds, book 49, page 174) he purchased a three-eighths interest in two lots of land on the shore with a wharf. This property was located in Boston on the Charles River, not far from the present site of the Massachusetts General Hospital. The wharf went into decay, for there being no clear channel the larger vessels could not be accommodated at it. Later the building of the West Boston Bridge and the closer connection with Cambridge and the inland towns brought this region into a new prominence for development, though then we find another the owner of the whole property.

Tomlinson was made a Mason on January 13, 1735, in the First Lodge in Boston and was later accepted in the Masters Lodge, although he was not raised here. He was chosen Master of the First Lodge in Boston on St. John the Baptist's Day, 1736, and at the Festival of St. John the Evangelist was appointed Deputy Grand Master by Henry Price, being succeeded by Thomas Oxnard as Master of the Lodge. His commission as Provincial Grand Master from the Earl of Loudoun, etc., Grand Master of the Free and Accepted Masons of England, dated December 7, 1736, was received here by Tomlinson on April 20, 1737, and in June he celebrated the Festival of St. John the Baptist.

During 1738 Tomlinson went to England by way of Antigua "where finding some old Boston Masons went to Work and made the Governour and sundry other Gentlemen of Distinction Masons, whereby from Our Lodge sprung Masonry in the West Indies." (This extract from the Massachusetts records is possibly in part in error. He undoubtedly founded a new Lodge in Antigua as related but it is believed that in Antigua, Parham Lodge was constituted January 31, 1737; Court House Lodge November 22, 1738; Baker's Lodge March 14, 1738/9; and another Lodge at St. John not long after.) He attended the meeting of the Grand Lodge of England held at the Devil Tavern near Temple Bar on Wednesday, January 31, 1738/9, *q.v.*

In May, 1739, Tomlinson returned to Boston and holding a Grand Lodge received the congratulations of the Brethren in Due Form.

On December 27th of that year Tomlinson appointed Thomas Oxnard as Deputy Grand Master, and we find the official minute in the Massachusetts record book,

"Nothing further Remarkable Occur'd this Year, only the Craft Continued flourishing."

Shortly thereafter Tomlinson returned to Antigua, where he soon died. The burial register of St. John's, Antigua, contains the following entry, viz.: "1740 July 16 Robert Tomlinson, Merchant, from Boston."

Benjamin Hallowell, a prominent member of the Fraternity who rose to the rank of Deputy Grand Master, evidently was very closely associated with Tomlinson and had reason to believe that on July 15, 1740, at Antigua, Tomlinson had made his will. This will was lost and has never been found, although strenuous exertions were made to discover it, various persons being carefully examined who were suspected of having sequestered it. In September, October, and November, 1740, Hallowell caused the following advertisement to be published in several issues of the *Boston Evening*

Post, the *New England Weekly Journal*, and the *Boston Weekly Post Boy:*

"WHEREAS: Robert Tomlinson, late of Boston, Merchant, at the Island of Antigua, on the 15th of July last made his Will, touching his estate in the West Indies, and thereby directed the Executors of that will (after payment of his debts and Funeral expenses and other disbursements), to transmit the Remainder of his estate to me, Benjamin Hallowell, of Boston, to be disposed of as his Will there (in Boston) directs; and the said Robert soon after died, but his Will last mentioned has not yet been found: These therefore, are earnestly to desire to such persons (if any such there be) as hath in his possession that Will, by the said Testator declared to be in Boston, to carry the same to the Hon. the Judge of the Probate of Wills for the County of Suffolk, or to the Registers Office, or to give me notice thereof, that so the Will of the deceased Gentleman may be lawfully proved, and afterwards fulfilled.

"BENJAMIN HALLOWELL."

Brother Hallowell's appointment as Administrator is still on file in the Suffolk Probate office, though there are no records of inventory, account, or distribution of the estate. The following is the advertisement in three successive issues of the *Boston News Letter*, beginning December 4, 1740, of Benjamin Hallowell as Administrator of the estate:

"All Persons indebted to the Estate of Robert Thomlinson, late of Boston, Merchant, deceased, are desired forthwith to pay their respective Debts to Benjamin Hallowell of said Boston, Administrator on said Estate, without further Notification than this Advertisement; and such as have any Demands on said Estate, are also desired speedily to bring in their Accounts to the said Administrator, in order to a Settlement."

I have recently discovered Brother Tomlinson's will. It was made in London, April 11, 1739, while he was on his last visit there. The following is extracted from the Principal Registry of the Probate, Divorce and Admiralty Division of the High Court of Justice in the Prerogative Court of Canterbury.

I, ROBERT THOMLINSON of Boston in New England in America Merchant do make and declare this to be my last Will and Testament and do hereby revoke all other Wills by me heretofore made   First my Will is that all my just debts be fully paid and satisfied Also I give all the rest and residue of my estate after my debts are paid to my brother Richard Thomlinson my sister Isabel Robinson and sister Catherine Robinson to be equally divided amongst them share and share alike In WITNESS whereof I have hereunto set my hand and seal the eleventh day of April in the year of our Lord 1739.— ROB^t THOMLINSON (LS)—Sealed published and declared in the presence of—ROB^t YORK—M. ROBINSON.—

Administration (with Will)
    granted 29th January 1740
    Fos 4 HJT.
    22. Spurway.

On the Twenty-ninth day of January in the Year of our Lord one Thousand and fforty[1] Administration with the Will annexed of the Goods Chattles and Credits of Robert Thomlinson late of Boston in New England in America Batchelor[2] deceased was granted to Richard Thomlinson the natural and lawfull Brother of the said deceased and one of the Residuary Legatees named in

[1] Old Style. This would be 1741, New Style. It is the January following his death (July, 1740).
[2] He was a widower, not a bachelor.

the said Will (for that no Executor is named therein) being first sworn duly to administer the same.

The most careful search has so far failed to bring to light any portrait of Brother Tomlinson.

1737, April 24, Boston.
Meeting of the First Lodge. Brother Richard Wolfe admitted.
P.L.

1737, April 25, Boston.
The *Boston Gazette* contains the following item of news, *viz.*

"That the Order of Free Mafons, eftablifhed long fince in England, has become lately much in Vogue at Paris, there being great ftriving to be admitted, even at the Expence of ten Louis d'Ors; 18 or 20 Perfons of great Diftinction have been lately created Mafons, amongft whom was the Marfhal d'Eftrees; and five Lodges are already eftablifhed, which makes fo great a Noife, and gives fo much Offence to People ignorant of their Mifteries, that it's expected they will fpeedily be fupprefs'd as they have been in Holland."
P–t.

1737, After April 28, and before April 27, 1738.
London—West Indies.
The Earl of Darnley, Grand Master of England, issued a Deputation to Captain William Douglas, as Provincial Grand Master on the coast of Africa and in the Islands of America; excepting such places where a Provincial Grand Master is already deputed. He also

issued one to James Watson, Esq., as Provincial Grand Master for Montserrat.

Preston (Portsmouth, 1804) 187.
Entick (1756 Ed.) 333.
Anderson (1738 Ed.) 195.
P.C. (2nd London Ed.) 116.

1737, May 3,   Philadelphia.
Entries in L. B. indicate a meeting.

1737, May 11,   Boston.
Meeting of the First Lodge. Alexander French made and Brother John Maxwell admitted.

P.L.
B.MS.

1737, May 12,   Philadelphia.
The *Pennsylvania Gazette* has an account of the election of the Grand Master of Scotland.

1737, May 26,   Charleston, S. C.
"The Recruiting Officer" was acted at Charleston for the entertainment of the Fraternity "who came to the play-house . . . in the usual manner." The Entered Apprentice's and Master's songs were sung, the Masons in the Pit joining in the chorus. "After the play, the Masons returned to the Lodge at Mr. Shepheard's in the same order observed in coming to the play-house."

South Carolina Gazette for May 28, 1737.

This is the first reported Masonic procession in America, though it does not appear that any regalia was worn.

1737, June 2,   Philadelphia.

The *Pennsylvania Gazette* has an account of a Masonic funeral in London.

1737, June 6,   Philadelphia.

L. B. charges the entrance fees of Dr. Thomas Cadwalader, Michael Cario, William Deering, Thomas Esdaile, David Humphrey, John Jones, and Henry Lewis.

1737, June 8,   Boston.

Meeting of the First Lodge. Captain Edward Clerke (Clarke) of New York and Albert Dennie made.

　　　P.L.

　　　B.MS.

1737, June 9,   Boston.

The *Boston Weekly News Letter* has the following curious item:

"The Humour of entring into the Society cal'd Free Mafons, runs fo high in France that there are no lefs than nine Lodges conftituted in Paris, a vaft many young Noblemen are become Members of the Order, particularly the Prince of Conti, and even the Minifter for the Marine Affairs, as well as feveral General Officers and two Bifhops. The Ladies pufh forward for an inftitution of this Kind, in order for an engraftment but the Princefs of Carignan is the only Woman yet discovered that can fteep (*sic*) a secret, fo that the Female Mafonry, it's thought, will fall to the Ground.—juft now we have Advice that Monfieur Blarer the noted Flute Player, and Monfieur Leclainlee, the famous Fidler, with feveral other Men of Science, and Poets of all Sizes were admitted Members, but as the old Cure of St. Sulpice the Great Pro ector (*sic*), and Father Tournemin the celebrated preacher and Jesuit, were going to initiate themfelves, out comes an Order from the King, like a Thunderbolt, and throws down the Babel Building."

P–t.

1737, June 16,   Philadelphia.

The *Pennsylvania Gazette* publishes an item copied in the *Boston Evening Post* of June 27, 1737, the *New England Weekly Journal* of June 28, 1737, and the *Boston Weekly News Letter* of June 30, 1737. It is as follows:

"Philadelphia, June 16.

We hear, that Monday night laft, fome People pretending to be Free Mafons, got together in the Cellar, with a young Man who was defirous of being made one, and in the Ceremony, 'tis faid, they threw fome burning Spirits on him, which burnt him fo that he was obliged to take to his bed, and died this Morning."

Immediately after this event there was published as an advertisement in the *Pennsylvania Gazette* and the *American Weekly Mercury* the following:

Penn'a, SS., Hopkinson, Grand Master.

Whereas, fome ill-difposed Perfons in this City affuming the Name of *Free-Mafons*, have for some years paft impofed upon feveral well-meaning People, who defirous of becoming true Brethren, perfuading them, after they had performed certain ridiculous Ceremonies, that they were really become Free-Mafons, and have lately, under the Pretence of making a Young Man *a Mafon*, caused his Death, as 'tis faid, by Purging, Vomiting, Burning, and the Terror of certain horrid and diabolical rites: It is thought proper, for preventing fuch

Impofitions for the future, and to avoid any unjust Af-
perfions that may be thrown on the Antient and Honourable Fraternity on this Account, either in this city or
any other Part of the World, to publifh this Advertife-
ment, declaring the Abhorance of all true Brethren to
fuch Practices in general, and their Innocence of this
Fact in particular: and that the Perfons concerned in this
wicked Action are not of our Society, nor of any Society
of *Free and Accepted Mafons*, to our knowledge or Belief.

Signed in Behalf of all the Members of St. John's
Lodge, at Philad'a the 16th day of June, 1737.

> Thomas Hopkinfon, Grand Mafter.
> Will. Plumftead, Deputy Mafter.
> Joseph Shippen ⎱ Grand Warden
> Henry Pratt ⎰

The attestation of this document tends to confirm what
has been hinted above, to the effect that there was up to
this date but one Lodge in Philadelphia and also that
the Lodge and the Grand Lodge there were one and the
same.

1737, June 23,   Philadelphia.

The *Pennsylvania Gazette* publishes the result of the
coroner's inquest on the matter referred to under 1737,
June 16, *supra*, to the effect that the throwing of the
spirits was accidental.

> See also *Boston Weekly News Letter* for July
> 7, 1737.

1737, June 24,   Boston.

The *Boston Gazette* for June 27, 1737, publishes the
following account of the Festival on this day:

"Friday laſt being the Feaſt of St. John the Baptiſt, the annual Meeting of the Free and Accepted Maſons, they accordingly met. The right worſhipful Mr. Robert Thomlinſon G. M. nominated and appointed his grand Officers for the Year enſuing, viz Mr. Hugh McDaniel D.G.M. Mr. Thomas Moffatt, (Doctor of Medicines) S.G.W. Mr. John Osborne J.G.W. Mr. Benjamin Hallowell, G.T. Mr. Francis Beteillie (Beteilhe) G.S. after which the Society attended the G.M. in Proceſſion to his Excellency Governour Belcher, & from thence the Governour was attended by the G.M. and the Brotherhood to the Royal Exchange Tavern in King-Street, where they had an elegant Entertainment. It being the firſt Proceſſion in America, they appeared in the proper Badges of their Order, ſome Gold, the reſt Silver. The Proceſſion was cloſed by the Grand Wardens."

P–t.

1 Mass. 6.

This item was copied in the *St. James Evening Post*, London, for August 20, 1737.

1 Mass. 470.

This was perhaps the first American procession of a Lodge as such in regalia.

But see 1737, May 26, *supra*.

Philadelphia.

William Plumstead was chosen Grand Master of Pennsylvania at a Grand Lodge held at the Indian King.

Pennsylvania Gazette for June 30, 1737.

Boston Weekly News Letter for July 14, 1737, *q.v.*

William Plumstead.

William Plumstead was a son of Clement Plumstead, Provincial Councillor, and was born in Philadelphia,

November 7, 1708. In 1724, he was taken abroad by his father. He became a Common Councilman of the City in 1739, and upon his return from a voyage to England in 1741, was suggested for the Provincial Council. He was chosen Register of Wills in 1735; 1748, Alderman; 1750, Judge of the Orphans' Court; 1754, Mayor of the City, and 1764, President Judge of the Court of Quarter Sessions. He was chosen Senior Grand Warden in 1735; Deputy Grand Master in 1736; Grand Master in 1737; and Grand Treasurer in 1755. He renounced Quakerism, and became an Episcopalian, and was one of the founders of the St. Peter's Church at Third and Pine Streets, Philadelphia. He died, August 10, 1765, and was buried in St. Peter's churchyard.

1 O.M.L.P. 40.

1737, June 27,   Boston.

The *Boston Evening Post* publishes the item referred to under 1737, June 16, *supra*.

    P–t.

1737, June 28,   Boston.

The *New England Weekly Journal* publishes the item referred to under 1737, June 16, *supra*.

1737, June 30,   Boston.

The *Boston Weekly News Letter* publishes the item referred to under 1737, June 16, *supra*.

    P–t.

1737, July 2,   Charleston, S. C.

The *South Carolina Gazette* announces the arrival at Charleston of the "Free-Mason," from Providence, referring to it as a sloop.

1737, July 4, Boston.

The *Boston Gazette* publishes the following item of news from London:

"April 26. Yefterday at Noon the Earl of Darnley Grand Mafter elect of the Antient and Honourable Society of Free Mafons in a Chariot drawn by fix fine Horfes, attended with upwards of an hundred Coaches & Chariots, went from his Lordship's Houfe in Pall-Mall, where the Company Breakfafted, which coft his Lordfhip two hundred Pounds, and then proceeded thro' the City to Fifhmonger's Hall, where a Grand Entertainment was provided: There were three Pair of Kettle Drums, fix Trumpets, and eight French Horns, properly difpos'd in the Proceffion."
P–t.

1737, July 11, Boston.

The *Boston Evening Post* publishes the following extract of a private letter from Paris:

"The Court has taken fuch Offence at the vaft and fudden Increafe of the Society of Free Mafons, that the King has forbid their Meeting at any of their Lodges, and looks with an indifferent eye on thofe who have been forward in entering into a Society, that even the States of Holland would not fuffer amongft them."
P–t.

1737, July 14, Boston.

The *Boston Weekly News Letter* publishes the following item quoted from the *Pennsylvania Gazette* of June 30, 1737:

"Friday laft was held, at the Indian King in this City, a Grand Lodge of the Free and Accepted Mafons; when

WILLIAM PLUMSTEAD

William Plumstead was unanimously chofen Grand
Mafter of this Province, for the Year enfuing; who appointed Jofeph Shippen, jun. to be his Deputy, and
Meffrs Henry Prat, and Philip Syng, were nominated
and chofen Grand Wardens."

P–t.

1737, July 21,   Charleston, S. C.

The *South Carolina Gazette* publishes the following:

"Last Thurfday, (21st July, 1737), John Hammerton, Efq., Receiver General of his Majefty's Quit-rents,
Secretary and one of his Majefty's Honourable Council,
who has been the firft Mafter of the Lodge of the
Ancient and Honourable Society of Free Mafons in this
place, and intending to embark on board the ship Molly
Galley, John Caruthers, Mafter, for London, at a Lodge
held that evening, refigned his office, for the true and
faithful difcharge of which he received the thanks of
the whole Society, who were 30 in number. James
Graeme, Efq., was then unanimoufly chofen Mafter in
his room, and having been duly inftalled into that office
with the ufual ceremonies, was pleafed to chufe and
appoint James Wright, Efq., who was Junior Warden,
to be Senior Warden, and Maurice Lewis, Efq., Junior
Warden."

Concerning the new Master, shortly to become Provincial Grand Master, Brother Mackey in his "History
of Freemasonry in South Carolina" says:

"James Graeme, who was an attorney at law, held, at
the time of his appointment as Master of the new Lodge,
the position of Commissioner of the Market. Afterwards he was appointed a Lieutenant in the Second Company of Militia, which was enrolled in November, 1738,
for the defence of the Province against an anticipated

attack of the Spaniards of Florida. Subsequently he was a Representative from Charleston in the Commons House of Assembly and finally received from the Crown the appointments of Chief Justice of the Province, Judge of the Court of Admiralty, and a seat in his Majesty's Council, offices which he held until his death, which took place on Saturday, 29th of August, 1752.

S. Car. Gazette, 1st Sept. 1752."

James Wright, afterwards Senior Warden, Master and Provincial Grand Master, will be referred to hereafter.

Maurice Lewis was the progenitor of a large family, many of whose members have held elevated positions in South Carolina. He himself was, in 1738, appointed one of the Commissioners to build up the curtain line before Charleston Bay.

Philadelphia.

The *Pennsylvania Gazette* copies from the *Boston Gazette* the item referred to under 1737, July 4, *supra*.

1737, July 27,   Boston.

 Meeting of the First Lodge. Thomas Pearson made.
   P.L.
   B.MS.

1737, August 10,   Philadelphia.

 Franklin charges the Lodge at Brother Hubard's for "Freight of limes, 3.0."
     F.J.

It is surmised that the Lodge put these limes to a use which would be unlawful in the United States to-day.

1737, August 18,   Charleston, S. C.

The *South Carolina Gazette* for Saturday, the 20th of August, 1737, contains the following important paragraph:

"On Thurſday night laſt, (18th of August,) at the Solomon's Lodge in Charles-Town, a Deputation from the Right Worſhipful and Right Honourable John, Earl of Loudoun, conſtituting and appointing a Provincial Grand Maſter of South Carolina, was read, when James Graeme, Eſq., the preſent Grand Maſter of the ſaid Province, propoſed James Wright, Eſq., to be Maſter of the Solomon's Lodge, which was unanimouſly agreed to by the Lodge."

In this news item the Lodge, for the first time is referred to as "Solomon's Lodge."

1737, August 24,   Boston.
Meeting of the First Lodge.   Brother Richard Wolfe admitted.
       P.L.

1737, September 12,   Boston.
The *Boston Evening Post* quotes "From *the Political State* for May, 1737," the following item:

"The 28th Inſtant at Noon the Society of Free Maſons, went with uncommon Splendor from the Houſe of their Grand Maſter the Earl of Darnley, in Pall Mall, to Fiſhmonger's Hall; his Lordſhip appeared on this Occaſion in a Superb Chariot drown by ſix fine Grey Horſes, Kettle Drums, French Horns, Trumpets, were properly diſpoſed in the Proceſſion which conſiſted of above a hundred Coaches and Chariots, all filled with Perſons of Eminence, and the Breakfaſt at his Lordſhip's Houſe coſt upwards of Two Hundred Pounds, all which are undeniable Marks of the Wealth and Wiſdom of the preſent Age!"

P–t.

1737, October 12,   Boston.

Meeting of the First Lodge.   Brother Nathaniel Derby admitted.

P.L.

1737, October 24.   Boston.

The *Boston Evening Post* under the heading of "London, August 5" publishes the following two items among others, *viz:*

"It ſeems they reſolv'd at Paris to go thro' Stitch with the Free Maſons: The Lientenant General of the Police ſent to an Engliſhman's Lodging in the Hotel de Bourgogne, Fauxbourge St. Germain, and his Meſſengers brought away not only the Utenſils, Figures, &c. belonging to the Free Maſons, but alſo the Statutes of their Order, and every thing that ſeem'd to have any Relation to it.   In the Year 1734 the French Miniſtry would have confider'd better of the Matter before they inſulted an Engliſh Free Maſon, for fear of ruffing the P—of B—; but Adieu Panniers, Vendanges: ſont faites."

"We hear that a Deputation from the Society of Free and Accepted Maſons of this Kingdom is to be ſent to Germany, to congratulate (a Royal Brother) the Duke of Lorrain on his Acceſſion to the Dutchy of Tuſcany."

P–t.

1737, October 26,   Boston.

Meeting of the First Lodge.   Andrew Hill made and Brother John Waghorn admitted.

P.L.

1737, November 9,   Boston.

Meeting of the First Lodge. John Tucker and Peter Buckley made, and Brother John Saint admitted.

P.L.

1737, November 11,   Boston.

Meeting of the First Lodge. Joseph Smith made.

P.L.

1737, November 14,   Boston.

Meeting of the First Lodge. Erasmus James Phillips made, and Brother J. Sheriff admitted.

P.L.

1737, November 15,   New York.

Capt. Richard Riggs was this day appointed Provincial Grand Master for New York by the Earl of Darnley, Grand Master of England. It is believed that he authorized the formation of one Lodge before September 24, 1739, because in the *New York Gazette* for that date is a notice of its meeting.

Anderson (1738 Ed.) 195.

Entick (1756 Ed.) 333.

P.C. (2nd English Ed.) 116.

S. & H. 255.

IV Gould 414.

1737, November 28,   Boston.

The *Boston Evening Post* contains a notice of the meeting of Lodge No. 9, in London, on September 21, 1737.

P–t.

New York.

Article in *New York Gazette* on the "New and unusual sect or society of persons of late appeared in our native country and at last has extended to these parts of America" and complaining that "this society, called Freemasons, meet with their doors shut and a guard at the outside." It will be noted that this was just after Provincial Grand Master Riggs' appointment but before news of the appointment could have reached New York. Captain Riggs arrived in New York some months later (May 21, 1738).

1737, December 1,   Philadelphia.

The *Pennsylvania Gazette* reports the appointment of a Provincial Grand Master for the Leeward group of the West India Islands.

1737, December 5,   Boston.

The *Boston Gazette* contains the following advertisement concerning the Pro. G. M.:

"Mr. Robert Thomlinſon being bound ſpeedily for England, deſires all Perſons that have any Demands on him forthwith to apply for Payment; and alſo Requeſts thoſe Indebted to him not to delay the ſame."
    P–t.

1737, December 8, Charleston, S. C.

The *South Carolina Gazette* announces the arrival of the "Free Mason" from New York.

1737, December 12,   Boston.

The advertisement of December 5 (*q.v.*) is repeated.

1737, December 14,   Boston.
  Meeting of the First Lodge. Stephen Deblois made.
  P.L.

1737, December 19,   Boston.
  The advertisement of December 5 (q.v.) is repeated.

1737, December 27,   Boston.
  The Festival is celebrated and shortly thereafter Provincial Grand Master Thomlinson leaves for England by way of Antigua.
      1 Mass. 6.

Charleston, S. C.
The *S. C. Gazette* for December 29, 1737, says:

"On Tuefday laft, being St. John's day, all the members of the Ancient and Honourable Society of Free and Accepted Mafons in this place met at Mr. Seaman's, Mafter of Solomon's Lodge, from whence they proceeded, all properly clothed, under the found of French horns, to wait on James Graeme, Efq., Provincial Grand Mafter, at his houfe in Broad Street, where they were received by all the members of the Grand Lodge. After a fhort ftay there, they all went in proceffion and with the enfigns of their Order into the Court-Room at Mr. Charles Shepheard's houfe, making a very grand fhow. Here, to a numerous audience of Ladies and Gentlemen, who were admitted by tickets, the Grand Mafter made a very elegant fpeech in praife of Mafonry, which we hear was univerfally applauded. Then the Grand Lodge withdrew in order to proceed to the election of a Grand Mafter for the ensuing year, when James Graeme, Efq., was unanimoufly re-chofen Grand Mafter, who appointed James Wright, Efq., Deputy Grand Mafter, Maurice Lewis, Esq., Senior Grand Warden, John Crookfhanks, Efq., Junior Grand Warden, James

Mitchie, Efq., Grand Treafurer, and James Gordon, Efq., Grand Secretary.

The fame day Mr. James Crokatt was unanimously chofen Mafter of Solomon's Lodge."

James Crokatt was evidently a citizen of some distinction for the succeeding June he was appointed "one of His Majesty's Honourable Council."

1737/8, January 24, New York.

Gould states that the earliest Lodge in New York "of which any record has been preserved was in full working order, and had probably existed for some time" before this day.

IV Gould 260.

1737/8, January 25, Boston.

Meeting of the First Lodge. James Carrel Tabbs and Thomas Walker made and Brother John Hutchinson admitted.

P.L.

1737/8, January 26, Charleston, S. C.

In the *South Carolina Gazette* for this day we find the following important record:

"We hear that at Mr. William Flud's, at the fign of the Harp and Crown, is held a Lodge of the Ancient and Honourable Society of Free and Accepted Mafons, belonging to the Lodge of St. John. Dr. Newman Oglethorpe being chofen Mafter."

Mackey's "History of Freemasonry in South Carolina" comments interestingly upon this item of news as follows:

"Perfectly to understand the character of this Lodge, it will be necessary to refer to the history of Masonry in another part of the Continent. In the year 1733, Viscount Montacute, then Grand Master of England, granted a Warrant, or more properly a Deputation, appointing Henry Price, of Boston, Provincial Grand Master of North America. Under this authority he opened a Provincial Grand Lodge in Boston on the 30th of July, 1733, and appointed his Deputy and Wardens. The Grand Lodge thus organized, assumed and was recognized by the appellation of 'St. John's Grand Lodge,' and proceeded to grant Warrants for instituting regular Lodges in various parts of North America. Webb,[1] from whom this account is taken, mentions South Carolina as one of the places in which these new Lodges were instituted. But until I met with the paragraph above cited from the *Carolina Gazette* I had found no other account of the Lodge instituted in South Carolina by St. John's Grand Lodge of Boston, than the mere announcement in *Webb's Monitor* that such a Lodge had been constituted. There is, however, no longer any doubt that the Lodge said to have been held in 1738 in Charlestown, at 'the Harp and Crown,' received its warrant from St. John's Grand Lodge of Boston, and hence the journalist calls it a 'Lodge of St. John.' The phraseology of the paragraph seems to indicate that it had an existence anterior to the date of the notice. It was probably organized late in the year 1737, and was thus the second Lodge established in the Province. But as its Constitution was manifestly an interference with the prerogatives and jurisdiction of the Provincial Grand Lodge, it must have been soon abandoned, and hence it is that we find no further account of it in the subsequent Masonic proceedings of the Province."

See page 146.

1737/8, January 31,   Antigua.

Lodge Constituted at Parham, Antigua, first given in

[1] *Webb's Monitor*, Ed. 1808, p. 299.

the Official English List for 1740, appearing as No. 154.

    P.C. (2nd Eng. Ed.) 378.

    Entick (1756 Ed.) 337.

    L.M.R. 74.

    L.H.B. 40.

1737/8, February 13.   Boston.

The *Boston Evening Post* copies from the *London Magazine* an article reading as follows:

"This Writer ſuppoſes, that this Fraternity might as well be call'd the Society of Carpenters, Joiners, Chimney-Sweepers, or Rat-Catchers, as Maſons; and endeavours to prove this parodoxical Truth, That the Maſons are no Maſons.

Agatharcbus the Athenian, Archimedes, Virtruvius, &c as well as the later Architects and Mathematicians, have deliver'd their Knowledge in this Science freely, generally and publickly.   How then can this be the Art, that is kept ſecret in the Breaſts of the Members of the modern Lodges? as the Constitution Book affects, that altho' this Society is poſſeſs'd of many Arts (curious ones, no doubt) yet do they dwell ſecurely in the Breaſts of the Brethren.

Nor does it appear by their Performances, that they are taught in the Lodges to hew, mould ſtone, lay a Level, or raiſe a Perpendicular.   How then can they be ſaid to be Maſons?   Is a Drawer a Maſon, becauſe he keeps his Reckoning ſquare?   Or a Tinker, becauſe he rings his Kettle by Rule?   If a Lawyer can compoſe his Cauſe, or a Bookſetter erect monumental Volumes; if a Porter ſtand ſtrong as a Coloſſus, and an Apothecary can temper his electuarial Mortars and Cements, to new-frame, and, as it were, rebuild our animate edifices: Yet cannot I perceive the leaſt Tincture of Vitruviſm, Euclidiſm, or Burlingtonism in any of theſe.

Laſtly, if the Art of Maſonry be really and truly

vefted in this Society, how comes it to pafs, that the Brethren build no better than fome of the monied Gentry among the Grubs, who, I own, feldom build any Thing but Caftles in the Air?

Having thus shewn what they are not, let us confider what they are, and from whence the Word Mafon, as applied to this Club, may be corrupted. The Society I allow to be a very antient one; and, I believe, they will not thank me for acknowledging, that fuch a ftrange Society may have been even as old as Chaucer; in whofe Dayes the Word mafe was ufed to fignify a Whim, or Fancy; And what could be more natural, than to diftinguifh a Society by this Name, which hath fo many peculiar whimfical Oddities? Doubt not then candid Bavy that the Word Mafon is a corruption of this Mafe; Which will appear ftill more probable, if thou wilt take a Ride or Walk to Devonshire; where, to this Day they call any Perfon whom they imagine to be mad, a Mafe, or Maze, Man or Woman. Some wicked Perfons, I know, would derive this Name from the popifh Mafe, which, I own is of very intricate Nature: Yet muft I reject fuch a malevolent Suppofition, if it was only becaufe so many zealous Protestants, nay even Jews, the conftant Enemies to Tranfubftantiation, are accepted Brethren.

A. H. F. G. S."

P–t.

1737/8, February 14, Philadelphia.

The *Philadelphia Gazette* publishes an account of the trial of those concerned in the mock initiation in Philadelphia which is copied in part in the *Boston Evening Post* for March 6th, *infra* (*q.v.*), the *New England Weekly Journal* for March 7th, and the *Boston Weekly News Letter* for March 9th.

The *American Weekly Mercury* published February 14th, at Philadelphia starts an anti-Masonic campaign by a letter based upon the events of the trial. Franklin in the *Gazette* of the same date (though issued the next day) replies.

Bradford in the *Mercury* is so bitter that he even refers to a band of negro thieves as a Lodge of Free Masons, and, utterly without foundation, accuses Franklin of conniving in the mock initiation.

1737/8, February 21, Philadelphia.

The *Pennsylvania Gazette* publishes an account of a Masonic Celebration in Charleston, S. C., and a notice of a Lodge in New York.

In the *American Weekly Mercury* is a rejoinder to Franklin's reply of February 14th.

1737/8, February 23. Boston.

The *Boston Weekly News Letter* publishes the following in an extract of a letter from Paris repeated from London under date of October 5, 1737, viz.:

"You have no doubt the Account of an Act of arbitrary Power of a very high Strain, I mean the forcing open the Doors of the French Free Maſons Lodge here by the Lieutenant-General of Police. Various are the Diſcourſes upon this Occaſion: Some ſay that the Inquiſition of Florence has tortur'd out Confeſſions from the Brethren of the Order impriſon'd ſome Weeks ago in that City, and ſent our Court an Account of their Diſcoveries; but whether there is any Truth or not in this Report, the Clergy here have decided open War againſt all Free-Maſonry, and upon this Declaration of the Clergy, the People look upon all Free-Maſons to be rank Hereticks, and dangerous to common Society. But, not to lay any Streſs on theſe Opinions, the Free-Maſons

were doubtlefs a Parcel of Madmen, to think of eftab-
lifhing Lodges under an arbitrary Government, efpecially
in any Country where there is an Inquifition or a Baf-
tile."

P–t.

1737/8, March 6,   Boston.

The *Boston Evening Post* quotes from the *Pennsylvania Gazette* the article referred to under date of February 14, 1737/8, *supra*, as follows:

"Philadelphia, Feb. 7. On Wednefday laft, at the
Court of Oyer and Terminer then fitting here, came on
the Trial of Evan Jones, Chymift, for being a Principal
concern'd in the death of D. R. a young Man who had
been his Apprentice, and was but juft free, in June laft.
The Trial began at Nine o'Clock in the Forenoon, and
lafted till almoft Two next Morning. The Jury found
him guilty of Manflaughter, and he was accordingly
burnt in the Hand, and order'd to find sufficient Security
for his good Behaviour. There was the greateft Throng
of People to hear the Trial, that perhaps ever appear'd
at any Trial in this Province. By the Evidence, fome
of whom were deeply concern'd in the Affair, it appear'd,
That the Deceafed, having made known to his Mafter
his Defires of being a Free-Mafon, he and fome of his
Affociates, contriv'd to make themfelves Mirth, by im-
pofing on the young Fellow, and making him believe
that they were Free-Mafons: The unwary young Man
was too foon prevail'd with to believe them, fuffer'd fuch
Impofitions (befide that of his Treating them) as at
length terminated in his Death. He was perfuaded to
repeat, after one of the Company, what was call'd an
Oath of Secrecy, but as vile, ftupid, and prophane (to
fay no worfe of it) as ever was invented; after which,
he being Blindfold, they gave him Phyfick to Drink;
and then led him to, and made him Kifs, the bare Pof-
teriors of one of their Company. After all this, viz. on

the 13th of June, at Evening, the Company, who call'd themfelves a Lodge, met again, at Dr. Jone's, in order, as the Deceafed was made to believe, to make him a compleat Free-Mafon. After Supper, the Company retir'd to the Cellar, and then this unhappy Perfon was led down blindfold to them, and there unveil'd: They had prepar'd a Pan of burning Spirits, with Raifins at the Bottom, and were ftanding round, dipping in their Hands for the Raifins, and flirting the Flames about. This was call'd Snap-Dragon. One of the Company was wrap'd in a Hide to represent the Devil, which, with the ftrange Countenances that the Light of the burning Spirits caus'd, made Things there look ghaftly, frightful, devilifh. However, this it seems did not terrify him as was expected, and he had not been long in the Cellar, when the whole Pan of burning Spirits was thrown on him, at which he cry'd out, Mafter, I'm kill'd, I'm kill'd; and, notwithstanding they immediately ftrove to extinguifh the Flames, he was fcorch'd to that Degree that he died on the 16th of the fame Month, in a miferable Manner. It was fworn, that the Doctor was the Perfon who flung or fpilt the Liquor; but no premeditated Malice could be proved, fo he came off with only burning in the Hand, as before related.

And on Thurfday F—R—g—n, Attorney at Law, and E—W— Taylor, were tried for being prefent at, and concern'd in, the faid Affair. The former was found Guilty of Manflaughter, but was pardon'd. The other the Jury acquitted."

P–t.

See also *Boston Weekly News Letter* for March 16, 1737/8.

1737/8, March 7,   Boston.

The *New England Weekly Journal* publishes the account quoted under 1737/8, March 6, *supra*.

P–t.

1737/8, March 9,   Boston.

The *Boston Weekly News Letter* publishes the account last referred to.

   P–t.

1737/8, March 13, Boston—Nova Scotia.

The *Boston Gazette* publishes the following paragraph:

"We are inform'd That Major Phillips is Appointed Provincial Grand Mafter over the Free and Accepted Mafons, in the Province of Nova Scotia, and that a Deputation is getting ready for that purpofe."

   P–t.

   See 1739, April 11, *infra*.

It has been heretofore thought that the above appointment was made about 1740.

Erasmus James Phillips.

Erasmus James Philipps (Phillips), the first Provincial Grand Master of Nova Scotia, was a nephew of Col. Richard Philipps, Governor of Nova Scotia from 1716 to 1749, being a son of his brother Erasmus, and was born April 23, 1705. The father, Erasmus, was the Captain of the "Blandford," a frigate lost with all hands in March, 1719.

Erasmus James entered the 40th regiment of Foot when a young man and was successively ensign, lieutenant, captain and major. This regiment, known as "the Fighting Fortieth," was organized at Annapolis on August 25, 1717 (its first Colonel being Col. Richard Philipps) and garrisoned the fort from that year until 1755 and probably till 1758, when it formed part of the expedition against Louisburg.

While an ensign in 1726, Philipps was selected by the acting governor, with Captain Joseph Bennett of the same regiment, to accompany the French deputies to Minas to tender oaths of allegiance to the habitans in that district. Owing to the prevalence of unfavourable weather they failed to reach the settlements there and the matter was postponed to a future day.

On February 23rd, 1729, he was appointed Advocate of the Vice-Admiralty of the Province of Nova Scotia or Acadia by the British Government, a position which he held until July, 1749.

The minutes of the Council of the Province, held at Annapolis Royal on December 7th, 1730, record that "His Excellency likewise acquainted ye Board that there not being Councillors enough upon ye spot to make up a Quorum he thought proper, with their advice to appoint Mr. Eras. Jas. Philipps a member thereof, who was sworn accordingly." He seems to have acted as Secretary of the Council for several months, and continued a member of the Council until his death in 1760.

In November, 1734, Philipps and thirty-five others, including all the members of the Government in England and of the Council of the Province, were made proprietors and patentees of some mines discovered in the Province, "as a Recompense of their many years Service at this Board." Such a resolution in these days would be regarded with some suspicion and would be the subject of investigation, but none of the proprietors seem to have grown rich as a result of their action.

In August, 1736, a grant was made to Philipps (at that time Captain in the 40th Regiment) and others of 50,000 acres of land "at Norwich, in the County of Norfolk, in Nova Scotia." This tract of land was situated at or near Chignecto, in what is now Cumberland County and was afterwards escheated and revested in the Crown in 1760.

In the archives of New Hampshire under date of August 1st, 1737, there is a record to the effect that Dr. W. Skene, E. J. Philipps and Otho Hamilton of H. M. Council of Nova Scotia, met at Hampton, N. H., with four commissioners from Rhode Island to mark out and settle the boundaries between the Province of Massachusetts Bay and the Colony of Rhode Island. He was in Boston from August, 1737, to June, 1738. A later commission, dated September 4, 1740, reappointed the same commissioners and several others for a similar purpose. He left Annapolis for New England in April, 1741, and was at Providence, Rhode Island, until June, 1741.

About 1740 he married Ann, eldest daughter of John Dyson and Alice his wife, by whom he had four children, Ann, who married Col. Robert Fenwick, R. A.; John Erasmus, born at Annapolis, April 30, 1741, Capt. 35th Regiment, died at New York, December, 1776; Elizabeth, who married Capt. Horatio Gates; and Dorothy, unmarried.

In the fall of 1746, the government decided on the military occupation of Grand Pré and a detachment of 470 men of the Massachusetts forces was sent to that place, disembarking on the day before Christmas day, where they were quartered on the inhabitants. The force was under the command of Colonel Arthur Noble and Major Philipps, and Edward How accompanied them as commissioner in charge of the administration of civil affairs and as commissary. The news of the occupation reached the French commander De Ramezay at

Chignecto on January 8, 1747, and he at once decided on an attack. A force of 300 men under Coulon de Villiers marched overland, reaching Grand Pré on February 11th, and attacked the sleeping New England forces at night in a blinding snow storm. The battle which followed was perhaps the most stubbornly contested fight in the history of Acadia. Colonel Noble and his brother were killed, Edward How was wounded and taken prisoner and after several hours' resistance during which the Massachusetts men fought in their shirts in hand-to-hand conflicts in the snow storm, with great losses, they capitulated on honourable terms at daybreak. They were allowed to march out of the village with the honours of war and permitted to retire to Annapolis, on making a declaration not to bear arms against the French for six months.

After the Treaty of Aix-la-Chapelle in 1749 we find Philipps among the claimants for compensation for losses sustained in consequence of the destruction of buildings torn down by the order of the Commander-in-Chief for the better defence of the place in the recent war. In the same year, 1749, Major Philipps resigned his office as King's Advocate in the Court of Vice-Admiralty, giving as the reason that "it would henceforth be impossible for him to attend and execute the duties of said office." He continued to live, however, at Annapolis.

On the 1st January, 1751, Governor Cornwallis issued a special commission to Mr. Philipps as Judge of Probate and Wills to prove the will of Edward How, who had been treacherously murdered by the French and Indians at Chignecto in October, 1750. The document sets forth that it is done "by reason of the distance between Annapolis Royal and the said town of Halifax, the inclemency of the weather and the difficulty of travelling through the country at this time would be attended with great inconvenience and danger to the person or persons on whom the proof of the said Will depends." In conclusion it required him "to transmit the original Will of the said Edward How together with this Commission and your proceedings thereon to me at Halifax as soon as convenient may be."

From 1753-60 Philipps was Commissary of Musters for the garrison at Annapolis.

In 1758 he was honoured by a vote of thanks of the Council for services rendered in 1757 in making prisoners of a number of French habitans who having managed to avoid capture at the time of the expulsion of the Acadians had formed a temporary settlement on the shores of St. Mary's Bay, Digby County.

On the retirement of Mascarene, Major Philipps became commander of the forces at Annapolis, in which capacity he acted until his death, 1760.

In 1759 Major Philipps was chosen a representative in the House of Assembly, for Annapolis County, Colonel Jonathan Hoar being his colleague, but his legislative career was of short duration, as he died suddenly of apoplexy at Halifax in 1760, while on a visit to that town.

Major Philipps was undoubtedly an able, energetic and efficient officer, in both his military and civil employments and managed with judgment public affairs requiring the exercise of skill and tact, always acquitting himself with credit and success.

Erasmus James Philipps, along with J. Sheriff, was made a Mason in The First Lodge at Boston, November

14, 1737, on the occasion of his first visit as a commissioner to settle the boundaries of Massachusetts and Rhode Island. The records of this lodge also show his presence at meetings held on April 11, May 9, November 28, December 26, 1739, and August 12, 1741. In the minutes of April, 1739, he appears as "Rt. Wpfull Bro'r Erasmus James Philipps, G. M. de Nov. Scot."

On his return to Annapolis in 1738 he established a lodge there which it is said was called the Annapolis Royal Lodge and Philipps was its first W. M.

On June 12, 1750, the Hon. Edward Cornwallis and others at Halifax petitioned Erasmus James Philipps as Pro. G. M. for a warrant or deputation to establish a lodge at Halifax. The warrant was received and the first meeting held July 19, 1750, Cornwallis being the first Master.

On March 18, 1751, the second lodge was formed at Halifax.

On Dec. 27, 1757, a Grand Warrant, signed by the Earl of Blessington, G. M. of the "Antients" was issued to Philipps, probably without any request on his part, constituting him "Provincial Grand Master of Novia Scotia and the territories thereunto belonging." This warrant was probably never acted upon, as Philipps' original authority, that of the Grand Lodge of Massachusetts, was the authority of the "Modern" Grand Lodge of England. The warrant from the "Antients" was written by Lawrence Dermott, Grand Secretary, and neither it nor two lodge warrants accompanying it were ever acted upon by Philipps or any one else, but lay dormant until 1784 when the Provincial Grand Lodge of Nova Scotia was formed.

On his death in 1760 Major Philipps was succeeded in

his position of Pro. G. M. by the Hon. Jonathan Belcher, Lieut. Governor of the province.

Major Philipps was thus the founder and first great figure of Freemasonry, not only in Nova Scotia, but in all of Canada.

> 1 Nova Scotia Lodge of Research 44.
>
> 1 Mass. 7.
>
> Ross's History of Freemasonry in Nova Scotia, 19.
>
> IV Gould 331.
>
> 1 Robertson's History of Freemasonry in Canada, 140-152.

1737, Maryland.

There is a tradition of a Lodge at Georgetown, Md., during this year, but without any supporting evidence.

> IV Gould 262.

Boston.

It may be interesting to note in this connection that during this year Provincial Grand Master Henry Price's portrait, the original of which has been destroyed by fire, although copies are preserved, was painted.

> 1871 Mass. 285, 295.
>
> See frontispiece.

Antigua.

Some time during this year Provincial Grand Master Thomlinson while at Antigua found some old Boston Masons and went to work, making the Governor and sundry other gentlemen of distinction Masons.

> 1 Mass. 6.
>
> L.M.R. 483.
>
> See page 117.

Cape Breton, Louisburg and West Indies.

There is a record in a registry book of the **Grand Lodge of England,** that in 1737 William Douglas, Commander of H.M.S. Falmouth, was appointed Provincial Grand Master for the coast of Africa and the islands of America, and Capt. Robert Comins (Commins; Cumins) for Cape Breton and Louisburg. What was meant by the islands of America was, of course, the West Indies, where Commander Douglas touched now and then in the discharge of his naval activities.

See closing items of Chapters **XII** and **XX.**

Chapter XII

1738

1738, April 6,   South Carolina.

"John Hammerton, Esq., P.G.M. of S. Carolina," visited the Grand Lodge of England.

      X Q.C.A. 295.

      Anderson (Ed. 1738) 138.

1738, April 13,   Philadelphia.

Benjamin Franklin writes a letter, the original of which is still preserved, to his father and mother that they are unduly exercised and that Freemasons "have no principles or practices that are inconsistent with religion and good manners."

      See Franklin's "Common-place Book" in the
         Dreer Collection of the Historical Society
         of Pennsylvania.

1738, April 18,   Boston.

The *New England Weekly Journal* published under its news from London:

"We hear that the principal Members of the Society of Free and Accepted Mafons intend to wait on the Prince of Wales, with an humble Requeft to his Royal Highnefs, to accept of the Grand Mafterfhip of that Ancient and Honourable Body for the Year enfuing."

      P.-t.

1738, April 26,   Boston.
 Meeting of the First Lodge. Ebenezer Swan made.
   P.L.

1738, May 21,   New York.
 Provincial Grand Master Riggs' arrival at New York is announced in the *New York Gazette* for this date.

1738, June 2,   Philadelphia.
 The last known meeting of the Lodge at Philadelphia, about which we have learned much from "Libr B," occurs on this date.
   L.B.

1738, June 24,   Boston.
 Celebration of the Festival. Benjamin Hallowell chosen Master of the First Lodge.
   1 Mass. 6.

Savannah, Ga.
 Rev. George Whitefield in his journal records under this date, "Was enabled to read prayer and preach with power before the Freemasons, with whom I afterwards dined."
   Whitefield's Journal.
   Mackey 1518.
   IV Gould 261.

Philadelphia.
 The *Pennsylvania Gazette* for July 6, 1738, recounts the choosing of Joseph Shippen as Grand Master of Pennsylvania at a Grand Lodge held at the Indian King this day and the last entry in "Libr B" bears this date.

The prejudice induced by the mock initiation heretofore referred to was so great that the activities of the Fraternity in Pennsylvania utterly ceased so far as we can learn until June 28, 1749, (*q.v.*) with the exception of a single meeting June 24, 1741 (*q.v.*).

See also

> 1914 Mass. 262.
> 1906 Mass. 90.
> 1903 Mass. 49.

Joseph Shippen.

The Joseph Shippen here mentioned was undoubtedly Joseph Shippen, Jr., born November 28, 1706, a son of Joseph Shippen, a son of the president of the Provincial Council and first Mayor of Philadelphia under Penn's Charter of October 25, 1702. He went in the family by the name of "Gentleman Joe." He served as Junior Grand Warden in 1735, Senior Grand Warden in 1736, Deputy Grand Master in 1737, Grand Master in 1738. He was elected, October 5, 1742, to the City Council, in which he served for many years. In 1755, he again served as Junior Grand Warden. He subsequently removed to Germantown. He died in 1793, and was buried in Christ Church burying ground.

> 1 O.M.L.P. 42.

1738, June 26,   New York.

The *New York Gazette* publishes a song for the Freemasons and a parody on the same for the ladies. They are not worth reprinting, but they never would have found their way into a newspaper unless Freemasonry had become enough of an element in the life of the city to attract public attention.

1738, August 3,   Boston.

Meeting of the First Lodge.   John Cunningham made.
        P.L.

1738, August 23,   Boston.

Meeting of the First Lodge.   John Cunningham admitted.

        P.L.

1738, August 28,   Boston.

The *Boston Evening Post* publishes the following paragraph:

"A Conftitution by the Pope is publifhed at Rome, which forbids the affociating of the Free Mafons upon Pain of Excommunication; and that in the mean time thofe Societies at Florence and Leghorn which were fupprefs'd in the Reign of the late Duke, have open'd their Lodges again without fear of the Inquifition, becaufe the Prefent Great Duke is a Brother; and they write from Conftantinople, Smyrna, and Aleppo, that the Societies there are very much increafed; and that they have admitted feveral Turks of Diftinction."
        P–t.

1738, September 11,   Boston.

The *Boston Evening Post* publishes the following:

"They write from Florence, that the Pope judging the Fraternity of the Free Mafons to be highly deferving of the Ecclefiaftical Cenfures, his Hollinefs has iffued a Bull of Excommunication againft that Society, the fubftance of which is as follows:

In the midft of the Cares of the Apoftlefhip, and the continued Attention we have to extirpate Herefies, and maintain the Lord's Vineyard in all its Purity; we have

JOSEPH SHIPPEN

heard with Grief and Bitterneſs of Soul, that a certain
Society, who ſtile themſelves the Fraternity of Free
Maſons, after making Progreſs in several States in Europe, have likewiſe ſpread into Italy, and even had ſome
Increaſe. We have conſidered that the impenetrable
Secret of this ſo Myſterious Society is the eſſential Part,
and as it were the Baſis of its Inſtitution; and that being
thereby become ſuſpicious to the Temporal Powers, ſeveral of them have proſcribed it in their Dominions. We
have likewiſe conſider'd, that by much ſtronger Reaſons
it ought to be ſuſpicious to the Spiritual Power, whoſe
Charge it is to have an ever watchful Eye to every Thing
that may concern the Salvation of Souls. For theſe
Reaſons, and animated by our Paſtoral Care, we have
condemn'd, and do condemn by the preſent Bull the Societies of Free Maſons, as perverſe, contrary to publick
Order, and having incurr'd the Major Excommunication
in its utmoſt Extent, forbidding all Perſons, of what
Rank, Quality, or Condition ſoever, who profeſs the
Catholick Apoſtolick, and Roman Religion, to cauſe
themſelves to be written down, or received into that Society, to frequent any of its Members, or hold Corre-
ſpondence with them, or to ſuffer or tolerate any Aſſemblies of Free Maſons in their Houſes, under Penalty
to the Contraveners of incurring likewiſe the ſaid Excommunication; reſerving to ourſelves alone the Right of
taking it off, except in Caſe of Death, &c.

Given at Rome, May 29, 1738."

P–t.

1738, September 18,   Boston.

The *Boston Evening Post* publishes the following:

"Letter from Florence, dated May 24.

The Free Maſons Lodges which had been interdicted
here, during the Life of the late Great Duke, are now held
again with all the Liberty and Freedom imaginable; and
without any Dread of the Inquiſition, which has no

Right to attack a Society of which the new Sovereign is a Member. (This is falſe Logick; a Sovereign may be a Member of a very illegal and evil Society: But the Streſs lies in this point; the Inquiſition has Power over the Sovereign himſelf in Matters of Religion, Etc.)

The Free Maſons of Leghorn have alſo re-open'd their Lodges; and we hear from Conſtantinople, that the Lodges at smyrna & Aleppo are greatly encreas'd, and that ſeveral Turks of Diſtinction have been admitted into them. This is falſe again; the Free Maſons ſure are Men of too much Honour, Religion and Good-Senſe, to receive the declar'd Enemies of Jeſus Chriſt into their Society."

     P–t.

1738, September 28,   Boston.

    Meeting of the First Lodge. John Tanner made.

        P.L.

1738, October,   Boston.

    Pro. G. M. Tomlinson sails for England by way of Antigua.

        1 Mass. 6.

1738, October 9,   Boston.

    The *Boston Gazette* publishes an elaborate account of the laying of the Corner-stone of the new Royal Infirmary at Edinburgh, Scotland, by the Fraternity on August 2, 1738.

        P–t.

1738, October 11,   Boston.

    Meeting of the First Lodge. Brother Alexander Woodrop and Alexander Bowman admitted.

        P.L.

1738, November 8, Boston.

Meeting of the First Lodge. Peter Pelham made.

P.L.

Re Peter Pelham, see 1744, August 8.

1738, November 22, Antigua.

On this date a Lodge was Constituted at St. John, Antigua. This became "The Great Lodge" April 4, 1744, *q.v.*

O.L.

L.M.R. 81.

Entick (1756 Ed.) 337.

P.C. (2nd Eng. Ed.) 378.

Prichard 28.

1738, December 9, Boston.

The accounts of the Masters Lodge which are written in the back of their First Book of Records begin by showing that upon this date there was bought of Beteilhe & Price "4 yds. Green Coating and 3 1-4 yds. Scarlet Riband," in preparation for Institution.

O.R.; A.B.

The members of this firm from 1736 to 1741 were Francis Beteilhe and Henry Price.

1738, December 22, Boston.

The Masters Lodge was constituted on this date, and Regulations or By-Laws were offered by a committee.

The original record book of this Lodge beginning on this day is in the archives of the Grand Lodge of Massachusetts. On its first pages it bears the report of this committee and annexed thereto are the original signatures of Hallowell, Oxnard, and Overing.

    O.R.

    See also O.R. for December 7, 1753.

    See page 33.

1738, December 27.   Boston.

Meeting of the First Lodge in Boston. The earliest original records of the First Lodge in Boston now known to have been preserved begin on this date with the "VI" meeting of the quarter.

The volume is a folio of two hundred and seventy pages bound in sheepskin. The secretary evidently felt the importance of his position and the dignity of the Lodge because this book is quite an elaborate affair. The fly leaf bears the following inscription set forth in imposing text:

THIS

BOOK OF REGISTERS

BELONGING TO THE ANCIENT AND HON^{ble}. SOCIETY OF

FREE AND ACCEPTED MASONS

IN

BOSTON NEW ENGLAND

WAS PRESENTED BY

BRO^r. THOMAS WALKER, SENIOR WARDEN.

———

Anno Domini 1738,
And of Masonry 5738.

Then follows a copy of the Deputation of Henry Price. Next are the quaint and curious By-Laws beginning:

"The following Regulations or By-Laws were unanimously Voted and agreed upon by the Brethren of the first Constituted Lodge in Boston New England at their Meeting October 24, 1733-5733 and are as follows. . . . Viz."

See page 104, *supra*.

Next is a copy of the deputation granted by the Earl of Loudoun December 7, 1736, as Grand Master of England, to Robert Thomlinson, as successor of Henry Price.

This is followed by the record of a meeting of the Lodge, being the "VI" meeting of the quarter. The secretary during the first year was Ebenezer Swan, a school master. We should have expected better chirography from a school master. Swan was succeeded by Peter Pelham as secretary on December 26, 1739, *q.v.* The Lodge opened a new account book on this date also, the first entry being "to a Ball^ce brought from a former book," etc.

O.R.; A.B.
See page 33.
1883 Mass. 159.
1900 Mass. 126.
The Grand Lodge also celebrated the Festival.
1 Mass. 6.

Charleston, South Carolina.

The *South Carolina Gazette* for December 28, 1738, contains the following interesting account of the celebration of the festival:

"Yefterday being the Feftival of St. John the Evangelift, the day was ufhered in with firing of guns at fun-

rife from feveral fhips in the harbour, with all their colours flying. At 9 o'clock all the members of Solomon's Lodge, belonging to the Ancient and Honourable Order of Free and Accepted Mafons, met at the houfe of the Honourable James Crokatt, Efq., Mafter of the faid Lodge, and at 10, proceeded from thence, properly clothed with the Enfigns of their Order, and Mufic before them, to the houfe of the Provincial Grand Mafter, James Graeme, Efq., where a Grand Lodge was held, and James Wright, Efq., elected Provincial Grand Mafter for the enfuing year, then the following officers were chofen, viz: Maurice Lewis, Efq., Deputy Provincial Grand Mafter; Mr. George Seaman, Senior Grand Warden; James Graeme, Efq., Junior Grand Warden; James Michie, Efq., Grand Treasurer, and Mr. James Gordon, Grand Secretary.

At 11 o'clock, both Lodges went in procefsion to Church to attend Divine Service, and in the same order returned to the houfe of Mr. Charles Shepheard, where, in the Court-room, to a numerous afsembly of ladies and gentlemen, the newly elected Provincial Grand Mafter made a very eloquent fpeech of the ufefulnefs of focieties, and the benefit arifing therefrom to mankind. The afsembly having been difmifsed, Solomon's Lodge proceeded to the election of their officers for the enfuing year, when Mr. John Houghton was chofen Mafter; Dr. John Lining, Senior Warden; Mr. David McClellan, Junior Warden; Mr. Arthur Strahan, Secretary, and Mr. Alexander Murrary, Treafurer. After an elegant dinner all the brethren were invited by Capt. Thomas White on board the Hope; there feveral loyal healths were drank, and at their coming on board and return to fhore, they were faluted by the difcharge of 39 guns, being the fame number obferved in each of the different falutes of this day, so that in all there were about 250 guns fired. The evening was concluded with a ball and entertainment for the ladies, and the whole was performed with much grandeur and decorum."

FACSIMILE OF PAGE OF RECORDS OF FIRST LODGE
IN BOSTON FOR DECEMBER 1738 AND JANUARY 1738/9

James Wright.

James Wright was of eminent ancestry. His grandfather, Sir Robert Wright, Knight, was Chief Justice of the Court of King's Bench in the time of James II. His grandmother was the daughter of Matthew Wren, Lord Bishop of Ely, nephew of Sir Christopher Wren.

James' father was born in South Carolina, of which province his father, the Honourable Robert Wright, was Chief Justice. At an early age he was appointed Attorney General of the colony and ably discharged the duties of that office for twenty-one years.

In October, 1760, he went to Georgia as Lieutenant-Governor, where he served with distinguished ability, being granted full executive powers as Captain-General and Governor-in-Chief, March 20, 1761. He was an ardent loyalist, dissolving the Assembly instantly upon its signifying approval of the letters from Massachusetts and Virginia. For his zeal, wisdom and prudence he was created a Baronet in 1772 while on a visit to Great Britain. He deserved the honour.

"Diligent in his official duties, firm in his resolves, loyal in his opinions, courteous in his manners, and possessed of a vigorous and well-balanced mind, he was respected and loved by his people; and though he differed from a majority of them, as to the cause of their distresses and the means of their removal, he never allowed himself to be betrayed into one act of violence, or into any course of outrage and revenge. The few years of his administration were the only happy ones Georgia had enjoyed and to his energy and devotedness may be attributed its civil and commercial prosperity."

Upon the breaking out of the Revolution he was arrested, but escaped and sailed for England. Later he returned and re-established Royal government in 1779, but finally when all of Georgia except the City of Savannah was in American hands, Wright received orders, June 14, 1782, to evacuate the province, which he did.

He was adjudged guilty of high treason to the State of Georgia and his property to the amount of about $160,000 was confiscated. He was made President of the Board of Agents of the Loyalists in their attempt to gain reimbursement for their losses and the Parliamentary Commissioners reported in his favour, among others.

Sir James did not long survive his political misfortunes, as he died in England in 1786.

2 Stevens' History of Georgia, 18 *et seq.*

1738/9, January 2, Boston.

This is the date of the first regular meeting of the Masters Lodge, which had been Constituted December 22, 1738, *q.v.* It has been stated erroneously that it was founded this day. Some similar condition of affairs undoubtedly accounts for the dates of July 30 and August 31, 1733, having been assigned at different times as the Constitution of the First Lodge in Boston. Of the Masters Lodge, Henry Price was the first Master and Francis Beteilhe the first Secretary.

O.R.; A.B.

1 Mass. 7.

16 M.F.M. 135.

1871 Mass. 317.

With this date and until July 6, 1753, the Treasurer's accounts of the Masters Lodge are to be found in detail in the back of the original record book.

A.B.

1738/9, January 10, Boston.
Meeting of the First Lodge. Leonard Lockman made.
O.R.; P.L.; A.B.

1738/9, January 22, New York.
There is an advertisement in the *New York Gazette* announcing that the Lodge will for the future be held at the Montgomerie Arms Tavern. This would indicate that it had been meeting elsewhere for some time past. This Lodge was never shown upon the Official Lists.
L.M.R. 478.

1738/9, January 24, Boston.
Meeting of the First Lodge.
O.R.; A.B.

1738/9, January 31.
Robert Tomlinson, Esq., Provincial Grand Master of New England, attended a meeting of the Grand Lodge of England held at the Devil Tavern near Temple Bar. This communication was attended by many noted Masons, among whom were the Grand Master, the Marquis of Carnarvon; John Payne, Esq.; John Theophilus Desaguliers; The Earl of Darnley; Martin Clare; Past Grand Master the Earl of Loudoun from whom Tomlinson's commission had come; and John Hammerton, Esq., Provincial Grand Master of South Carolina.
X Q.C.A. 306.

1738/9, February 2, Boston.
The *Boston Gazette* for February 5 published the following article evidently intended as an answer to some criticisms of our Fraternity, *viz.:*

"To the Publifher of the Bofton Gazette,

S I R,

By inferting the following Lines in your Paper, you will greatly oblige your conftant Readers and humble Servants;

S I S.

Homo ad Societatem natus,   St. Augustin

Man is a focial Creature, and cannot poffibly enjoy any Comfort or Happinefs in a reclufe and retired Life, entirely deprived of Converfation or Society; for it is that which fweetens Life unto us and renders us fit for Converfe with Heav'n. By exercifing our Tho'ts, and by communicating that Knowledge we are invefted with to our Fellow-Creatures, we not only oblige ourfelves, but them; For we by thinking furnifh our Minds with more Knowledge, and by communicating to our Fellow Creatures we afford them Aid in their Search after Truth. And as no one will deny but that this is a glorious Practice, fo they muft allow that the Way for executing it muft be by Society, for without it what would become of the Minds of Men? Even the Body which is only the cortex of the Man could not fubfift without it. But then, How much greater Care ought to be taken of the Mind, which would inevitably fuffer without it, and come to nothing, but Unhappinefs and Confufion?

And is this the Cafe that we muft be in without Society? Let every Lover of Reafon then ftir himfelf up, and put forth all his Powers for fetting up fuch Societies for the invefting the Mind with Learning and true Knowledge. And if there are already any fuch Societies fet up among us, let the Members of fuch Societies confider that the Ends of Society is the good of the Perfons affociated, and that the keeping private the Secrets of fuch Societies is doing a great Benefit to the Society to which they belong. For it is to be fuppofed by all Men of Reafon, that every Society is governed by fome Law or other, and that the Members are to keep them with all

Care. But let the ignorant and unthinking Part of Mankind ſpit out all their Malice and Fury, and call Society
to Task for their convening together; the Way they ſhall
be anſwered is according to the Advice of Solomon the
wifeſt of Men—anſwer not a Fool according to his Folly,
left he be wife in his own Conceit.
   Boſton, Feb.
    2d 17; 8 9.   Philo-Mathes."
    P–t.

1738/9, February 6, Boston.
  Meeting of the Masters Lodge. George Monerieff
(Moncrief) raised.
    O.R.; A.B.
The Treasurer's account for this day shows the pur-
chase and engraving of Jewels, Rods, etc.
    O.R.

1738/9, February 14, Boston.
  Meeting of the First Lodge.
    O.R.; A.B.

1738/9, February 28, Boston.
  Meeting of the First Lodge.
    O.R.; A.B.

1738/9, March 6,   Boston.
  Meeting of the Masters Lodge.
    O.R.; A.B.

1738/9, March 14 Boston.
  Meeting of the First Lodge.
    O.R.

Antigua.

Baker's Lodge constituted at St. John, Antigua.

O.L.

Entick (1756 Ed.) 337.

L.M.R. 79.

Prichard 28.

This Lodge as No. 164 first appears on the Official English List in 1740. On the same list another Lodge appears at St. John as No. 170.

L.H.B. 40.

1738,   Annapolis.

Annapolis Royal Lodge constituted by Erasmus James Philipps, who became its first Master.

Cape Breton, Louisburg and West Indies.

The entry referred to under 1737 (page 202) is repeated under 1738 with the words added "excepting such places where a Provincial Grand Master is already deputed." What Commander Douglas may have done is unknown, but it is reasonably certain that Comins never exercised his deputation, at least until after 1749. This limitation of his authority is evidence of the recognition of the Provincial Grand Mastership of Philipps for Nova Scotia.

See closing items of Chapters XI and XX.

CHAPTER XIII

1739

1739, March 28,   Boston.
  Alexander Delavoux made.
        O.R.; P.L.; A.B.

1739, April 3,   Boston.
  Meeting of the Masters Lodge.
        O.R.; A.B.

1739, April 11,   Boston—Nova Scotia.
  Meeting of the First Lodge. The records report the presence as a visitor of "R^t W.pfull Br^o: Erasmus Ja^s: Phillips G: M. De Nov: Scot:"
        O.R.; A.B.
   See page 195.
        For notes concerning Pro. G. M. Philipps see
           page 195, *supra*.
  Provincial Grand Master Robert Thomlinson of Boston was in London, where this day he executed his will.
        For copy and record of its probate see page
        172.

1739, April 14,   Jamaica.
  Lodge Constituted at Kingston, Jamaica.
        O.L.
        Entick (1756 Ed.) 337.
        L.M.R. 82.
        Prichard 28.

1739, April 25,   Boston.
Meeting of the First Lodge.
        O.R.; A.B.

1739, May,   Boston.
Pro. G. M. Thomlinson returns to Boston from London.
        1 Mass. 7.

1739, May 1,   Boston.
Meeting of the Masters Lodge.
        O.R.; A.B.

1739, May 9,   Boston.
Meeting of the First Lodge.
        O.R.; A.B.

1739, May 15,   Boston.
Meeting of the First Lodge.   Capt. William Morris made.
        O.R.; P.L.; A.B.

1739, May 23,   Boston.
Meeting of the First Lodge.   Brother Clement Vincent admitted.
        O.R.; A.B.

1739, June 5,   Boston.
Meeting of the Masters Lodge.
        O.R.; A.B.

1739, June 13,   Boston.
Meeting of the First Lodge.   Hugh McDaniel chosen Master.
        O.R.; A.B.
        1 Mass. 7.

1739, June 14, Boston.

The *Boston Weekly News Letter* publishes the following passage, *viz.*:

"We hear from Rome, that about a Month ſince, by Order of the Inquiſition, was burnt there, in the open Place before the Church of Santa Maria ſupra Minerva, with great Solemnity, a Piece wrote by the Chevalier Ramſay (Author of the Lives of Cyrus, Fenelon Archbiſhop of Cambray, &c) in Defence of Free-Maſonry, (of which he was a member) entitled, Relation Apologique et Hiſtorique de la Secrets dès Francs-Maſons, par J. G. D. M. F. M. A Dublin chez Patriae Odonoko, 1738. This was publiſhed at Paris in Anſwer to a pretended Catechiſm printed there by Order of the Lieutenant de Police, much of the ſame Nature and Authority of that printed in Engliſh by one Pritchard and paraded into the World by the ſame ſolemn Oaths; though the one is as little credited as the other."

P–t.

1739, June 21, St. Christopher.

The Mother Lodge held at Scotch Arms, Basseterre, St. Christopher, Constituted.

O.L.

Entick (1756 Ed.) 337.

L.M.R. 78.

1739, June 22, Boston.

Meeting of the First Lodge. Capts. John Pringle and John Akins made.

O.R.; P.L.; A.B.

1739, June 25, Boston.

The *Boston Evening Post* contains the following paragraph:

"We hear, that the Society of Free and Accepted Mafons belonging to the Lodge in this Town, intend to Morrow in the Afternoon, to walk in Proceffion in all their Formalities, with a pair of Kettle Drums before them, from the South End of the Town, to the Houfe of Mr. Luke Vardy in Kingftreet, where a moft elegant Supper will be provided."

P–t.

1739, June 25,   Savannah, Ga.

William Stephens, who was sent to Savannah as "Secretary to the Trustees in Georgia," wrote in his diary under this date:

"Monday. This being the Grand Anniversary of the Free Masons every where (as it is said) the Brethren with us would not let it pass without due Observance. Mr. Norris accordingly was asked to give them a Sermon, which had been customary with his Predecessors; and he made them an ingenious Discourse, with a decent and proper application: From Church they marched in solemn Order to Dinner at a publick House, the Warden, Dr. Tailfer (who likes Pre-eminence as well as any Man) attended by four or five with Wands, and Red Ribbands in their Bosoms as Badges of their several Offices, took Place foremost; but the Train that followed in white Gloves and Aprons, amounted only to about Half a Dozen more; which some, who are apt to burlesque the Order, turned into Ridicule."

IV Colonial Records of Georgia, 361.

1739, June 26,   Boston.

An account of the elaborate celebration of the Festival of Saint John the Baptist on this day appears in the *Boston Gazette* for July 2, 1739, *viz.:*

"Tuefday laft being the Day appointed by the Right Worfhipfull Robert Thomlinson Grand Mafter of the ancient and honourable Society of the Free and Accepted Mafons, in and of New England, for the Celebration of a Feftival, in Commemoration of their Patron Saint John the Baptist: The fame was obferved here with the utmoft Decency, and Solemnity, by the Gentlemen of that Society.

At three in the Afternoon They affembled at the Houfe of their Brother John Wagborn, from whence they walk'd in Proceffion to His Excellency's Houfe, properly Cloathed, and Diftinguifhed, with Badges, and other Implement pertaining to the feveral Orders and Degrees of the Society, proceeded by a Compleat band of Mufick, confifting of Trumpets, Kettle Drums, &c.

The Society was elegantly entertain'd at the Governour's, from whence they walk'd in the fame Order with his Excellency their Brother, to their Brother Stephen Deblois Houfe, where they were entertain'd with a fine Concert of Mufick: After which they walk'd to the Royal Exchange Tavern in Kingftreet, where a fumptous Supper was provided, to which were invited many Gentlemen of Diftinction, Civil, and Military."

> P–t.

> See also *Boston Weekly News Letter* for July 5, 1739.

The following account of the celebration in doggerel appeared in the *American Apollo*, a magazine printed in Boston, upon the first printing press manufactured in that city:

"Messrs. Printers,
The following historical scrap, *written by the late* Joseph Green, *Esq.*, *claims a place in the Apollo.* J. M.
We insert this, by particular desire, according to the original form.

A true and exact account of the celebration of the Festival
of St. John the Baptist, by the Ancient and Honourable
Society of Free and Accepted Masons, at Boston in
New England, on June the 26th, 1739, taken
from the Boston Gazette, and rendered into Metre, that children may commit it to
and retain it in their
memory.

'They might distinguish different noise
Of horns, and pans, and dogs, and boys,
And kettle drums whose sullen dub,
Sounds like the hooping of a tub.'

                                        HUDIBRAS.

In Roman callendars we find,
Saint John the Baptist's feast assign'd,
To June the twenty-fourth, and he,
(For so all Masons do agree)
A famous Lodge in days of old,
In Jordan's wilderness did hold.
For this as legends us acquaint,
They made a *Patron*, of the Saint;
Right worshipful Bob THOMLINSON,[1]
Having *this* duly thought upon;
The Lodge on Tuesday last did call,
To celebrate the festival;
For June the twenty-fourth was Sunday,
And Brother BELCHER[2] fasts on Monday;
So for the sake of eating dinner,
He *trick'd* the Saint to *please* the Sinner,
The Brethren, soon as this was known,
All met to walk about the town.

[1] Robert Tomlinson, Provincial Grand Master.
[2] His Excellency Jonathan Belcher, Esq., Governour of his Majesty's
Province of Massachusetts Bay.

First Brother WAGHORN [1] was their choice,
Waghorn of sounding *fame* and *voice;*
At three, they to his house repair,
And having staid a little there,
Proceeded onwards through the street,
Unto his Excellency's seat;
For as *this* Waghorn was a Brother
His Excellency was another.
Unlucky *name* it grieves full sore,
Waghorn and Belcher—but no more.
Here, having drank and giv'n the *sign,*
By which he was oblig'd to join,
From hence in *leather apron* drest
With tinsel *ribbons* on their breast
In pompous order march'd the *train,*
First *two,* then *three,* then *two* again;
As thro' the street they pass'd along,
All *kinds* of *music* led the throng;
Trumpets and kettle drums were there,
And *horns too in the front* appear.
Thus they went on thro' various noises
To hear them *fiddle* at DEBLOIS's—
And thence came thro' another street,
To Brother LUKE's [2] to drink and eat;
For Luke was ordered to prepare,
Plenty of every dainty fare;
Tongues, hams, and lambs, green peas and chickens,
So that, in short, 'twas '*pretty* pickings.'
Girls left their needle, Boys their book,
And crowded in the street to look;
And if from *laughing* we guess right,
They were much pleased with the sight.
All this by land—now follows after
The gallant show, upon the water.
The ship, that HOLLOWELL is named,
From HOLLOWELL, for building famed;

[1] Mr. Waghorn, Grand Sword Bearer.
[2] Luke Vardy, Innholder.

Of which their Brother Alexander
French was part owner and Commander;
Soon as appeared the Eastern Beam
This ship, haul'd off into the stream,
Red baize was tacked on the top,
And all the colours hoisted up,
And on the mizzen peak was spread,
A *leathern apron*, lin'd with *red*.
The men on board all day were glad,
And drank and smoked like any mad.
And from her sides three times did ring,
Great guns as loud as *anything*,
But at the setting of the sun
Precisely, ceas'd the noise of gun,
All ornaments were taken down,
Jack, ensign, pendant and APRON."

1739, June 27,　　　　Boston.
Meeting of the First Lodge. Brother Peter Prescott admitted.
　　　　O.R.; A.B.

Antigua.
Meeting of Grand Lodge at St. John.
See 1739, August 8, *infra*.

1739, June 28,　　　　Boston.
The *Boston Weekly News Letter* prints the following paragraph, viz.:

"There are Letters from Poland * * * * *
They add, that the Society of Free Maſons ſpreads ſo faſt at Poſen that the Clergy there have thought it their Duty to oppoſe it, and that a Bull of Excommunication has been publiſh'd againſt that Fraternity, not only in all the Churches there, but in other Parts of Poland."
　　　　P–t.

1739, July 3,   Boston.

Meeting of the Masters Lodge. Brothers John Hamilton and St. Clair raised.

      O.R.

1739, July 10,   Boston.

Meeting of the Auditing Committee of the First Lodge.

      A.B.

1739, July 11,   Boston.

Meeting of the First Lodge.

      O.R.; A.B.

1739, July 25,   Boston.

Meeting of the First Lodge.

Robert Jenkins and Lincy Wallis made and admitted. That they were made this night does not appear on the original records, but the record for July 11th shows their election and the record for this night shows their admission; therefore the Pelham List must be correct notwithstanding the omission in the records. Both the Pelham List and the original records show the admission of James Montier and John Nappier. The original records also state that Brothers John Pringle, John Akins, and Albert Dennie were admitted.

      O.R.; P.L.; A.B.

1739, August 7,   Boston.

Meeting of the Masters Lodge.

"The Lodge being opened Bro. Peter Napper (Nappier) desireing to be raised, was accordingly examined,

and being found a good Fellow-Craft to the Satisfaction of the Lodge, was unanimously Voted in, and Raised a Master in due manner & form and paid 30/. for Entrance & quarteridge."
Election.
O.R.; P.L.

Following the record of this meeting are two blank pages. This was the time when the Secretary, Brother Beteilhe, apparently became incapacitated (see page 36), although his partnership with Price was not dissolved until 1741. No other records of this Lodge appear until December 2, 1743, *q.v.* The Pelham List, however, gives proof that meetings were held during the interval, for it gives the names of four Brethren who were raised and seven who were admitted during the unrecorded period.
O.R.; P.L.

1739, August 8,   Boston—Antigua.
Meeting of the First Lodge. Upon the records appears the following letter:

"Right Worshipfull
        Worshipfull
Thrice Worthy & Ever Dear Brethren
We with the utmost Pleasure recd: your hearty congratulation Upon the Establishment of Masonry in this our Island, And return thanks to Our Worthy Brethren of Boston for the good Opinion they entertain of the virtues of Our Countrymen, which we hope will be continualy encreasing as the Royal Craft comes every day to flourish and gain ground among us, not only by the Accession of numbers of New Brethren, but especially under the happy Influence of our thrice Worthy Right Wor-

shipfull Grand Master his Excellency William Mathew, whom we boast of as a true good, Mason & a sincere lover and encourager of our inestimable craft.

We take kindly our Dear Brethrens offer of a friendly correspondence and should before this time have signified the pleasure we hope to reap from it, by an answer to yours of the 4th of April last but that we waited for an Opertunity of sending our sincere and hearty good wishes to our Brethren and Fellows by the hands of one who might in our name greet you in a Brother like manner.

We are now so happy as to enjoy this wishd for Opertunity by Our well beloved Brother Majr. John Murrys intending for Boston in a Very few Days, whom we commend to you as a Worthy upright Master Mason who has for some time past. Executed the office of SW of one of our Lodges to the entire satisfaction of all his Brethren and Fellows.

All the Brethren here salute you well beloved with the greeting of St. John, wishing that all Prosperity may attend you, and that no Malicious Cowan may ever with profane ears & eyes approach even the lowest step of your Worshipfull Lodge, in Order to listen to the Wisdom or pry into the Beauty or Disturb the order & harmony thereof.

From the Grand Lodge held at the Court House in St. Johns the 27th June A L 5739.	We are Dear Brethren Your Sincer Effectionate Brethren and Humble Servants.

Signed by the Command
of the Rt. W :pfull the Grand Master

William Mercer   G S"

O.R.; A.B.

1739, August 22,   Boston.
Meeting of the First Lodge.

O.R.; A.B.

1739, September 12,   Boston.
   Meeting of the First Lodge. Caleb Phillips made.
         O.R.; P.L.; A.B.

1739, September 24,   New York.
   The *New York Gazette* has an advertisement that the Lodge will meet on Wednesday, September 26th, at 6.00 P.M.

1739, September 26,   Boston.
   Meeting of the First Lodge. Thomas Smith and Capts. James Underdown, Narias Vaughn, and Edward Calior (Keller) made.
         O.R.; P.L.; A.B.

1739, October 8,   Boston.
   The advertisement of John Dabney appears in *The Boston Evening Post* offering for sale, among other things, Freemason's jewels.
         P–t.

1739, October 11,   Boston.
   Meeting of the First Lodge.
         O.R.; A.B.

1739, October 15,   Boston.
   The *Boston Evening Post* contains the following paragraph:

                    "Friday, June 1ſt, was interred in Burnhill Fields, the Corpſe of Dr. Anderſon, a Diſſenting Teacher, in a very remarkable deep Grave. His Pall was ſupported by five Diſſenting

PETER PELHAM

Secretary of the First Lodge in Boston, from December
26, 1739 to Sept. 26, 1744

Teachers and the Rev. Dr. Defaguliers: It was followed by about a Dozen of Free Mafons, who encircled the Grave; and after Dr. Earle had harrangued on the Uncertainty of Life, &'c the Brethren, in a moft folemn difmal Pofture, lifted up their Hands, figh'd, and ftruck their Aprons three Times in Honour to the deceafed."

Dr. Anderson was the compiler and publisher of the first printed Constitutions of the Grand Lodge of England. To Dr. Desaguliers, more than any other person, we owe the casting of our ritual in substantially its present form.

The signs given will be recognized by the Brethren of some jurisdictions as in use to-day though their meaning and original purpose have generally been forgotten.

1739, October 24,   Boston.
Meeting of the First Lodge. Brother James Monk admitted.
      O.R.; P.L.; A.B.

1739, October 31,
      Portsmouth, New Hampshire.
Meeting of the First Lodge at Portsmouth, N. H., at which "Regulations or By-Laws" were adopted as shown by the earliest volume now known of the records of this Lodge. It is not certain whether a record book, now lost, was kept prior to this date or not. Concerning this Lodge see 1735/6, February 5, *supra.*
      O.R.

1739, November 14,   Boston.
Meeting of the First Lodge. Hugh Surrey, John Lamport and Peter Dillon made.
      O.R.; P.L.; A.B.

1739, November 15,   Antigua.

Corner Stone of Fort James laid with Masonic ceremonies by Is^c Mathew, Pro. G. M.

> West Indies Circular, Vol. 23.
>
> 1916 Mass. 239.
>
> See page 170.

This is the first definite record of a Masonic corner
stone ceremony in the Western world. The stone, with
its inscription, is still visible.

1739, November 28,   Boston.

Meeting of the First Lodge.

> O.R.; A.B.

1739, December 12,   Boston.

Meeting of the First Lodge. Capt. Timothy Mc-
Daniel made.

> O.R.; P.L.; A.B.

Antigua.

Antigua Lodge, Courthouse Lodge, Lodge in Saint
Mary's Street, and Baſsatee (Basseterre) Lodge, each
stated as of Antigua (although the latter is of course the
Lodge in Saint Christopher) are reported on the records
of the Grand Lodge of England as making payment to
the Grand Treasurer for their Constitution.

> X Q.C.A. 322.

1739, December 26,   Boston.

Meeting of the First Lodge. Election. The records
for this meeting appear in a new handwriting and state
that Peter Pelham was elected Secretary.

> O.R.

FACSIMILE OF PAGE OF RECORDS OF THE LODGE AT
PORTSMOUTH, NEW HAMPSHIRE, FOR JANUARY 17, 1739/40

1883 Mass. 159.

1900 Mass. 122.

Re Peter Pelham, see pg. 290.

From this date to the end of the volume the entire record is in the beautiful penmanship of Peter and Charles Pelham. For a facsimile of one page, see 1740, April 23, *infra.*

1739, December 27,   Boston.

Celebration of the Festival by the First Lodge and Grand Lodge.

> O.R.
>
> 1 Mass. 7.

South Carolina.

Meeting of Solomon's Lodge and Provincial Grand Lodge at Charleston, South Carolina. Graeme again chosen Provincial Grand Master. Benj. Smith elected Master of the Lodge.

> *South Carolina Gazette* for December 31, 1739.

1739/40, January 1,

Portsmouth, New Hampshire.

Meeting of the Lodge at Portsmouth, N.H., when the By-Laws adopted October 31, 1739, *q.v.*, were approved, being subscribed by Geo. Mitchell, Master; N. Fellows, S.W.; Robert Hart, J.W.; Henry Sherburn, Treas.; Jon^a Loggin, Sec. pro tem, and other Brethren. These By-Laws in the original record book bear the signatures of fifty one Brethren, although most of them signed after this date.

> O.R.

1739/40, January 9,   Boston.
Meeting of the First Lodge.
O.R.

1739/40, January 17, New Hampshire.
Meeting of the Lodge at Portsmouth.   Pro. G.M.
Robert Tomlinson of Boston was present.
O.R.

1739/40, January 23,   Boston.
Meeting of the First Lodge.
O.R.

1739/40, February 13,   Boston.
Meeting of the First Lodge.
O.R.

1739/40, February 27,   Boston.
Meeting of the First Lodge.
O.R.

1739/40, March 12,   Boston.
Meeting of the First Lodge.
O.R.

Barbados.

St. Michael's Lodge Constituted at Bridgeton, Bar-
bados.
O.L.
Entick 337.
L.M.R. 86.

Chapter XIV

1740

1740, March 26,   Boston.

Meeting of the First Lodge. At this meeting a committee was appointed "to prepare a Remonstrance," to lay before the Lodge on the matter of increasing the initiation fee.

     O.R.

     See 1740, April 9, *infra*.

1740, April 3,   Boston.

Meeting of the First Lodge. John Webster and Capt. Thomas Durfey made.

     O. R.; P.L.

Portsmouth, N. H.

Meeting of the Lodge. William Wentworth made.

     O.R.

1740, April 7,   Boston.

Meeting of the Committee on the "Remonstrance" referred to under 1740, March 26, *supra*.

     O.R. 1740, April 9.

1740, April 9,   Boston.

Meeting of the First Lodge. The use of the words "humble Remonstrance" in the Oxnard petition of October 7, 1751 (see page 369), has been misinterpreted because of the present common use of the word. As showing the true use of the word in those days as well as because of its general interest the record of the First Lodge for this meeting is quoted as follows:

Wednesday April 9th: 1740.   Being Lodge Night
The following Brethren Mett.
The Rt.W: Bro: Robert Tomlinson G M
The Rt.W: Bro: Hugh McDaniel M.   Bro; I Waghorne
   S W.
The Rt.W: Bro: T: Oxnard. D: G: M Pd: 20/.
Bro: I Farrel J W Pd: 20/.

Bro: Benjn: Hollowell	Bro: T: Walker
Bro: Fran: Johonnot	T. Pd: 20/.
Bro: John Hutchinson	Bro: H. Surrey Pd: 20/.
Bro: Henry Price	Bro: Durfee Visr: Pd: 5/.
Bro: T: Moffatt	Bro: I: Webster " Pd: 5/.
Bro: Luke Vardy	Bro: S. Deblois PD: 20/.
Bro: Stevenson Tylar 3/.	Bro: P. Pelham S
	Recd: 56/6 . . . 2., 19., 6.

The Lodge being open'd, the Comms: Appointed last Lodge Night, to prepare a Remonstrance to lay before the Rt. W. Masr: and Brethren of this Society, were Introduced in due form; and Order'd to Present the same: Bro: T: Moffat one of the Sd: Comms: was desir'd to Read it, in Audience of the Rt W: Masr. & Brethren; And, after due Attention

Voted, Nemeni Con: that the Sd: Remonstrance be Ingross'd in the Book and to pass into a Law, that, for the Future, the Premium to be paid by Candidates, at their Initiation, to be Ten Pounds.

Voted, that the Sd: Comms: be Respectfully Thanked for their Care and Trouble in drawing up Sd: Remonstrance: Which was perform'd by the Rt W: Masr: & Brethren in due form.

Voted, that the Sd: Comms: be continued, and, that our W: Brothers Oxnard and Waghorne be added to them, in order to prepare a Remonstre: (as soon as posable) for the Benifit of the Bank Stock &c of this Society.

The Rt W: Masr: Hugh McDaniel, Propos'd and Nominated, Mr: Box, (Rope Mkr:) a Candidate: and to answer 40/s.

To the Rt W: Mastr:, and W: Wardens, and the rest of the Members of this Lodge.

We whose Names are hereunto Annex'd being a Committee appointed by this Lodge to consider, whether it be Expedient that a greater Premium than that now Stipulated by a Quandam Vote of this Society, be required from Candidates before Admission into our Lodge.

We, after due Deliberation upon the present Circumstances of this Lodge, and Treasury thereof, do think that it is now, not only Proper, but absolutely Necessary for preserving the Honour and Dignity of Masonry in General, and advancing the Interest of this Lodge in perticular: That the Sum paid by Novices before Intiation be Augmented, and that the said Augmentation when concurr'd to, & agreed on, may presently have the Sanction of a Law hence-forward.

We Your Said Committee are perswaded, that most of the Reasons which prevailed for then establishing the Inaugurating Fee at the present Rate, do not now Subsist; and consequently cannot be employ'd as Arguments against our Judgment, and Opinion, to abrogate, or alter that Decree. As that was a Resolution of this Lodge when in its Infant-state, and scarcely a sufficient Number to form One perfectly, much less to Maintain it with Spirit: We regard it only as a Result of Necessity, and good Policy, whereby the Society might be Encreased to a proper Number.

We Your Committee are convinced that if the Sum paid by Candidates was fixed at Ten Pounds, it would not prevent any Man of merit from making Application: on the Contrary—would Invite, and induce Them, inasmuch as it would discourage those of mean Spirits, and narrow, or Incumber'd Fortunes from Solliciting to Enter with Us: both which are Inconveniences which We cannot carefully enough avaoid, or provide against: because We apprehend the First to be a Disparagement to, and Prostitution of Our Honour; And the Latter are often a heavy Charge, and Burthen, in a General and Particular Respect.

We Your Committee observe that at Some Admissions, There has little or not part of the Money (after defraying incumbent Expenses) been applyed towards the encreasing of Our Publick Bank Stock—nay! that at Times, there has been Occasion Voluntarily to Contribute for discharging the Defficiency, or else Vote the Same out of the Treasury: by both which pernicious Practices, that Fund, which should be encouraged, & encreas'd by all honest Methods, & Means—is Lessen'd, & and the Noble Ends, & Purposes, for which it was destin'd, & appropriated—are frustrated, and rendered abortive.

Wherefore, We Your Committee move for Concurrence with Us in Opinion, whereby the General, & Perticular Interest: & Honour of Our Society may be advanced: and by which Men of Eminence may be encouraged; and those of base Spirits, & embarras'd Fortunes may be discouraged to Associate with Us—And by which our Fund, which ought to be invoilably sacred towards the Relief of Indigent & Distress'd Masons, their Wives, & Children—may be preserv'd and Encreas'd.

We Your Committee think there are Further Means, whereby all these Advantages might be further enlarged, and Secured, which We heartily wish.

Thos: Moffatt

April the 7th: 5740   Thos: Walker

Peter Pelham

O.R.

1740, April 22,   Barbados.
Charles Crawford, Esq., from Saint Michael's Lodge

at Barbados attended the Grand Lodge at London and paid ten guineas for charity.

> P.C. (2nd Eng. Ed.) 119.

1740, After April 22 and before March 19, 1740/41.
West Indies.

The Earl of Kintore, Grand Master of England, appointed Thomas Baxter, Esq., Provincial Grand Master of "Barbados and of all the Islands to the Windward of Guardaloup."

> Preston (Portsmouth, 1804) 191.
> Entick 334.
> P.C. (2nd Eng. Ed.) 120.

1740, April 23,   Boston.
Meeting of the First Lodge.
> O.R.

The records contained in this volume are so unusually attractive that a facsimile of the record of this meeting is presented herewith as a specimen.   It is the most ornate page of the book.

> 1 N.E.F. 57.

1740, May 14,   Boston.
Meeting of the First Lodge.
> O.R.

1740, May 28,   Boston.
Meeting of the First Lodge.
> O.R.

1740, June 11,   Boston.
Meeting of the First Lodge.   Election.
> O.R.; A.B.

1740, June 24,

Portsmouth, New Hampshire.

Meeting of the Lodge.   Brother Thomas Newmarch admitted.

O.R.

1740, June 24,   Barbados

A badly mutilated copy (but the only one known) of the *Boston Gazette* of August 11, 1740, contains the beginning and the ending of an account of the celebration of the Festival, in part as follows:

"Barbados, June 24th, 1740.

This being the Feaſt of St. John the Baptiſt, the Maſter and Brethren of the St. Michael's Lodge of Free and accepted Maſons, in a grand Proceſſion, went to St. Michaels Church in Bridge Town, to pay their Devotions, wher they heard a moſt excellent Sermon ſuitable to the Occaſion, preached by their Reverend Brother Huxley, Recter of St. Michaels, the Service of the Day being perform'd by their Reverend Brother Roſe, Rector of St. Thomas's.

*   *   *   *   *   *

After Sermon the Maſter and Brethren, with the other Gentlemen attendant on His Excellency in the Proceſſion, proceeded from Church, in the ſame order as above to the Lodge Houſe, where an elegant Entertainment was prepared for them, and the Ladies the Siſters; and in the Evening, they conducted the Ladies to the Aſſembly Room, where they gave a Ball to the Siſters, and other Ladies and Gentlemen, to whom Tickets had been given for that purpoſe.

The whole was conducted with great Order, and Deceency, and gave great Satisfaction to every Body.   As the like was never ſeen before in this Part of the World, the Town was crowded with People from all Parts of the Iſland to ſee the Solemnity."

P-t.

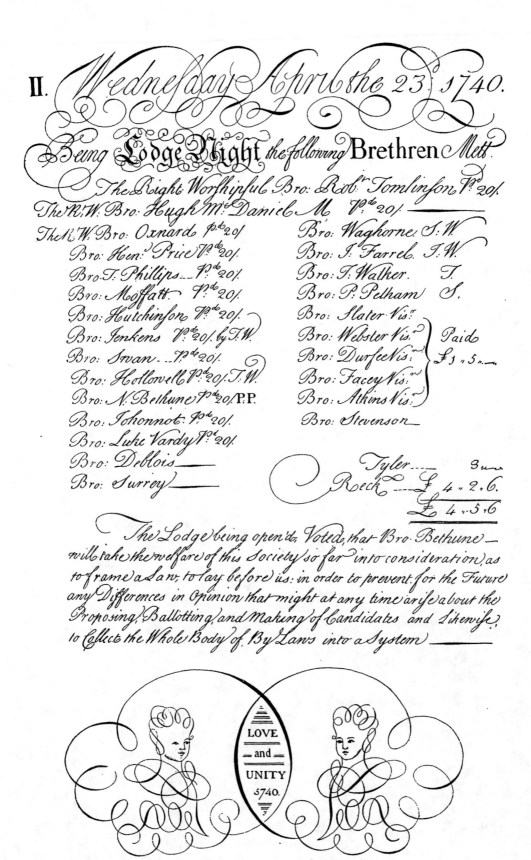

FACSIMILE OF RECORD OF FIRST LODGE IN BOSTON
FOR APRIL 23, 1740

1740, June 25,   Boston.
    Meeting of the First Lodge.
         O.R.; A.B.

1740, July 9,   Boston.
    Meeting of the First Lodge.
         O.R.; A.B.

1740, July 15 or 16,   Boston.
    Pro. G. M. Tomlinson died in Antigua. It was supposed that he made a will on the 15th, but it has never been found. He was buried on the 16th.
         See 1916 Mass. 241.

1740, July 23,   Boston.
    Meeting of the First Lodge. Robert Charles, John Box, John Rowe, and Capt. John Furney made.
         O.R.; P.L.; A.B.

1740, August 13,   Boston.
    Meeting of the First Lodge.
         O.R.; A.B.

1740, August 21,   Boston.
    The *Boston Weekly News Letter* publishes the following paragraph:
    "We have the forrowful News from Antigua, of the Death of Mr. Robert Tomlinfon, after Five Days Illnefs. He was Grand Mafter of the Lodge of Free and Accepted Mafons, in this Town. A Gentleman well refpected, and his Death is much lamented by his Brethren and Acquaintance among us."
         P-t.

1740, August 25,   Boston.

The *Boston Gazette* publishes the paragraph last quoted.

> P-t.

1740, August 27,   Boston.
> Meeting of the First Lodge.
> > O.R.; A.B.

1740, September 10,   Boston.
> > O.R.; A.B.

Meeting of the First Lodge. Capt. Samuel Waterhouse made. Brothers John Rickman, P. Hall, and H. Wethered admitted.

> > O.R.; P.L.; A.B.

1740, September 24,   Boston.
> Meeting of the First Lodge.
> > O.R.; A.B.

1740, October 8,   Boston.

Meeting of the First Lodge. John Wright (Right) and Patrick Tracy made.

> > O.R.; P.L.; A.B.

1740, October 22,   Boston.
> Meeting of the First Lodge.
> > O.R.; A.B.

1740, November 12,   Boston.
> Meeting of the First Lodge.
> > O.R.; A.B.

1740, November 18,
>Charleston, South Carolina.

A large part of Charleston was destroyed by fire.   The Fraternity there contributed two hundred and fifty dollars to the relief fund.
>*South Carolina Gazette.*

1740, November 26,   Boston.
Meeting of the First Lodge.   Capt. George Ladain (Leddain) made and accepted.
>O.R.; P.L.; A.B.

1740, December 10,   Boston.
Meeting of the First Lodge.
>O.R.; A.B.

1740, December 24,   Boston.
Meeting of the First Lodge.   Election.   Capt. Edward Oliver made.
>O.R.; P.L.; A.B.
>1 Mass. 7.

1740, December 27,
>Charleston, South Carolina.

The Fraternity of Charleston again celebrated the Festival in a most imposing manner.

"Saturday last being the Festival of St. John the Evangelist, the day was ushered in with firing of guns at sunrise, from several ships in the harbour, with all their colours flying.   At 9 o'clock all the members of Soloman's Lodge, belonging to the Ancient and Honourable Society of Free and Accepted Masons, met at the house of Mr. Benjamin Smith, Master of the said Lodge;

and at 10, proceeded from thence, properly clothed, with the ensigns of their Order to the house of the Provincial Grand Master, James Graeme, Esq., where a Grand Lodge was held, and Mr. John Houghton was elected Provincial Grand Master for the ensuing year, then the following officers were chosen, *viz:*

Mr. George Seaman, Deputy Provincial Grand Master;
Mr. Benjamin Smith, Senior Grand Warden;
Mr. James Graeme, Junior Grand Warden;
James Mitchie, Esq. Grand Treasurer;
James Wright, Esq. Grand Secretary.

At 11 o'clock both Lodges went in procession to church to attend Divine Service; and in the same order returned to the house of Mr. Charles Shepheard, where Soloman's Lodge proceeded to the election of their officers for the ensuing year, when

    Mr. Alexander Murray was chosen Master;
    Mr. Hugh Anderson, Senior Warden;
    Mr. Samuel Prioleau, Junior Warden;
    Mr. John Gwin, Treasurer;
    Mr. John Oyston, Secretary.

After an elegant dinner, all the brethren being invited, went on board the Lydia, Capt. Allen, and from thence on board the John and William, Capt. Fishbourne, where several loyal healths were drank under the discharge of a great many guns. The above ships were on this occasion, decked out with a great many colours, and illuminated at night with a great number of lights, regularly disposed on the yards, both of which made a very grand and agreeable appearance. In the evening the brethren adjourned to Mr. Shepheard's again, where they concluded the day suitable to the occasion. The whole was conducted with the utmost order and decency."
South Carolina Gazette for Jan. 1, 1740/1.

John Houghton, the new Provincial Grand Master, was a leading merchant of Charleston.
1921 South Carolina 195.

1740, December 29,   Boston.

Celebration of the Festival of Saint John the Evangelist at Boston by Thomas Oxnard as Deputy Grand Master and "a great number of Brethren." He opened a Grand Lodge and appointed his officers.

O.R. and A.B. of the First Lodge.

1740/1, January 14,   Boston.
   Meeting of the First Lodge.
      O.R.; A.B.

1740/1, January 28,   Boston.
   Meeting of the First Lodge. Peter Pelham directed to have a copper plate engraved for blank summonses.
      O.R.; A.B.

1740/1, January 29,   London.
   Provincial Grand Master Tomlinson's will probated in London.
      1916 Mass. 242.
      See page 172, *supra.*

1740/1, February 11,   Boston.
   Meeting of the First Lodge. Charity Committee appointed. Edward Tothill (Tuthill) made and admitted.
      O.R.; P.L.; A.B.
      1883 Mass. 165.

1740/1, February 25,   Boston.
   Meeting of the First Lodge. Peter Cade and Capts. Thomas Dunster and Robert Rand made and admitted. "The other candidate not attending forfeited his praemium."
      O.R.; P.L.; A.B.

1740/1, March 5,

> Portsmouth, New Hampshire.

Meeting of the Lodge, "being the Third Night of the Quarter." Brother Jno. Nailor admitted, Jno. Tufton made.

> **O.R.**

The above quotation shows that records have not been preserved of every meeting for we have no such between June 24, 1740 and March 5, 1740/1. Similar hiatuses are to be found later.

1740/1, March 11,   Boston.

Meeting of the First Lodge.

> **O.R.; A.B.**

CHAPTER XV

1741

1741, March 25,   Boston.
  Meeting of the First Lodge.
      O.R.; A.B.

1741, April 2, Portsmouth, New Hampshire.
  Meeting of the Lodge.
      O.R.

1741, April 8,   Boston.
  Meeting of the First Lodge.
      O.R.; A.B.

1741, April 22,   Boston.
  Meeting of the First Lodge.   The ballot on an application showed "More Nay's than Yea's."
      O.R.; A.B.

1741, May 7, Portsmouth, New Hampshire.
  Meeting of the Lodge.
      O.R.

1741, May 13,   Boston.
  Meeting of the First Lodge.
      O.R.

1741, May 25,   Boston.
  The *Boston Post Boy* has the following interesting item of News from London:

"London, March 20. Yefterday the antient and honourable Society of Free and Accepted Mafons had their grand annual Feaft at Haberdafhers-Hall. The Conclave was very grand, (more Noblemen and Gentlemen attending than has been known for many Years) the Entertainment in the moft elegant Tafte, mang'd with the niceft Decorum, and the Evening fpent as became the Brothers of that Society.

Yefterday fome Mock Free-Mafons march'd thro' Pall-Mall and the Strand, as far as Temple-bar, in Proceffion; firft went Fellows on Jack-Affes, with Cows Horns in their Hands, then a Kettle-Drummer on a Jack-Afs, having two Butter-Firkins for Kettle-Drums; then followed two Carts drawn by Jack-Affes, having in them the Stewards, with feveral Badges of the Order; then came a Mourning-Coach, drawn by fix Horfes, each of a different Colour and Size, in which were the Grand-Mafter and Wardens, the whole attended by a vaft Mob; they ftaid without Temple-bar till the Mafons came by, and paid their Compliments to them, who return'd the fame with an agreable Humour, which poffibly difappointed the Contriver of this Mock-Scene, whofe Misfortune is, that tho' he has fome Wit, his subjects are generally fo ill-chofen, that, he lofes by it as many Friends, as other People, of more Judgment, gain."

P-t.

XVIII A.Q.C. 129, 130.

1741, May 27,   Boston.

The record says, "The house being all taken up and engaged on some publick affairs, there was no Lodge held."

O.R.

1741, June 1,   Norfolk, Virginia.

It has been stated by several Masonic historians that

St. John's Lodge No. 117 was Chartered for Norfolk, Virginia, by the Grand Lodge of Scotland on this date.

> Dove's History of the G. L. of Virginia.
> IV Gould 379.
> S. & H. 298.

No proof of this statement can be found and it is evidently incorrect. Neither the Lodge at Norfolk nor any other Lodge in America warranted from Scotland prior to St. Andrew's Lodge in Boston (1756) is to be found in the Official List of Lodges Removed from the Roll, published with the 1904 edition of the Constitutions and Laws of the Grand Lodge of Scotland (pgs. 198-207); nor in the Edinburgh edition of the *Pocket Companion* of 1761, 1763, or 1765. Brother Dove says that on the Scottish Register it is given as No. 111, Constituted in 1741. It is found on the Scottish lists, however, only as No. 117, Instituted 1763.

> Constitutions of Grand Lodge of Scotland, 1904 Ed., 199 and 1852 Ed., 86.
> P.C. (3rd Edinburgh Ed. 1772) 143.

1741, June 2, Portsmouth, New Hampshire.
Meeting of the Lodge.   Election.
> O.R.

1741, June 10,   Boston.
Meeting of the First Lodge.
> O.R.; A.B.

1741, June 15,   Boston.
The *Boston Evening Post* publishes an interesting article relative to the mock Masons in London, as follows:

March 28.   *By the Right Worſhipful the* Grand Maſter, Grand Officers, Stewards *and* Brethren *of the*
SCALD MISERABLE MASONS.

A   *M A N I F E S T O.*

WHEREAS it hath been maliciouſly and impudently
inſinuated that *Our Proceſſion* of the 19th Inſtant, was intended as an unkind and ungenerous Reflection on the *Cavalcade of Our younger Brethren* the
Free Maſons.   Let this ſatisfy the Public, that We had
no ſuch Intention, bearing always the greateſt *Brotherly
Love* and *Friendſhip* towards Our ſeperated Brethren.
But Our Reaſons are.

Primo, That We are the True Original *SCALD MIS-
ERABLE MASONS,* as We can prove by the Records
of the *Ancient Lodges of RAGG-FAIR, HOCKLEY in
the HOLE,* St. *GILES's, BRICK-STREET,* and the
GOOSE and *GRIDIRON* in St. Paul's Church-Yard.

Secundo, That we were inconteſtibly one Body at the
ÆRA of the *Grand Maſterſhip* of Mr. *A-YER* now
Tyler, or Porter to their Grand and ſeveral other of
their Lodges,

Tertio, Becauſe ſeveral of the *Gentry,* without our
Privity, have crept in among Us who had more *Money*
than *Wit,* and more *Nicety* than *Good Fellowſhip,* and
have ſet up, themſelves as a diſtinct Body, under the
Name of *FREE MASONS,* in open Violation of our
Ancient Conſtitution.

Quarto, Becauſe We have heard it inſinuated, that
our diſcontinuing the *Annual Proceſſion* was urged as a
proof of our Non Exiſtence; or, at leaſt, was a Tacit
Reſignation of Right of Elderſhip to our *Younger-
Brothers,* the *FREE MASONS.*

Wherefore, We have at this time thought fit, according to the *known Conſtitutions* of the above *ancient
Lodges,* to re-aſſume our *Proceſſional Ceremony.*

And that All whom it may concern may Judge of the
Juſtneſs of our Pretenſions, We have annexed a Scheme

of our *Proceſſion*, and their *Cavalcade*, and ſubmit to
the Public which wa' moſt becoming the *Dignity* and
Solemnity of ſo *Ancient* and ſo *Venerable* a *Society*.

PROCESSION of the Scald Miserable Masons.

Two *Sackbutts*, vulgarly call'd *Cow's Horns*, in Liveries.

An Aſs, in proper Habiliments, led by two Pages, in
the *Liveries* and *Ribbons* of the *Stewards* Colour; carrying a Pair of *Butter Firkins*, on which a Youth in a neat
Attire beat, with a Pair of *Marrow-Bones*.

A dextrous one legged Man riding on an *Aſs*, and play-
ing on a *Tinkling Cymbal*, viz. a *Salt Box*.

The TYLER, in a long Robe or Veſtment, compleatly
arm'd; on his Head a Cap of Maintenance, on which was
Hieroglyphically depicted the myſtical Emblems of the
CRAFT; in his Hand a wooden Sword, riding on a *Lean,
Lame*, cropt Sorrel Nagg.

Three Stewards in *Proper Cloathing*, with *Jewels* and
Wands, in a *GUTT CART*, drawn by Three Aſſes
beautifully adorned, with Ribbons and Cockades. A
Poſtilion on the firſt, which was led by two *Pages*.

Three more *Stewards* in a *SAND CART*, drawn as
before.

GRAND GARDER, or *Tyler*, to the Grand Lodge, in
a *Huge Cap* of Skins, in his Hand a Truncheon; his
Shoulders from both Sides *ornamented* with *LAY-
BANDS*, like a *Hamlet Collonel*, riding on a *Fine*
prancing Steed, well managed *in a Grain Cart*.

RAGGED BRETHREN in proper Cloathing, walk-
ing according to the Ancient Conſtitutions, *THREE,
THREE* and *THREE*.

The Right Worſhipful *GRAND MASTER* with his
GRAND OFFICERS in a *ſuperb magnificent, ſable
State Coach*, drawn by *Spavin Splint, Swiſhtail, Bobtail,
One eye*, and *None-eye*, all of various Colours, and be-
decked with *Azure Ribbons*.

This *Grand* and *Illuſtrious* Proceſſion, was finiſh'd by

vaſt Numbers of different Inſruments, which all together compoſed a *detectable* Symphony of *ROUGH MU-SICK.*

The ∴ Mark of the right worſhipful

PONEY
Grand Maſter

P-t.
XVIII A.Q.C. 129, 201.

1741, June 24,   Boston.
Meeting of the First Lodge. Election. Thomas Oxnard as Deputy Grand Master held a Grand Lodge to celebrate the Festival and appointed his officers.

O.R. of the First Lodge.
1 N.E.F. 64.

Pennsylvania.

A Grand Lodge for the Province of Pennsylvania was held at the Indian King, Philadelphia, and Philip Syng was chosen Grand Master.

Pennsylvania Gazette for June 25, 1741.

See 1738, June 24, *supra;* and 1749, July 10, *infra.*

Philip Syng.

Philip Syng was born in Ireland, September 29, 1703. He sailed with his father (a goldsmith), from Bristol, England, arriving at Philadelphia, July 14, 1714, where he learned the trade of silversmith, married Elizabeth Warner in 1730, and there spent the remainder of his days. Brother Syng held the following positions and offices:

Original member of the Philadelphia Library Company;

Original member of American Philosophical Society;

Vestryman of Christ Church (1747-1749);

Promoter of the Association Battery (1748);

Warden of the Port (1753);

Treasurer of the City of Philadelphia from 1759 to 1769;

Trustee of the Academy from its foundation until 1773;

SILHOUETTE OF BRO. PHILIP SYNG

From *Old Masonic Lodges of Pennsylvania*

Provincial Commissioner of Appeals (1765);

Member of Franklin's Junto;

Contributor to the Pennsylvania Hospital.

He became a member of St. John's Lodge in 1734, Junior Grand Warden in 1737, Deputy Grand Master in 1738, and Grand Master in 1741. He died in 1789, and was buried in Christ Church ground. Brother Syng was an expert artisan and made the silver inkstand (still preserved in Independence Hall) used by the signers of the Declaration of Independence. He lived and had his shop on the west side of Front Street, a few doors below the coffee house.

    1 O.M.L.P. 43.

1741, July 9,   Boston.
    Meeting of the First Lodge.
        O.R.; A.B.
The Lodge should have met on the 8th, but the house was "fill'd by the members of the General Court, and no possibility of a proper room to hold a lodge," &c.
        O.R.
        1 N.E.F. 64.

1741, July 18,   Boston.
    The Masters Lodge bought 2 1/4 yds. of Double Gold Lace.
        A.B.

1741, July 22,   Boston.
    Meeting of the First Lodge.
        O.R.; A.B.

1741, August 12,   Boston.
    Meeting of the First Lodge.   William Maul made.
        O.R.; P.L.; A.B.

1741, August 26,   Boston.
    Meeting of the First Lodge.
        O.R.; A.B.

1741, September 9,   Boston.
    Meeting of the First Lodge.   Daniel Hooper made and admitted.
        O.R.; P.L.; A.B.

1741, September 23,   Boston.

Meeting of the First Lodge. The records contain the following:

"Our R^t Worship^l Mas^r recommended to the Brethren, that it was his opinion, some perticular order should be observed in toasting the health of our R^t W: Bro: the Honble Mr Belcher: and that a Committee might be appointed as soon as possable to wait upon him, with acknowledgements from the Lodge, of his past favours, and to return our thanks &c.

Voted, that next after the G: M. the Late Govern^r of this Province, is to be toasted in the following manner, viz: To our R^t W: Bro: the Honble Mr Belcher, Late Governour of N.E. with $\frac{3}{\frac{3}{3}} = 9.$

Voted, that Our R^t W: Bro: Oxnard D.G.M. Bro^{rs} Phillips, Row, Price, Hallowell, Forbes, McDaniel and Pelham, be a Committee to form a speech, and wait upon the Honble Mr Belcher in behalf of this Society, and to make report of their proceeding the next Lodge."

O.R.; A.B.
1 Mass. 388.
1883 Mass. 160.

1741, September 25,   Boston.

The records of the First Lodge contain the following:

"On Fryday Septem^r 25. 1741, the Committee appointed by this Lodge waited upon the Honble Mr Belcher &c., and made the following Speech:
Thrice Worthy Brother.

We being a Committee by the Mother Lodge of N. England held in Boston to wait on You, take this Oppertunity to Acknowledge the many favours You have always shewed (when in Power) to Masonry in General, but in a More Especial manner to the Breth^r of this Lodge, of which we shall ever retain a most grateful Remembrance.

As we have had your Protection when in the most Exalted Station here, so we think it is Incumbent on us to make this Acknowledgement, having no other means to testify our Gratitude but this; And to wish for Your future Health and Prosperity which is the Sincere desire of Us, and those in whose behalf We appear, and permit us to assure You we shall ever remain

Honoured Sir

Your most Affectionate Breth^r

& Humble Servants.

PETER PELHAM Sec^r

in behalf of the Committee.

To which, we receiv'd the following Answer:
Worthy Brothers.

I take very kindly this mark of your Respect. It is now Thirty Seven years since I was admitted into the Ancient and Honble Society of Free and accepted Masons, to whom I have been a faithful Brother, & well-wisher to the Art of Masonry.

I shall ever maintain a strict friendship for the whole Fraternity; & always be glad when it may fall in my power to do them any Services.

J. BELCHER."

O.R. of First Lodge.

I Mass. 389.

1883 Mass. 161.

1 N.E.F. 66.

Boston Gazette for September 28, 1741.

1741, October 2, Portsmouth, New Hampshire.
  Meeting of the Lodge.
        O.R.

1741, October 13, Portsmouth, New Hampshire.

Meeting of the Lodge. "Capt. Andrew Tombes was made a Mason and *raised* to a Fellow Craft."

O.R.

1741, October 14, Boston.

Meeting of the First Lodge. A committee was appointed to wait upon His Excellency William Shirley, the new Governor of the Province.

O.R.; A.B.
1 Mass. 389.
1883 Mass. 162.
1 N.E.F. 66.

1741, October 23, Boston.

Evidently the new Governor, William Shirley, succeeding Brother Belcher, was not a member of the Fraternity but they, nevertheless, attested their allegiance to the Government as disclosed by the following record from the minute book of the First Lodge:

"On Fryday October the 23ᵈ 1741. The Committee appointed by this Lodge, waited upon his Excellency William Shirley Esqʳ and presented him with the following Address:

May it please your Excellency,

We being a Committee appointed by the Ancient and honᵇˡᵉ Society of Free & accepted Masons of the MOTHER LODGE of AMERICA held in Boston, presume to wait upon you with the utmost Sincerity, to congratulate your Advancement to the Government of this Province, and to assure your Excellency that our Desire is that your Administration may be successful and easy.

We have had hitherto the Honour of His Majesty's Governor being one of our ancient Society, who was ever a well-wisher & faithful Brother to the Royal Art of Masonry.

And as it has been the Custom for men in the most exalted Station to have had the Door of our Society's Constitutions always opened to them (when desired) we think it our Duty to acquaint your Excellency with that Custom, and assure you, that we shall chearfully attend your Excellency's Pleasure therein; and as we are conscious that our Society are loyal and faithful Subjects to His Majesty, so we may reasonably hope for your Excellency's Favour and Protection, which is the Request of
Your Excellency's
most obedient humble Servants,
PETER PELHAM Secr.
in behalf of the Society.

To which His Excellency was pleas'd to return the following Answer:
Gentlemen.

I Return the ancient and honourable Society my Thanks for their Address, and Invitation of me to the Mother Lodge of Free and Accepted Masons in America: And they may rest assur'd that their Loyalty and Fidelity to his Majesty will always recommend the Society to my Favour and Protection.

W. SHIRLEY.

Voted, that the above Address to His Excellency Wm Shirley Esqr &c. with his Excellency's Answer, be printed in one of the Publick papers next Monday."
O.R. of First Lodge.
1 Mass. 390.
1914 Mass. 263, *et cit.*
Boston Gazette for November 3, 1741 (P.–t).
1 N.E.F. 279.

For many years following we shall learn little from the newspapers about the membership or doings of the Lodge. This is probably due to a resolution passed this

year by the Grand Lodge of England forbidding, under
penalty, any brother to print or cause to be printed, the
proceedings of any Lodge, or any part thereof, or the
names of the persons present at such Lodge, except by
the direction of the Grand Master or his Deputy. When
this resolution was communicated to the Colonies, it must
have had a strong influence. From the above publication
until January 1749/50, I can find but two newspaper
items in all the colonies giving local news of the craft.
These two are the accounts of the celebration of the
Festival of St. John the Evangelist in Charleston in 1741
and 1742, *q.v.* In these early days there was a woful
neglect to keep records. Of those which were recorded,
most have been lost or destroyed by casualty or careless-
ness. Add to all this, the resolution against newspaper
publication and it is not strange that our sources of information are few.

1741, October 28,   Boston.
     Meeting of the First Lodge. George Ruggles and Ed-
ward Cahill made.
     Report of Shirley Committee.
          O.R.; P.L.; A.B.
          1 N.E.F. 279.

1741, November 6,
               Portsmouth, New Hampshire.
     Meeting of the Lodge.
          O.R.

1741, November 11,   Boston.
     Meeting of the First Lodge. George Ruggles ad-
mitted.
          O.R.; A.B.

1741, November 25,   Boston.
  Meeting of the First Lodge.
        O.R.; A.B.
        1883 Mass. 163.
        1 N.E.F. 280.

1741, November 27,   Boston.
  Meeting of the First Lodge.
        O.R.; A.B.

1741, December 4,
        Portsmouth, New Hampshire.
  Meeting of the Lodge.
        O.R.

1741, December 9,   Boston.
  Meeting of the First Lodge.
        O.R.; A.B.

1741, December 23,   Boston.
  Meeting of the First Lodge.   Election.
        O.R.; A.B.
        1 Mass. 7.
        1 N.E.F. 280.

1741, December 27,
        Charleston, South Carolina.
  Elaborate celebration of the Festival. The account in the *South Carolina Gazette* for January 2, 1741/2, reads as follows:

"On Monday laſt, the brethren of the Provincial Grand Lodge and of Solomon's Lodge, proceeded in their proper clothing from the Provincial Grand Mafter's houfe to church, where a fermon fuited to the occafion was preached by the Rev. Brother Durant, and the brethren returned in the due order of Mafons, to Mr. Shepheard's houfe, where an elegant entertainment was prepared for them and fome other gentlemen of diftinction, invited by the Grand Mafter.

The following officers were chofen for the enfuing year, viz:

Of the Provincial Grand Lodge:

The Hon. John Hammerton, Efq. Provincial Grand Mafter;

Mr. George Seaman, Deputy Grand Mafter;

Mr. Benjamin Smith, Senior Grand Warden;

James Mitchie, Efq., Junior Grand Warden;

James Wright, Efq., Grand Treasurer;

Mr. Alexander Murray, Grand Secretary.

Of Solomon's Lodge:

Mr. Hugh Anderfon, Mafter;

The Hon. Richard Hill, Efq., Senior Warden;

Mr. John Gwynn, Junior Warden;

Mr. John Oyfton, Treafurer;

Mr. Samuel Bowman, Secretary;

Mr. Samuel Rofs ⎱
Mr. William Lowndes, ⎰ Stewards.

Great numbers of guns were difcharged from the fhips in the harbour during the procefion and afterwards; and the whole was conducted with the greateft order and decency, the night concluding with the illumination of the vefsels of the brethren in the harbour, and a ball to the ladies."

1741/2, January 1, Portsmouth, New Hampshire.

Meeting of the Lodge. Capt. Henry Darling made and "raised Fellow Craft."

O.R.

1741/2, January 13,   Boston.
  Meeting of the First Lodge.
        O.R.; A.B.

1741/2, January 27,   Boston.
  Meeting of the First Lodge. Samuel Rhodes, Benjamin Marlow, Charles Price, and Bagwell Irish made.
        O.R.; P.L.; A.B.

1741/2, February 3,   Boston.
  Meeting of the First Lodge. William Bishop made.
        O.R.; P.L.; A.B.

1741/2, February 4, Portsmouth, New Hampshire.
  Meeting of the Lodge.
        O.R.

1741/2, February 10,   Boston.
  Meeting of the First Lodge. Thomas Kelby (Kilby), Esq., made.
  It was voted that a petition to the Grand Lodge of England be sent with all speed for the appointment of Thomas Oxnard as Provincial Grand Master.
        O.R.; A.B.

1741/2, February 24,   Boston.
  Meeting of the First Lodge.
        O.R.; A.B.

1741/2, March 4, Portsmouth, New Hampshire.
  Meeting of the Lodge.
        O.R.

1741/2, March 10,   Boston.

Meeting of the First Lodge. George Diamond made. Brothers Samuel Rhodes, Benjamin Marlow, and William Bishop admitted.

      O.R.; P.L.; A.B.

1741/2, March 24,   Boston.

Meeting of the First Lodge. Phillip O'debart (Audibert), John Lee, and Henry Smithson made and admitted.

      O.R.; P.L.; A.B.

Chapter XVI

1742

1742, April 14, Boston.
Meeting of the First Lodge. Charles Gautier and Peter Cossett made.

      O.R.; P.L.; A.B.

1742, April 22, Portsmouth, New Hampshire.
Meeting of the Lodge. Capt. Eliakim Bickford made and "raised Fellow Craft."

      O.R.

1742, after April 27 and before May 2, 1744, Jamaica.
Lord Ward, during his term as Grand Master of England, in addition to Oxnard as Provincial Grand Master for North America (September 23, 1743), appointed Ballard Beckford, George Hynde, and Alexander Crawford, Esqrs., Provincial Grand Masters for Jamaica and one Provincial Grand Master for Bermuda.

      Preston (Portsmouth, 1804) 192.
      Entick 334.
      P.C. (2nd Eng. Ed.) 123.

1742, April 28, Boston.
Meeting of the First Lodge. Brothers Peter Cossett and Francis Johonott (Johonnott) admitted.

      O.R.; A.B.

1742, May 12,   Boston.
Meeting of the First Lodge.
        O.R.; A.B.

1742, May 26,   Boston.
Meeting of the First Lodge.
        O.R.; A.B.

1742, June 9,   Boston.
Meeting of the First Lodge.   Election.
        O.R.; A.B.
        1 Mass. 7.

1742, June 16,   Boston.
Meeting of the Auditing Committee of the First Lodge.
        A.B.

1742, June 17,   West Indies.
Lodge Constituted at Old Road, St. Christopher, by
Grand Master of England.
        O.L.
        L.M.R. 87.

1742, June 23,   Boston.
Meeting of the First Lodge.   Abraham Orpin, William
Ball, and William Starkey made.   "Brother William
Foy, Rais'd F. C. & Mem^r."
        O.R.; P.L.; A.B.

1742, June 24,   Boston.
Meeting of the Grand Lodge and celebration of the
Festival by about forty Brethren.
        O.R. of First Lodge.
        1 N.E.F. 280.

Portsmouth, New Hampshire.
Meeting of the Lodge.   Election.
O.R.

1742, June 28,   Boston.
Meeting of the First Lodge. Brother Thomas James Gruchy (Luchy) admitted. Henry Lawrence of South Carolina made.
O.R.; P.L.; A.B
1883 Mass. 164
1 N.E.F. 280.

1742, July 14,   Boston.
Meeting of the First Lodge. Lewis Vassal made.
O.R.; P.L.; A.B.

1742, July 28,   Boston.
Meeting of the First Lodge.
O.R.; A.B.

1742, August 11,   Boston.
Meeting of the First Lodge. James Brunette made and Brother Edward Cahill admitted.
O.R.; P.L.; A.B.

1742, August 25,   Boston.
Meeting of the First Lodge.
O.R.; A.B.

1742, September 8,   Boston.
Meeting of the First Lodge.
O.R.; A.B.

1742, September 22,   Boston.
Meeting of the First Lodge.
        O.R.; A.B.

1742, October 8,
            Portsmouth, New Hampshire.
Meeting of the Lodge.
        O.R.

1742, After October 11, Jamaica.
Lodge Constituted at Port Royal.
        O.L.
        Entick 337.
        L.M.R. 88.

1742, October 13,   Boston.
Meeting of the First Lodge.   Brother Thomas Camp-
ling admitted.
        O.R.; P.L.; A.B.
        1883 Mass. 165.
        1 N.E.F. 280

1742, October 14,
            Portsmouth, New Hampshire.
Meeting of the Lodge at which it was voted that it
meet the first and third Thursday in every month.
        O.R.

1742, October 27,   Boston.
Meeting of the First Lodge.
        O.R.; A.B.

1742. November 4,
> Portsmouth, New Hampshire.
Meeting of the Lodge.
> O.R.

1742, November 10,   Boston.
Meeting of the First Lodge.
> O.R.; A.B.

1742, November 24,   Boston.
Meeting of the First Lodge.   James Sprowll made.
> O.R.; P.L.; A.B.

1742, December 8,   Boston.
Meeting of the First Lodge at which rules were adopted concerning the issuance of letters of recommendation for Brothers intending to travel in foreign countries.
> O.R.; A.B.
> 1 N.E.F. 281.

1742, December 22,   Boston.
Meeting of the First Lodge.   Election.   Joseph Smythurst (Smithurst) made.
> O.R.; P.L.; A.B.

1742, December 28,   Boston.
Celebration of the Festival by the Grand Lodge.
> O.R. and A.B. of First Lodge.

Charleston, South Carolina.
The Festival was again celebrated in an imposing manner.   In Charleston this festival was evidently a

great civic event. The account from the *South Carolina Gazette* for January 3, 1742/3, reads:

"Monday laſt being the anniverſary meeting of the Ancient and Honourable Society of Free and Accepted Maſons, the members of Solomon's Lodge met at the house of Worſhipful Mr. Hugh Anderſon, Maſter of the Lodge, at 9 o'clock in the morning; from thence they walked in proceſsion to the houſe of the Right Worſhipful John Hammerton, Eſq., Provincial Grand Maſter, and there joined the members of the Grand Lodge, and from thence, (being properly clothed,) both Lodges proceeded regularly, with the enſigns of their Order, and muſic before them, to Church, where they heard a very learned ſermon from their brother, the Rev. Mr. Durant (Durand); then returned in due order to the house of Mr. Charles Shepheard, where an elegant entertainment was prepared, and the Lodges being called, the following gentlemen were choſen officers for the enſuing year:

R.W.Mr. Benjamin Smith, Provincial Grand Maſter;

James Michie, Eſq., Deputy Provincial Grand Maſter;

Mr. Alexander Murray, Senior Grand Warden;

Mr. Hugh Anderſon, Junior Grand Warden;

James Wright, Eſq., Grand Treaſurer;

James Graeme, Eſq., Grand Secretary.

The Worſhipful Mr. John Gwinne, Maſter of Solomon's Lodge;

Mr. John McKenzie, Senior Warden;

Mr. John Oyſton, Junior Warden;

Mr. Thomas Smith, Treaſurer;

Mr. Kenneth Michie, Secretary;

Mr. Henry Harramond, } Stewards.
Mr. Robert Blyth

During all this time great numbers of guns were fired from the ſhips in the harbour, and after dinner ſeveral loyal toafts were drank. The whole was conducted with the greateft order and decency and the evening concluded, fuitable to the occafion, with a ball to the ladies."

Benjamin Smith.

Hon. Benjamin Smith was born in 1718. Member Assembly, 1748-1762; Speaker, 1755, 1760, 1762. Associate Justice Common Pleas, 1766. Died at Newport, R. I., July 28, 1770, and buried there in Trinity Church.
1921 So. Car. 195.

There is no further account known of Masonic meetings in South Carolina until 1751, except as noted under "1743" *infra;* page 283. For the probable reason see page 258. The next accounts (*South Carolina Gazette* for January 10, 1751/2, and January 8, 1752/3, and *Timothy's Gazette* for March 30, 1752) show abundant signs of continuity.

See Mackey's History of Freemasonry in South Carolina, 21.

1742/3, January 6,
  Portsmouth, New Hampshire.
  Meeting of the Lodge.
  O.R.

1742/3, January 12,   Boston.
  Meeting of the First Lodge.
  O.R.; A.B.

1742/3, January 26,   Boston.
  Meeting of the First Lodge.
  O.R.; A.B.
  1 N.E.F. 281.

BENJAMIN SMITH
From Portrait Painted by Theus, Charleston, 1760.

1742/3, February 9,   Boston.
Meeting of the First Lodge.
O.R.; A.B.

1742/3, February 23,   Boston.
Meeting of the First Lodge.
O.R.; A.B.

1742/3, March 9,   Boston.
Meeting of the First Lodge.
O.R.; A.B.

1742/3, March 23,   Boston.
Meeting of the First Lodge.
O.R.; A.B.
1883 Mass. 165.
1 N.E.F. 281.

Chapter XVII

1743

1743, April 13,   Boston.
    Meeting of the First Lodge.
       O.R.; A.B.

1743, April 27,   Boston.
    Meeting of the First Lodge. Joseph Murry (Murray) and Edmund Lewis (Ellis) made.
       O.R.; P.L.; A.B.

1743, May 11,   Boston.
    Meeting of the First Lodge. Brothers William Ball, Edmund Lewis (Ellis), and Archibald Spencer admitted, and Lewis Turner and George Wilson made.
       O.R.; P.L.; A.B.

1743, May 25,   Boston.
    Meeting of the First Lodge. Brothers Benjamin Franklin and Henry Price both attended this meeting.
       O.R.; A.B.
       1 Mass. 390.
       1888 Mass. 153.

1743, June 8,   Boston.
    Meeting of the First Lodge. Brother Lewis Turner

admitted. Brother Benjamin Franklin was also present at this meeting.

O.R.; A.B.

1743, June 20, Boston.

The *Boston Evening Post* publishes the following item, *viz.*:

"Extract of a Letter from Vienna, dated March 20, N.S.

The Affair of the Free-Mafons, ftill makes a great Noife here, becaufe of the Perfons of high Rank concerned in it. By a Lift handed about here, it appears that the Lodge was compofed of a young Prince of an illuftrious Houfe, two other Princes, fix Counts of the greateft Families of Auftria, four Generals, a Foreign Minifter, well known in the learned World, and three Priests, befides others of inferior Note. Among them there were Roman Catholicks, Proteftants, and Lutherans, the Free-Mafons admitting all Sort of Religions among them, not even excepting Mahometans; but what we moft wonder at, is, to have found Priefts in this Society. The latter are clofe confined in the Prifon of the Archbifhoprick, and have been interrogated feveral Times already, but abfolutely refufed to give any Eclairciffement concerning the Secret of the Fraternity: Cardinal Collonitz, our Archbifhop, is charged to profecute them. Among other Things found in the Lodge, there was a Book, in which thefe Words are wrote; Our Orders, the moft illuftrious that ever was known, is of as great Antiquity as the World itfelf, for Adam was the firft Free-Mafon, &c. Upon which it is further to be obferved, that when the Guards broke the Door of the Lodge, they found a Bible on the Table, open at the firft Chapter of Genefis; but as to the Report of their having a Death's Head and black Tapers, is a mere In-

vention of the Populace, who take the Free-Mafons to be Magicians."
P–t.

1743, June 20,   Boston.
Meeting of the First Lodge.   Election.   Capt. John Shannon made.
O.R.; P.L.; A.B.

1743, June 23,   Boston.
The *Boston Weekly News Letter* publishes the following item:

"We have Letters from Lisbon which fay, that the Inquifitors having difcover'd that there were Free-Mafons in that City, found Means to take up about 18 of them; that they examin'd them about the Secret of the Society; but upon their refufing to reveal it, the Inquifitors dec'ear'd to them, that they fhould remain in the Prifons of the Inquifition until they give fatisfactory Anfwers on that Head."
P–t.

1743, June 24,   Boston.
Celebration of the Festival by the Grand Lodge.
O.R. of First Lodge.
1 Mass. 7.

1743, July 13,   Boston.
Brothers Hall, Phillips, Allen, and Thomas Rind admitted.   Thomas Aston made.
O.R.; P.L.; A.B.

1743, July 27,   Boston.
Meeting of the First Lodge.   John Amil and John Vanhartburger made.
O.R.; P.L.; A.B.

1743, August 10,   Boston.

Meeting of the First Lodge.   Daniel Perchard and Benjamin Ives made.

This record contains the first American reference to the actual issuance of a "dispenceation."

See page 106, IIII^{ly}.

A committee was appointed to invite Governor Belcher.

      O.R.; P.L.; A.B.

      1883 Mass. 162.

      1 N.E.F. 281.

1743, August 24,   Boston.

Meeting of the First Lodge.

      O.R.; A.B.

      1883 Mass. 165.

      1 N.E.F. 281.

1743, September 14,   Boston.

Meeting of the First Lodge.

      O.R.; A.B.

1743, September 23,   Boston.

Deputation issued by Lord Ward, Grand Master of England, to Thomas Oxnard as Provincial Grand Master for North America.   A copy of this Deputation certified by Peter Pelham, Grand Secretary, on May 29, 1744, is in the archives of the Grand Lodge of Massachusetts.

      See page 279.

      1 Mass. 8.

      The Picture of Philadelphia, (1811) 289.

1743, September 28,   Boston.
Meeting of the First Lodge.
   O.R.; A.B.
   1 N.E.F. 282.

1743, October 12,   Boston.
Meeting of the First Lodge.
   O.R.; A.B.

1743, October 26,   Boston.
Meeting of the First Lodge.
   O.R.; A.B.

1743, November 9,   Boston.
Meeting of the First Lodge. Dr. Edward Ellis made.
   O.R.; P.L.; A.B.

1743, November 23,   Boston.
Meeting of the First Lodge. Capt. John Boutin (by Dispensation) and Henry Johnson made.
   O.R.; P.L.; A.B.

1743, December 2,   Boston.
Meeting of the Masters Lodge. This is the first record after August 7, 1739, *q.v.* This record is in the handwriting of Peter Pelham, Secretary, who left two blank pages upon which to write the omitted meetings.
   O.R.; A.B.

1743, December 14,   Boston.
Meeting of the First Lodge. Brother Edward Cahill admitted.
   O.R.; A.B.

OXNARD'S DEPUTATION AS PROVINCIAL GRAND
MASTER FOR NORTH AMERICA; SEPTEMBER 23, 1743

1743, December 27,   Boston.
    Celebration of the Festival by the Grand Lodge.
        O.R. of First Lodge.
        1883 Mass. 165.
        1 N.E.F. 282.

1743, December 28,   Boston.
    Meeting of the First Lodge.   Election.
        O.R.; A.B.

1743/4, January 6,   Boston.
    Meeting of the Masters Lodge.
        O.R.; A.B.

1743/4, January 9,   Boston.
    The *Boston Evening Post* contains an account of the
recent formation in Avignon of the Knights and Knight-
esses of the Order of Felicity soon after the Freemasons
were suppressed there, and the mandate of the Arch-
bishop against the new society.
        P–t.

1743/4, January 11,   Boston.
    Meeting of the First Lodge.   Joseph Holbrook made.
Brother Abraham Reller admitted.   Under this date the
Treasurer paid for binding a book for the laws and list
of the members of the Lodge.   (This book has been lost.)
        O.R.; P.L.; A.B.

1743/4, January 26,   Boston.
    Meeting of the First Lodge.
        O.R.; A.B.

1743/4, February 3,   Boston.
Meeting of the Masters Lodge.   Election.
O.R.; A.B.

1743/4, February 8,   Boston.
Meeting of the First Lodge.   Vote concerning the entertainment of Governor Belcher.
O.R.; A.B.
1 N.E.F. 282.

1743/4, February 9,   Boston.
Meeting of the First Lodge.   Entertainment of Governor Belcher who attended with about forty of the Brethren.
O.R.; A.B.
1 Mass. 391.
1883 Mass. 162.
1 N.E.F. 282.
He soon thereafter sailed for England.   See 1744, September 26, *infra*.

1743/4, February 22,   Boston.
Meeting of the First Lodge.   Jonathan Pue made.
O.R.; P.L.; A.B.

1743/4, March 2,   Boston.
Meeting of the Masters Lodge.   Brothers Thomas Aston, John Boutin, and Philip Audibert raised.
O.R.; P.L.; A.B.

1743/4, March 6,   Boston.
Thomas Oxnard received his Deputation as Provincial Grand Master of North America.   The original records

of the First Lodge contain a copy of this Deputation, together with an account of his holding a Grand Lodge and appointing his officers. The Deputation reads as follows:

J: Ward (SEAL) G: M.

To all and every, Our R^t Worsh^l and Loving Brethren We John Lord Ward Baron of Birmingham in the County of Warwick Grand Master of the Honourable Society of Free and Accepted Masons

SENDETH GREETING,

Whereas Application hath been made unto us by several of Our Brethren Residing in North America praying that We would appoint a Provincial Grand Master for North America in the Room of our Bro Robt Tomlinson Esqr Deceas'd late Provincial Grand Master,

Now KNOW YE That We John Lord Ward have Nominated Constituted and Appointed, and by these Presents do Nominate Constitute and Appoint Our Well beloved Bro^r Thomas Oxnard Esqr To Be Provincial Grand Master of North America with full power to Nominate and Appoint his Deputy Grand Master and Grand Wardens, and in Our Name and stead to Constitute Lodges in North America he the said Thos Oxnard Esqr taking special care that all and every Member, or Members of any Lodge or Lodges so to be Constituted have been or shall be made Regular Masons, and that he cause all and every the Regulations contain'd in the Printed Book of Constitutions (except so far as they have been alter'd by the Grand Lodge at their Quarterly Communications) to be kept and Observ'd, and also all such other Rules and Instructions as shall from time to time be Transmitted to him by us or Sr Robt Lawley Bart: our Deputy Grand Master, or the Grand Master or his Deputy for the time being, and that he the said Thos Oxnard Esqr do send an Acco^t in Writing to us or our Deputy, or the Grand Master for the time being of all and every the Lodge or Lodges, he shall Constitute with the Date of their Constitution and Days of Meeting and Names of their Members, and their place of abode, also Two Guineas for the General Charity and half a Guinea for other Expences from every Lodge he shall Constitute, and also to hold four Quarterly Communications in a Year, one of them upon the Feast of St John the Evangelist or as near that time as Conveniently may be. Given unto Our Hand and Seal at London This Twenty Third Day of September, One Thousand Seven Hundred and Forty Three, and of Masonry Five Thousand Seven Hundred and Forty Three.

By the Grand Masters Command
      sign'd

JOHN REVIS, G: S.

    O.R. of First Lodge.
    See 1743, September 23, *supra.*
    1 Mass. 7, 8, 387.
    1871 Mass. 313, 350.
    1 N.E.F. 283.

Thomas Oxnard.

Provincial Grand Master for North America, March 6, 1743/4 to June 25, 1754.

Thomas Oxnard was born about 1703 in the Bishopric of Durham in England. The date of his emigration to this country has not been ascertained. On January 21, 1735/6, he was made a Mason in the First Lodge in Boston of which he was chosen Master at the Feast of Saint John the Evangelist, 1736. He was one of the founders of the Masters Lodge on January 2, 1738/9, and frequently attended its meetings. At the Feast of Saint John the Evangelist in 1739 he was appointed Deputy Grand Master. He succeeded Tomlinson as Grand Master, his Commission being dated September 23, 1743, and being received in Boston on March 6,

1743/4. He was specifically appointed by his original warrant to be Provincial Grand Master of North America, with full power to constitute lodges in North America. In the exercise of that power he constituted Lodges not only in and about Boston, but also in Newfoundland, Rhode Island, Maryland, Connecticut, and elsewhere. We know that he was in England in 1752 (1 Mass. 19) and he was probably absent for some time because he did not attend the Communications of the Grand Lodge from October 11, 1751, until October 13, 1752. During his absence, however, he was evidently in communication with the Grand Lodge for in January, 1752, Brother McDaniel was Deputy Grand Master, while in June of the same year we find that Alexander Lord Colvill had been deputized as Deputy Grand Master.

A contemporaneous estimate of him as an experienced merchant, an upright dealer, an affectionate husband, a tender parent, a sincere friend, and a kind master, is recorded on the records of the Grand Lodge under date of July 1, 1754, together with an account of the Masonic ceremonies at his funeral (1 Mass. 33).

Oxnard and his wife's father, John Osborn, were partners in business. Mr. Osborn had many public offices, and doubtless Oxnard was a chief factor in the management of the affairs at the store and on the wharf. His mansion was at the northerly corner of Tremont and Winter streets, having been bought in 1742 of Adam Winthrop, Esq. This property is diagonally across Tremont street from Park Street Church. Full statements concerning his family may be found in the references given.

His widow, Madam Sarah Oxnard, married, second, April 10, 1756, the Honourable Samuel Watts, Esq.

She was evidently a shrewd business woman, for it would appear from the settlement of the Oxnard Estate that she charged her second husband, Judge Watts, for four years' use of her house in Boston from 1756 to 1760, about which time the family removed to Chelsea where Judge Watts died in 1770. Her portrait was painted by John Singleton Copley and is still in existence. Unfortunately no portrait of Thomas Oxnard is known. *The Boston Post Boy* for Monday, July 1, 1754, contains an account of his death and funeral identical with that recorded in the records of the Grand Lodge above referred to. The *Boston Gazette* of Tuesday, July 2, 1754, has the following intelligence:

"Last Tuesday died here Thomas Oxnard, Esq., a noted merchant of this town, in the fifty-first year of his age, and was decently interred on Friday last."

There is also a note in the *Gentlemen's Magazine* of London for 1754, page 388, reading:

"At Boston in New England, Thomas Oxnard, Esq., an eminent merchant, Grand Master of the Society of Freemasons in North America."
>   1871 Mass. 642.
>   6 N. E. Historical and Gen. Reg. 375.
>   26 N. E. Historical and Gen. Reg. 3.
>   Willis' History of Portland.

1743/4, March 14,   Boston.
Meeting of the First Lodge. Louis Demoulin made. A vote is passed to procure a new book for the By-Laws. (This book lost.)
>   O.R.; P.L.; A.B.

1743, South Carolina.

Prince George Lodge Constituted at George Town (Winyaw) South Carolina.

L.M.R. 89.

IV Gould 395.

Chapter XVIII

1744

1744, March 28,   Boston.

Meeting of the First Lodge. Brother Benjamin Hallowell admitted.

> O.R.; A.B.

1744, April 4,   Antigua.

Francis Byam, D.D., Master and in behalf of Court-House Lodge, Antigua, petitioned the Grand Lodge in London that as they had built a new Lodge-room sixty feet long and thirty feet wide, with a small room adjoining, the said new built Lodge might be entered on the Register as "The Great Lodge of St. John's." The petition was granted with the alteration that the name should be "The Great Lodge at St. John's in Antigua."

> Entick 242.
> Preston (Portsmouth 1804) 192.
> P.C. (2nd Eng. Ed.) 123.
> 1738, November 22, *supra.*

1744, April 6,   Boston.

Meeting of the Masters Lodge.

> O.R.; A.B.

1744, April 11,   Boston.

Meeting of the First Lodge.

> O.R.; A.B.

1744, April 25,   Boston.
  Meeting of the First Lodge.
          O.R.; A.B.

1744, May 4,   Boston.
  Meeting of the Masters Lodge.
          O.R.; A.B.

1744, May 9,   Boston.
  Meeting of the First Lodge.   Richard White made.
          O.R.; P.L.; A.B.

1744, May 23,   Boston.
  Meeting of the First Lodge.
          O.R.; A.B.

1744, May 29,   Boston.
  Grand Secretary Peter Pelham certified a copy of
Thomas Oxnard's commission as Provincial Grand Mas-
ter of North America.
          See page 279.

1744, June 1,   Boston.
  Meeting of the Masters Lodge.   Brothers Jonathan
Pue, Henry Johnson, and Timothy McDaniel raised.
          O.R.; P.L.; A.B.

1744, June 13,   Boston.
  Meeting of the First Lodge. Election. Brother W.
Starkey admitted.   Daniel Plaister and Samuel Winslow
made.
          O.R.; P.L.; A.B.

1744, June 26,　　　　Boston.
Celebration of the Festival by the Grand Lodge.
　　　　O.R. and A.B. of First Lodge.

1744, June 27,　　　　Boston.
Meeting of the First Lodge.
　　　　O.R.; A.B.

1744, July 6,　　　　Boston.
Meeting of the Masters Lodge.　Election.
　　　　O.R.; A.B.

1744, July 11,　　　　Boston.
Meeting of the First Lodge.
　　　　O.R.; A.B.

1744, July 25,　　　　Boston.
Meeting of the First Lodge.
　　　　O.R.; A.B.

1744, August 2,　　　　Boston.
The *Boston Weekly News Letter* publishes an account of the burlesque procession by the mock Masons which we reproduce as follows:

From the St. James's Evening-Poft.
L O N D O N, May 3.

YESTERDAY the Cavalcade of Scald Miferable-Mafons, went in Proceffion from the Place of Meeting thro' the Strand to Temple-Bar, and on returning back to meet the Free and Accepted Mafons, they were put into Diforder near Somerfet-Houfe, by the High Conftable of Weftminfter, attended by a large Body of inferior Officers, who prefs'd Dag A—e

Jack, Poney and feveral others, to the Number of 20, whom they fecur'd in St. Clement's Church and Round Houfe, for his Majefty's Service.

A Key to the Proceffion of the Scald-Miferable Mafons.

WHEREAS by our Manifefto of laft Year, dated from our Lodge in Brick-Street, we did, in the moft explicit Manner, vindicate the ancient Right and Privileges of this Society, and by inconteftable Arguments evince our fuperior Dignity and Seniority to all other Inftitutions, whether Grand-Volgi, Gregorians, Hurlothrumbians, Ubiquarians, Hiccubites, Lumber-Troopers, Hungarians, or Free-Mafons; yet neverthelefs, a few Perfons under the laft Denomination, ftill arrogate to them the ufurped Titles of Moft Antient and Honourable, in open Violation of Truth and Juftice,—— ftill endeavour to impofe their falfe Myfteries (for a Premium) on the Credulous and Unwary, under Pretence of being Part of our Brotherhood, and ftill are determin'd with Drums, Trumpets, gilt Chariots and other unconftitutional Finery to caft a Reflection on the primitive Simplicity and decent Oeconomy of our Ancient and Annual Peregrination: We think therefore proper, in Juftification of Ourfelves, publickly to Difclaim all Relation or Alliance whatfoever, with the faid Society of Free Mafons, as the fame muft manifeftly tend to the Sacrifice of our folemn Myfteries: And further, to convince the Publick of the Candour and Opennefs of our Proceedings, We here prefent them with a Key to our Proceffion ; and that the rather, as it confifts of many Things Emblematical, Myftical, Hieroglyphical, Comical, Satirical, Political, &c.

And whereas many perfuaded by the Purity of our Conftitution, the nice Morality of our Brethren, and peculiar Decency of our Rites and Ceremonies, have lately forfook the grofs Errors and Follies of the Free-Mafonry, are now become true Scald-Miferables, it cannot but afford a moft pleafing Satisfaction to all who have any Regard for Truth and Decency, to fee our Proceſſion encreaſed with ſuch Number of Proſelytes, and behold thoſe, whoſe Vanity, but the laſt Year, exalted them into a borrow'd Equipage, now condeſcended to become the humble Cargo of a Sand-cart: But, ————. *Magna eſt Veritas, & prevalebit.*

Two Tylers, or Guarders

In yellow Cockades and Liveries, being the Colour ordain'd by the Sword-Bearer of State. They, as young-eſt enter'd Apprentices, are to guard the Lodge, with a drawn Sword, from all Cowens and Eves-droppers, that is Liſtners, leſt they ſhould diſcover the incomprehenſi-ble Myſteries of Maſonry.

A Grand Chorus of Inſtruments, viz.

Four Sackbutts, or Cow's Horns; ſix Hottentot Haut-boys; four Tinkling Cymbals, or Tea Caniſters, with broken Glaſs in them; four Shovels and Bruſhes; two Double Baſs Drippingpans; a Tenor Frying pan; a Salt-Box in De-la-ſol; and a Pair of Gut Tubs.

Two Pillars, Jachin and Boaz.

After the Proportion and Workmanſhip of the famous ones in the Porch of Solomon's Temple. Their Height, their Thickneſs, and their Capital. Adorn'd with Lilly-work, Net-work, and Pomgranet-work.

Three pair of Stewards.

With their Attendants, in Red Ribands, being their Colour, in three Gut-Carts drawn by three Aſſes each, their Aprons being lined with Red Silk, their Jewels pendant to Red Ribands, and their Heads properly adorned with emblematical Caps.

The true Original Maſon's Lodge,

Upon which poor old Hyram made all his enter'd Pren-tices.

The entered 'Prentices Token,

That is to ſay, the Manner in which the Novices, or thoſe lately admitted, ſhake each other by the Hand; and it is by putting the Ball of the Thumb of the Right Hand (for we never do any Act of Maſonry with the Left) upon the Knuckle of the third Joint of the firſt

Finger of the Brother's Right Hand, fqueezing it gently.

Ragged entered 'Prentices.

Properly cloathed, giving the above Token, and the Word, which is Jachin.

Three great Lights.

Myftically refembling the Sun and Moon, and the Mafter Mafon.

The Sun ; To Rule the Day. Hieroglyphial.

The Moon ; To Rule the Night. Emblematical.

A Mafter Mafon, To Rule his Lodge. Political.

The Letter G. The Fellow Craft's Token.

The Fellow-Craft, or Letter G. Men,

A Mafter's Lodge.

The Funeral of Hyram.

Grand Band of Mufick as before.

Two Trophies.

The Equipage of the Grand Miftrefs.

Attendants of Honour.

The Grand Secretary with his Infignia, &c.

Probationifts and Candidates clofe the whole Proceffion.

N. B. After the Proceffion was over, 5l. was fpent at one of the Lodges 4 l. 19 s. 4 d. in Geneva, and 3 d. in bread and Cheefe; fo the Night was concluded with Drinking, Swearing, Fighting, and all other Demonftrations of Difturbance.

P–t.

1744, August 3,   Boston.

Meeting of the Masters Lodge.

O.R.; A.B.

1744, August 8,   Boston.

Meeting of the First Lodge. William Coffin made. Charles Pelham proposed by Henry Price as a candidate for the purpose of making him Secretary of the Lodge; Peter Pelham desiring to withdraw from the office.

O.R.; P.L.; A.B.

Peter and Charles Pelham.

Peter Pelham came to America, from London, probably between 1724 and 1726. He was the first portrait painter and engraver known in New England. The earliest work in that line yet traced to him is his engraved portrait of Rev. Cotton Mather, dated 1727. It is inscribed: "P. Pelham ad vivum pinxit, ab origine fecit et excud." A print of this very rare mezzotint hangs in the Masonic Temple in Boston.

We learn from his advertisements in the newspapers of the day that from 1734 to 1748, and perhaps later, he kept a school where "Young Gentlemen and Ladies may be Taught Dancing, Writing, Reading, painting upon Glass, and all sorts of needle work," the last-named department probably being in charge of his wife.

On the 22d of May, 1747, he married, for his second wife, Mrs. Mary Singleton, widow of Richard Copley and mother of John Singleton Copley, the celebrated artist and father of Lord Lyndhurst who was three times Lord Chancellor of England.

Peter Pelham was made a Mason in the First Lodge in Boston on the 8th of November, 1738, five years after the Lodge was instituted. On the 26th of December, 1739, he was elected Secretary, and the record of that meeting is entered in a new and beautiful handwriting, the same style being continued for many years. He served in that office until September 26, 1744, when he was succeeded by his son Charles. On the 13th of April, 1750, the Third Lodge in Boston was represented in Grand Lodge by father and son, as Master and Junior Warden respectively. The records of Trinity Church, in Boston, where he had long worshipped, show that

Peter Pelham was buried December 14, 1751. For his portrait, see page 232.

Charles, the son of Peter and Martha Pelham, was baptized at St. Paul's, Covent Garden, London, on the 9th of December, 1722. He came to America with his parents, when three or four years old, and is said to have been educated as a merchant, but in the "Boston News Letter" of April 23, 1762, he advertises his intention "again to open a Dancing School" at Concert Hall. In April, 1765, he bought the homestead of Rev. J. Cotton, in Newton, with 103 acres of land, for £735. We are told that "he was represented by his neighbours to have been a very polite and intelligent man. He opened an academy at his own house and fitted scholars for College." "He was a stanch friend of the Colony, as will appear by the resolutions he prepared for the Town."

In 1766 we find him teaching school in Medford, where, on the 6th of December of that year, he married Mary, daughter of Andrew Tyler by his wife Miriam, a sister of the famous Sir William Pepperell. A daughter Helen married Thomas Curtis and was the mother of Charles Pelham Curtis, the senior member of the firm of C. P. & B. R. Curtis, for many years leading members of the Boston bar, the junior member of the firm serving during the later portion of his life as a Justice of the United States Supreme Court.

The stepmother of Charles died on the 29th of April, 1789, and her will named as her executor her "good friend, Charles Pelham, of Newton." Late in life he removed to Wilmington, N. C., where he died December 13, 1809. A portrait painted by his stepbrother, John Singleton Copley, is in the possession of the Curtis fam-

ily. Representatives of two generations of that family
now living bear the name of Charles Pelham, and it is
by their kindness that we are able to present portraits
of both Peter and Charles.

On the 8th of August, 1744, "Brother (Henry) Price
proposed Mr. Charles Pelham as a Candidate" in the
First Lodge in Boston. He was accepted on the 22d of
the same month, and on the 12th of September "was
made a Mason in due Form." On the 26th it was
"Voted That our late Sec^r. Bro. P. Pelham be paid Ten
Pounds, with the Thanks of the Society for his past
Services"; also "Voted, That Bro. Charles Pelham be
Secretary, in the Room of Our Late Secr^y, who has laid
it down." He served the Lodge in that capacity until
July 24, 1754, when the volume ends, and perhaps
longer. This is the only volume of early records of the
First Lodge now known to exist. It is the earliest book
of Masonic Lodge Records now known to be in exist-
ence on this continent, commencing December 27, 1738,
and ending July 24, 1754.

1744, August 22,   Boston.
    Meeting of the First Lodge.
            O.R.; A.B.

1744, September 7,   Boston.
    Meeting of the Masters Lodge.
            O.R.; A.B.

1744, September 12,   Boston.
    Meeting of the First Lodge.   Charles Pelham made.
            O.R.; P.L.; A.B.
            Re Charles Pelham, see page 291.

CHARLES PELHAM
Grand Secretary 1744—1754.

1744, September 26,   Boston.

Meeting of the First Lodge. Charles Pelham elected Secretary.

O.R.; A.B.
1900 Mass. 124.

On this same day Governor Belcher visits the Grand Lodge at London with a letter from the First Lodge in Boston.

O.R. of the Grand Lodge of England.
1871 Mass. 316.
1888 Mass. 156.

1744, October 5,   Boston.

The record book of the Masters Lodge under this date says: "No meeting this night, our R^t W: M. and several of the members being out of Town on Extraordinary Business."

O.R.

1744, October 10,   Boston.

Meeting of the First Lodge. Capt. Lewis Delabraz (Dolobaratz) a prisoner of war elected and, by dispensation, made, gratis, "as he might be serviceable (when at Home) to any Brother whom Providence might cast in his way."

O.R.; P.L.; A.B.

1744, October 24,   Boston.

Meeting of the First Lodge. Brother Pearson admitted.

O.R.; A.B.

1744, November 2,   Boston.
Meeting of the Masters Lodge.
        O.R.; A.B.

1744, November 14,   Boston.
Meeting of the First Lodge. Ballard Beckford, Pro.
G. M. of Jamaica, visited the Lodge. Peter Pelham, Jr.,
made.
        O.R.; P.L.; A.B.

1744, November 28,   Boston.
Meeting of the First Lodge.
        O.R.; A.B.

1744, December 7,   Boston.
Meeting of the Masters Lodge.   Brother William
Coffin raised.
        O.R.; P.L.; A.B.

1744, December 12,   Boston.
Meeting of the First Lodge.
        O.R.; A.B.

1744, December 17,   Boston.
The *Boston Post Boy* contains the following paragraph
under date of London, August 14, 1744.

"We learn by Letters from Lisbon, that there has been
lately Auto de Fe; after which feveral Jews were burnt,
and some French Men, who were Free Mafons, and have
been two Years in the Prisons of the Inquifition, appeared in the S. Benito on that Occafion."

1744, December 26,   Boston.
Meeting of the First Lodge.   Election.   Mr. Belviel
made.
> O.R.; P.L.; A.B.
> 1 Mass. 8.

1744, December 27,   Boston.
Celebration of the Festival by the Grand Lodge.
> O.R. of First Lodge.
> 1 Mass. 9.

1744/5, January 4,   Boston.
Meeting of the Masters Lodge.   Election.   Brothers
Edward Ellis and Lewis Demouline raised.
> O.R.; P.L.; A.B.

1744/5, January 9,   Boston.
Meeting of the First Lodge.
> O.R.; A.B.

1744/5, January 23,   Boston.
Meeting of the First Lodge.   Brother Robert Glover
admitted.   James Gough made.
> O.R.; P.L.; A.B.

1744/5, February 1,   Boston.
Meeting of the Masters Lodge.
> O.R.

1744/5, February 13,   Boston.
Meeting of the First Lodge.
> O.R.; A.B.

1744/5, February 27,   Boston.
   Meeting of the First Lodge.
       O.R.; A.B.

1744/5, March 1,   Boston.
   Meeting of the Masters Lodge.
       O.R.

1744/5, March 13,   Boston.
   Meeting of the First Lodge.   Richard Hood made.
       O.R.; P.L.; A.B.

1744/5, March 22,   Boston.
   Meeting of the Masters Lodge.   Brother Robert
Glover raised.
       O.R.; P.L.

Chapter XIX

1745

1745, March 27,   Boston.
  Meeting of the First Lodge.
          O.R.; A.B.

1745, April 10,   Boston.
  Meeting of the First Lodge.
          O.R.; A.B.

1745, April 24,   Boston.
  Meeting of the First Lodge.   Daniel Marquand made.
          O.R.; P.L.; A.B.

1745, May 2,   Boston.
  Meeting of the Masters Lodge.
          O.R.

1745, May 8,   Boston.
  Meeting of the First Lodge.
          O.R.; A.B.

1745, May 22,   Boston.
  Meeting of the First Lodge.   John Colson made.
          O.R.; A.B.

1745, June 7,   Boston.
  Meeting of the Masters Lodge.
          O.R.

1745, June 12,   Boston.
  Meeting of the First Lodge.
          O.R.; A.B.

1745, June 18,   Boston.
  "Stephen Greenleaf, Mathematical Instrument Maker,
in Queen Street, Boston, opposite to the Prison," advertises to make "Free Masons Jewels."
          Boston Gazette.

1745, June 24,   Boston.
  Celebration of the Festival by the Grand Lodge.
Thirty-three Brethren in attendance.
          O.R. and A.B. of First Lodge.

1745, June 26,   Boston.
  Meeting of the First Lodge.   Election.
          O.R.; A.B.

1745, July 1,   Boston.
  Meeting of the First Lodge.   Daniel Byles and Capt.
John (James) Heweton made.
          O.R.; P.L.; A.B.

1745, July 10,   Boston.
  Meeting of the First Lodge.   Richard Smith made.
          O.R.; P.L.; A.B.

1745, July 24,   Boston.
  Meeting of the First Lodge.   William Coffin, Jr.,
made.
          O.R.; P.L.; A.B.

1745, August 2,　　　Boston.

Meeting of the Masters Lodge. After this meeting the following is written in the record book: "Adjourned 'till Octo.^r ye 4th; for substantial reasons from time to time."
　　　O.R.

1745, August 14,　　　Boston.

Meeting of the First Lodge. Antho. D'Laboladree (D'Laboulerdree), and Peter Phill Chas. St. Paul made.
　　　O.R.; P.L.

The Pelham List furnishes the information that Thomas Cross was admitted. In this respect the list must be in error for he is recorded as a Visitor as late as November 13, 1745, on the Original Record.

1745, August 28,　　　Boston.

Meeting of the First Lodge.
　　　O.R.; A.B.

1745, September 11,　　　Boston.

Meeting of the First Lodge.
　　　O.R.; A.B.

1745, September 25,　　　Boston.

Meeting of the First Lodge.
　　　O.R.; A.B.

1745, October 4,　　　Boston.

Meeting of the Masters Lodge.
　　　O.R.

1745, October 9,　　　Boston.

Meeting of the First Lodge.
　　　O.R.; A.B.

1745, October 23,   Boston.
  Meeting of the First Lodge.
        O.R.; A.B.

1745, November 1,   Boston.
  Meeting of the Masters Lodge. Brothers Thomas
Cross and Charles Pelham raised. At the same meeting
Charles Pelham is elected Secretary and the handwriting
changes from Henry Johnson's to his.
        O.R.

1744, November 13,   Boston.
  Meeting of the First Lodge. Brother Price reported
that the Masters Lodge had voted a set of Candles to
this Lodge.
        O.R.; A.B.

1745, November 27,   Boston.
  Meeting of the First Lodge.
        O.R.; A.B.

1745, December 6,   Boston.
  Meeting of the Masters Lodge. Election.
        O.R.

1745, December 11,   Boston.
  Meeting of the First Lodge.
        O.R.; A.B.

1745, December 24,   Boston.
  Meeting of the First Lodge. Election. William Merchant made.
        O.R.; P.L.; A.B.
        1 Mass. 9.

1745/6, January 8,   Boston.

Meeting of the Masters Lodge. Brothers Thomas James Gruchy and James Gough raised.

O.R.; A.B.

The same evening the First Lodge met and immediately adjourned.

O.R.; A.B.

1745/6, January 22,   Boston.

Meeting of the First Lodge. The records state that the Lodge being opened, "Bro. Jones being but an Enter'd Apprentice (by his earnest desire) made a Fellow Craft in due Form & Voted Mem^r."

Brothers John Phillips and Richard Gridley admitted.

O.R.; P.L.; A.B.

1745/6, February 7,   Boston.

Meeting of the Masters Lodge.

O.R.; A.B.

1745/6, February 12,   Boston.

Meeting of the First Lodge.

O.R.; A.B.

1745/6, February 26,   Boston.

Meeting of the First Lodge.

O.R.; A.B.

1745/6, March 7,   Boston.

Meeting of the Masters Lodge.

O.R.; A.B.

1745/6, March 12,   Boston.
   Meeting of the First Lodge. Barnard Townsend and Benjamin Brimston (Brimsdon) made.
         O.R.; P.L.; A.B.

|1745/6, March 26,   Boston.
   Meeting of the First Lodge.
         O.R.; A.B.

Chapter XX

1746

1746, April 4, Boston.

Meeting of the Masters Lodge. Brother Richard Gridley raised.

1916 Mass. 30.

O.R.; A.B.

Richard Gridley.

Richard Gridley was born in Boston on January 3, 1710, the youngest of six children of Richard and Rebecca Gridley. As his elder brother had entered the law, it was the desire of his parents that Richard should enter a business career, and he was apprenticed to Mr. Atkinson, a wholesale merchant of Boston. Brother Huntoon says, "Apt and learned in the arts and sciences, he was one of the greatest mathematicians of his day; of romantic honour, chivalrous ambition, and adventurous bravery; nature made him a soldier, and art could not make him a merchant." He became a surveyor and civil engineer. He was the first, and for a long time the only gauger in America. He was the projector of Long Wharf, which was constructed according to his plan. He became proficient in military science in part through association with John Henry Bastide who became Director of His Majesty's Engineers and Chief Engineer of Nova Scotia.

In the southeastern part of Cape Breton was the city of Louisburgh. It was perhaps the best fortified city in America. To this city in 1745, the New England Colonists laid siege under the command of Colonel William Pepperrell. Gridley was commissioned "Lieutenant Colonel" and "Captain of Train and Company," and was given the command of the Grand or Royal Battery, which stood directly opposite the Harbour of Louisburgh and which was captured by His Majesty's forces on May 2, 1745. On August 1st Governor Shirley commissioned him First Bombardier, and he continued in the double capacity of First Captain of Artillery and First Bombardier until the end of the siege. Such was his skill that he succeeded on the third fire in dropping a shell directly into the citadel, which was the immediate cause of the surrender of the city. All of the Pepperrell batteries were erected by Gridley. In this command he won his first military laurels. Returning home, he drew the designs for a battery and other fortifications on Governor's Island in Boston Harbor, and then left the military service in 1749. Again taking up fortification work, in 1752 he erected Fort Halifax on the Kennebec River. In 1755 he was Chief Engineer of the Army and later in the year was appointed Commander-in-Chief of the Provincial Artillery and Colonel of Infantry, drawing pay in both positions. He joined the expedition against Crown Point and under his supervision all the fortifications around Lake George were constructed. On August 4, 1756, he was selected by General Winslow to attend him in a visit to His Excellency the Earl of Loudoun, Past Grand Master of the Grand Lodge of England, then Commander-in-Chief of His Majesty's forces in America. This year Paul Revere, who had just become of age, was commissioned Second Lieutenant in Gridley's Regiment.

Cape Breton having been restored to France, Louisburgh, in 1758, again became the seat of war. Gridley participated in the siege and was present at the second taking of the city. In 1759, he was appointed by General Amherst to command the Provincial Artillery, which was about to besiege Quebec. It was Gridley's corps that dragged up to the Plains of Abraham the only two field pieces which were raised to the Heights. Gridley stood by the side of General Wolfe when that gallant officer fell victorious. Gridley then went to England to adjust his accounts with the government. For his distinguished services he was given the Magdalen Isles, and one-half pay as a British officer. For several years thereafter he maintained his home upon these islands, but in 1762 purchased a house in Prince Street in Boston. In 1770, in connection with Edmund Quincy, he entered the business of smelting ore in Sharon, leaving there in 1773.

In 1774 he signed a secret agreement with his intimate friend, General Joseph Warren, pledging each other that in the event of hostilities with the Mother Country they would join the Patriot Army. When his British agent in England requested to be informed upon which side he would take up arms, he replied: "I shall fight for justice and my country," and cast his lot with the Patriots. April 21, 1775, he was summoned to attend the Committee of Safety, and was appointed to the command of the First Regiment of Artillery, the only artillery regiment in the Provinces at the opening of the war. On April 23rd he was appointed Chief Engineer of the Patriot forces and voted a pension for life. On April 26th he entered the service and planned the fortification of Bunker's Hill. On the 16th of June, 1775, the Patriot troops assembled on Cambridge Common and marched silently to Charlestown. Upon arrival acrimonious discussion arose as to whether Breed's Hill or Bunker's Hill was the proper one for fortifications. Gridley with all his force argued that Bunker's Hill was the only one whereon to erect breastworks. One of the Generals coincided with him, but the other was stubborn and determined not to yield. At length Gridley said to the latter, "Sir, the moments are precious, we must decide at once. Since you will not give up your individual opinion to ours, we will give it up to you. Action, and that instantly, only can save us." Gridley at once in person marked the place for the fortifications, gave orders, and even worked himself, spade in hand. Though this battle is generally known as the Battle of Bunker Hill, the fact is that the fortifications were erected and the fight staged on Breed's Hill. Military authorities tell us that Gridley's choice would have been much better. The next morning, the 17th of June, Gridley, owing to his age and the exhausting labour of the previous night, was sick and obliged to leave the hill, although he resolved so as to return later in the day and take command of his own battery, which consisted of ten companies and four hundred and seventeen men. It had only two brass pieces and six iron six-pounders. He was near to Warren when he fell. Almost at the same moment Gridley was struck by a musket ball and was unable to continue longer in the fight. Only two days after, however, assisted by one of his sons, he took charge of a battery at the Highlands.

To the skill and ingenuity of Richard Gridley America

is indebted for the first cannon and mortars ever cast in this country.

On September 20, 1775, he received from the Provincial Congress the rank of Major General. Washington said of him that there was no one better qualified to serve as Chief Engineer of the army. But the infirmities of age were creeping upon him. He was obliged to resign his commission, and the council of officers agreed that it was better to place the command of the artillery in younger hands. Nevertheless in March, 1776, he directed the fortifying of Dorchester Heights, and they were made so formidable that the British dared not attack them and deemed it best to evacuate Boston. After the evacuation, he was entrusted by Washington with the duty of demolishing the British intrenchments on the Neck, and after these were destroyed he laid out and strengthened various fortifications in and about the city.

On the 8th of April, 1776, the body of Major General Joseph Warren was reinterred, Bunker's Hill having again come into the possession of the Americans, and Richard Gridley was one of the pallbearers. Twelve days after, he was ordered by Washington to attend to the fortifications on Cape Ann and protect the harbour of Gloucester. His last military work which is historically demonstrable was upon the fortifications at Castle William and Governor's Island from March, 1778, to the first of January, 1781. The strength of his patriotism was certainly tested at this time for we find that in 1780 he wrote to Major General Heath that he had had no pay for thirteen months, and begged that something should be sent to him. His last appearance in public was in 1795, when he assisted in laying the corner-stone of the State House with Masonic ceremonies.

Our first knowledge of him Masonically is that on January 22, 1745/6 he was made or admitted a member of the First Lodge in Boston, receiving the Degree of Master Mason in the Masters Lodge on April 4, 1746. He was Junior Warden of the Masters Lodge in 1753 and 1754, Senior Warden of the Second Lodge in 1755, Master of the Masters Lodge in 1756, and Master of the First Lodge in 1757. In Grand Lodge he was Junior Grand Warden in 1758 and 1759 and Senior Grand Warden in 1760 and the early part of 1761. Again he appears as Master of the Masters Lodge in 1763 and 1764, serving during the same years as Senior Grand Warden of the Grand Lodge. When R. W. John Rowe was chosen Provincial Grand Master after the death of Jeremy Gridley he appointed on January 22, 1768, R. W. Richard Gridley, Past Grand Warden, to be Deputy Grand Master, and in this position Richard Gridley continued until after the death of John Rowe, and as late as August 4, 1787. On numerous occasions other than those already stated we find him constituting Lodges under special commissions.

Much has been said and written of his manly character, his urbanity, his uniform politeness, and graceful demeanor, as well as of his charitable and philanthropic disposition. His personal appearance was that of a handsome, remarkably tall, commanding presence, with a frame firm and vigorous, and a constitution like iron. His death, which occurred on June 21, 1796, was caused by blood poisoning, and on Thursday, the 23rd, he was buried in a small enclosure near his home. On October 28, 1876, his body was disinterred and conveyed to the cemetery in Canton, where the remains were reinterred and a monument was erected over his grave.

See oration (*et cit.*) by Daniel T. V. Huntoon at the Memorial Services of Commemoration Day, held in Canton, May 30, 1877, under the auspices of Revere Encampment, Post 94, Grand Army of the Republic; also
1 Mass. *passim.*

1746, April 9, Boston.
Meeting of the First Lodge.
O.R.; A.B.

1746, April 23, Boston.
Meeting of the First Lodge.
O.R.; A.B.

1746, April 29, Jamaica.
Lodge Constituted at St. Jago de la Vega (now Spanish Town), Jamaica.
O.L.
Entick 337.
L.M.R. 89.
Prichard 29

1746, May 2, Boston.
Meeting of the Masters Lodge.
O.R.; A.B.

1746, May 14, Boston.
Meeting of the First Lodge.
O.R.; A.B.

1746, May 29, Boston.
Meeting of the First Lodge. Robert Williams made.
O.R.; P.L.; A.B.

1746, June 6,   Boston.
Meeting of the Masters Lodge.
      O.R.; A.B.

1746, June 11,   Boston.
Meeting of the First Lodge.
      O.R.; A.B.

1746, June 24,   Boston.
Celebration of the Festival by the Grand Lodge, twenty-five Brethren in attendance.
      O.R. of First Lodge.

1746, June 25,   Boston.
Meeting of the First Lodge.
      O.R.; A.B.

1746, July 4,   Boston.
Meeting of the Masters Lodge.   Election.   Brother Joseph Holbrook raised.
      O.R.; P.L.; A.B.

1746, July 9,   Boston.
Meeting of the First Lodge.   Election.
      O.R.; A.B.

1746, July 23,   Boston.
Meeting of the First Lodge.
      O.R.; A.B.

1746, August 1,   Boston.
Meeting of the Masters Lodge.
      O.R.; A.B.

1746, August 13, Boston.
Meeting of the First Lodge.
O.R.; A.B.

1746, August 27, Boston.
Meeting of the First Lodge.
O.R.; A.B.

1746, September 5, Boston.
Meeting of the Masters Lodge.
O.R.; A.B.

1746, September 10, Boston.
Meeting of the First Lodge.
O.R.; A.B.

1746, September 24, Boston.
The records of the First Lodge state that by reason of
an "Alarm of French Fleet" the Lodge was not opened.
O.R.; A.B.
1883 Mass. 165.

1746, October 3, Boston.
Meeting of the Masters Lodge.
O.R.; A.B.

1746, October 8, Boston.
Meeting of the First Lodge. Rev. John Woods made.
O.R.; P.L.; A.B.

1746, October 13, Boston.
Meeting of the First Lodge. Robert McKennen
(Mackinen) made.
O.R.; P.L.; A.B.

1746, October 22,   Boston.
   Meeting of the First Lodge.
            O.R.
            A.B. records this meeting as the 24th.

1746, November 7,   Boston.
   Meeting of the Masters Lodge.   Brother Rev. John
Woods raised.
            O.R.; P.L.; A.B.

1746, November 12,   Boston.
   Meeting of the First Lodge.   Capt. John Bradford and
Joseph Sherburne made.   James Buck "made for a
Tylar."
            O.R.; P.L.; A.B.

1746, November 26,   Boston.
   Meeting of the First Lodge.
            O.R.; A.B.

1746, December 5,   Boston.
   Meeting of the Masters Lodge.   Election.
            O.R.; A.B.

1746, December 10,   Boston.
   Meeting of the First Lodge.   Fee for making raised
from 15 Pounds to 20 Pounds.
            O.R.; A.B.

1746, December 24,   Boston.
   Meeting of the First Lodge.   Election.
   Voted: "That all Visiting Bro[rs] who are Town inhabi-

tants shall pay 15/ each night, and Transient persons 10/."
      O.R.; A.B.

      Boston—Newfoundland.
Pro. G. M. Oxnard grants a Constitution for a Lodge to be held in Newfoundland.
      1 Mass. 9.
      L.M.R. 472.

1746/7, January 2,   Boston.
  Meeting of the Masters Lodge.
      O.R.; A.B.

1746/7, January 14,   Boston.
  Meeting of the First Lodge. James Day, Jonathan Prescott, Newcoming Herbert, Andrew Irwin, Andrew Dure, Joseph Aberry, and Estes Hatch made. Brother Jonathan Rush "made F. C." Brother Robert Cummins admitted.
      O.R.; P.L.; A.B.

1746/7, January 16,
      Portsmouth, New Hampshire.
  Meeting of the Lodge. Election. Capt. Nathaniel Pierce made.
      O.R.

1746/7, January 28,   Boston.
  Meeting of the First Lodge. Capt. William Day, Peter Hammond, William Martin, and Simeon Patter made and admitted. Rev. Brother Charles Brockwell, King's Chaplain, admitted.
      O.R.; P.L.; A.B.

1746/7, February 5,   Boston.
   Meeting of the Masters Lodge.
            O.R.; A.B.

1746/7, February 11,   Boston.
   Meeting of the First Lodge. Brother Benjamin Stans-
bury admitted.
            O.R.; P.L.; A.B.

1746/7, February 25,   Boston.
   Meeting of the First Lodge.
            O.R.; A.B.

1746/7, March 7,   Boston.
   Meeting of the Masters Lodge. Brothers Samuel
Waterhouse, James Day, John Colson (Collson), and
Robert Williams raised.
            O.R.; P.L.; A.B.

1746/7, March 11,   Boston.
   Meeting of the First Lodge.
            O.R.; A.B.

1746,   Nova Scotia.
   Lord Cranstoun, Grand Master of England, appointed
Robert Commins, Provincial Grand Master for Cape
Breton and Louisburgh.
            Preston (Portsmouth, 1804) 192.
            Entick 334.
            P.C. (2nd Eng. Ed.) 126.
Respecting Capt. Robert Commins little or nothing
is known. His name is not to be found in any naval
history nor is it in any account of the war operations

which preceded the capture of either Louisburgh or Quebec. Commins may have been an army officer although searches have not found his name in the army list of 1749. Along about this time there were many traders between New England ports and Louisburgh and Commins may have been one of these. With so little known about Commins and the practical certainty that he did not exercise his commission, we may with propriety dismiss him from further consideration.

1 Nova Scotia Lodge of Research 3, page 44.

Cf. Closing items of Chapters **XI** and **XII**; also 1746/7, January 14.

Chapter XXI

1747

1747, March 25,   Boston.
Meeting of the First Lodge.
      O.R.; A.B.

1747, April 3,   Boston.
Meeting of the Masters Lodge.
      O.R.; A.B.

1747, April 8,   Boston.
Meeting of the First Lodge.
      O.R.; A.B.

1747, April 22,   Boston.
Meeting of the First Lodge.
      O.R.; A.B.

1747, May 1,   Boston.
Meeting of the Masters Lodge.
      O.R.; A.B.

1747, May 13,   Boston.
Meeting of the First Lodge.
      O.R.; A.B.

1747, May 27,   Boston
Meeting of the First Lodge. Brother Andrew McKenzie admitted.
      O.R.; A.B.

The Pelham List says "pass'd F.C." But it is wrong. McKenzie was pass'd July 22, 1747.

    O.R.

The few errors which from time to time we find in the Pelham List, in the Beteilhe Manuscript, in the Barons Letter, and in the records prove their general correctness. In them there are no more errors than the average secretary or copyist makes in his work. The fact also that names are often differently spelled, although *idem sonans*, is a further indication that much of Pelham's information was obtained from other sources than the books now in our possession. The agreement, however, between the original Proceedings which we have and the Pelham List from January 10, 1738/9, to August 28, 1751, is the best possible evidence of the correctness of the List for the period from July 30, 1733, to November 8, 1738, a period for which we have no original records except now and then a document such as the petition of July 30, 1733, the Beteilhe Manuscript, and others cited *supra*. In this connection the surprisingly accurate agreement between the Pelham List, the Beteilhe Manuscript, and the Barons Letter for the periods when they overlap is worthy of special notice. All of these facts and others noted now and then *supra* give remarkable proof that we may rely upon the Pelham List except for such an occasional error as might be made by a reasonably accurate scrivener.

(NOTE. As a modern instance of just such errors creeping in, note instances in the article on The Establishment and Early Days of Masonry in America, found in 1914 Mass. 243 to 288, and in *The Builder* for the months of May, August and October, 1915, *q.v.* The date of Henry Price's commission is given as April 2,

1733, which should of course have been April 13, 1733. The Provincial Grand Lodge of New South Wales in June, 1727, was referred to. It should of course have been South Wales. The date of the Deputation to Philipps as Provincial Grand Master for Nova Scotia was stated as 1740 when it should have been 1738. The date of the Portsmouth petition was quoted as February 9, 1735/6, instead of February 5; and the establishment of the Second Lodge in Boston February 17 instead of February 15, 1750. The author has gone over this book dozens of times, yet some such errors may escape him and a number of other Brethren who have kindly assisted him by verifying citations, etc.)

Henry Price himself made a similar error on one occasion by stating that his extension of authority over all North America was in 1735 instead of 1734.

> 1914 Mass. 270.
> 1871 Mass. 330.
> See Chapter II, 4, c, and e;
> also 1739, July 25, *supra.*

1747, June 5,   Boston.
   Meeting of the Masters Lodge.
> O.R.; A.B.

1747, June 6,   West Indies.
   Lodge Constituted by the Grand Master of England at St. Eustatius.
> O.L.
> Entick 337.
> L.M.R. 90.
   Prichard says January 6, 1747, but he is wrong.

1747, June 10,   Boston.
Meeting of the First Lodge.   Election.
O.R.; A.B.

1747, June 24,   Boston.
Meeting of the First Lodge.
O.R.; A.B.

1747, July 3,   Boston.
Meeting of the Masters Lodge.   Election.
O.R.; A.B.

1747, July 8,   Boston.
Meeting of the First Lodge.
O.R.; A.B.

1747, July 22,   Boston.
Meeting of the First Lodge.   Capt. Archibald Gray-
ham made.
P.L.; O.R.
Brother Andrew McKenzie "Rais'd F.C. in due Form."
O.R.; A.B.

1747, August 7,   Boston.
Meeting of the Masters Lodge.
O.R.; A.B.

1747, August 12,   Boston.
Meeting of the First Lodge.
O.R.; A.B.

1747, August 26,   Boston.
Meeting of the First Lodge.   Committee appointed to

send congratulations to Governor Belcher upon his appointment as Governor of the Jerseys (New Jersey).

> O.R.; A.B.
> 1 Mass. 391.
> 1883 Mass. 162.

1747, September 3,   Boston.

Letter of congratulation sent from the Provincial Grand Master and from the First Lodge to Governor Belcher upon his safe arrival to assume his new office as Governor of the Jerseys (New Jersey).

> 1 Mass. 391.
> 1871 Mass. 376.
> O.R. of First Lodge for September 9, 1747.

1747, September 4,   Boston.

Meeting of the Masters Lodge.

> **O.R.; A.B.**

1747, September 9,   Boston.

Meeting of the First Lodge. John Ray (Rae) made.

The report of the committee appointed to send congratulations to Governor Belcher together with their letter is spread in full upon the records.

> O.R.; A.B.
> 1883 Mass. 163.

1747, September 18,

> Portsmouth, New Hampshire.

Meeting of the Lodge. Samuel Solly, Charles Gorwood, John Salmon, and Alexander Malcum made.

> O.R.

1747, September 23,   Boston.
Meeting of the First Lodge.
O.R.; A.B.

The Pelham List gives Robert Bowers as made, John Salmon as passed on this evening. The record is silent as to both.

See 1747, October 28, *infra.*

1747, September 24
Portsmouth, New Hampshire.
Meeting of the Lodge at which a vote was passed that application be made to Pro. G. M. Oxnard that there be a Provincial Grand Master for New Hampshire.
O.R.

1747, October 2,   Boston.
Meeting of the Masters Lodge.
O.R.; A.B.

1747, October 6,
Governor Jonathan Belcher from Kingswood House in the City of Burlington wrote to R. W. Thomas Oxnard, Esq., Provincial Grand Master of North America, and the Master, Wardens and Fellows of the First Lodge in Boston, a letter in acknowledgment of and thanks for the letter of September 3, 1747.
1 Mass. 392.
O.R. of First Lodge for November 11, 1747.

1747, October 14,   Boston.
Meeting of the First Lodge. Brothers John Salmon and Robert Bowers admitted.
O.R.; A.B.

1747, October 28,   Boston.
Meeting of the First Lodge. Brother Charles Gorwood passed.
        O.R.; P.L.
Brother John Salmon passed and Brother John Rowe
admitted.
        O.R.; A.B.

1747, November 3,   Boston.
Meeting of the First Lodge. John Conally (Conolly,
Connally), Hugh Hardgrove, and Sampson Hodge made.
        O.R.; P.L.; A.B.

1747, November 11,   Boston.
Meeting of the First Lodge. Letter of October 6,
1747, from Governor Belcher read and recorded.
        O.R.; A.B.
        1 Mass. 392.
        1883 Mass. 163.

1747, November 25,   Boston.
Meeting of the First Lodge. Brother Alexander Mal-
colm passed and admitted.
        O.R.; P.L.; A.B.

1747, December 9,   Boston.
Meeting of the First Lodge.
        O.R.; A.B.
        1 Mass. 9.

1747, December 23,   Boston.
Meeting of the First Lodge. Election. John Husk
(Huske) made.
        O.R.; P.L.; A.B.

1747/8, January 13,   Boston.

Meeting of the First Lodge. Rev. Alexander Malcom, Capt. Aeneas Mackay (McKay), Samuel Levins, Thomas Newton, and Samuel Stone ("Master of the House") made.

O.R.; P.L.; A.B.

1747/8, January 15,
           Portsmouth, New Hampshire.
Meeting of the Lodge.
           O.R.

1747/8, January 21,
           Portsmouth, New Hampshire.
Meeting of the Lodge.
           O.R.

1747/8, January 25,
           Portsmouth, New Hampshire.
Meeting of the Lodge.
           O.R.

1747/8, January 27,   Boston.

Meeting of the First Lodge. Capts. William Norris, Thomas Bogle, and Pat. Montgomery (Montgomerie) made.

O.R.; P.L.; A.B.

1747/8, February 5,   Boston.
Meeting of the Masters Lodge. Election.
           O.R.; A.B.

1747/8, February 10,   Boston.
Meeting of the First Lodge.   Jonathan Dwight and James Abercrombie made.
> O.R.; P.L.; A.B.

1747/8, February 24,   Boston.
Meeting of the First Lodge.   Capt. Paul Binney made.
> O.R.; P.L.; A.B.

1747/8, March 4,   Boston.
Meeting of the Masters Lodge.   Brother John Husk (Huske) raised.
> O.R.; P.L.; A.B.

1747/8, March 9,   Boston.
Meeting of the First Lodge.
> O.R.; A.B.

1747/8, March 23,   Boston.
Meeting of the First Lodge.   Benjamin Smithers made.
> O.R.; P.L.; A.B.

Chapter XXII

1748

1748, April 1,   Boston.
Meeting of the Masters Lodge. Brother Andrew McKenzie raised.
        O.R.; P.L.; A.B.

1748, April 13,   Boston.
Meeting of the First Lodge.
        O.R.; A.B.

1748, April 21,
        Portsmouth, New Hampshire.
Meeting of the Lodge.
        O.R.

1748, April 27,   Boston.
Meeting of the First Lodge.
        O.R.; A.B.

1748, May 6,   Boston.
Meeting of the Masters Lodge.
        O.R.; A.B.

1748, May 11,   Boston.
Meeting of the First Lodge. Jeremiah (Jeremy) Gridley and Belshr (Belthar) Bayard made.
        O.R.; P.L.; A.B.

Jeremy Gridley.

Jeremiah Gridley was born in Boston, March 10, 1701/2. We refer to him as Jeremy Gridley because during the larger part of his adult career he wrote his name that way, and by that name received his appointment as Provincial Grand Master of Masons in North America.

He graduated from Harvard in 1725 and became a school teacher, but while engaged in teaching and for some time afterwards he studied theology and general literature and occasionally preached. From Harvard he received the degree of A.M. on June 28, 1728. On October 26, 1727, he was elected usher or assistant to Dr. Nathaniel Williams in the public grammar school in Boston at a salary of thirty pounds per year, which was raised from time to time until he received a maximum of one hundred pounds per year from May 5, 1731.

While still teaching he married Abigail Lewis, the daughter of Hon. Ezekiel Lewis, a prominent Bostonian who was during his life a school teacher, selectman, representative, counsellor, and merchant. I am unable to find the date of the marriage, but its issue were Abigail, born August 8, 1731; Sarah, born April 4, 1736, and Rebecca, born April 25, 1741.

While still teaching he, in 1731, founded *The Weekly Rehearsal*, one of the earliest of the Boston newspapers. Past Grand Master Isaiah Thomas in his *History of Printing* (1810 edition, Volume 1, page 327) states that *The Weekly Rehearsal* "was carried on at the expense of some gentlemen who formed themselves into a political or literary club and wrote for it. At the head of this club was the late celebrated Jeremy Gridley who was the real editor of the paper." He ceased connection with this paper on April 2, 1733, when Thomas Fleet became its sole proprietor and publisher, who continued it until August 11, 1735, after which it was replaced by *The Boston Evening-Post.* Copies of all but four issues of *The Weekly Rehearsal* are known, most of them being in the library of the American Antiquarian Society at Worcester, Mass. This was the first newspaper or magazine published in America having any substantial claim to literary merit. High encomiums are paid by reviewers and critics to the elegant and classical style of Gridley's contributions.

Meanwhile he was studying law and was admitted to the Bar probably about the time of his resignation as usher in Mr. Nathaniel Williams's School where, on February 4, 1733/4, he was succeeded by Nathaniel Oliver, Jr.

Little is known about his early days at the Bar, except that he speedily rose to a commanding position. On March 17, 1741/2, the Selectmen of Boston voted to engage John Overing and Jeremy Gridley as Town Counsel in impending litigation which, by the way, the town lost. June 10, 1742, he was, for the first time, chosen Attorney General by both Houses of Assembly.

On April 13, 1748, he was proposed to the First Lodge by Past Grand Master Henry Price, was elected April 27 and made a Mason May 11. Almost immediately thereafter he went to England carrying a letter of recommendation from the Brethren in Boston.

On September 21, 1748, he presented in London to the Right Honourable the Lords Commissioners of the Treasury an important Memorial from the men of affairs in New England, with regard to the depreciation of the currency and the establishment of a stable basis of exchange. It may be found in *The Boston News Letter* for November 25, 1748.

Gridley did not attend Lodge in Boston again until December 7, 1750, when he was raised in the Masters Lodge.

Our customs differ much from those of the period of Gridley's life. Then very few progressed beyond the grade of Entered Apprentice. Occasionally a Brother was "raised Fellow Craft" and admitted a member of the Lodge. But the membership was small and limited. Many were made who never became members. Gridley, indeed, did not become a member of the First Lodge until January 25, 1753. Meantime he was active. Almost immediately after his raising he became a legal adviser to the Fraternity.

Thomas Fleet published in *The Boston Evening-Post* for January 7, 1751, some doggerel verse and a picture, both reflecting upon the Fraternity and too filthy and disgusting to be reproduced. It greatly disturbed the Brethren.

A meeting of the First Lodge was held on January 9, 1750/1, at which many Brethren not members were in attendance, among them Brother Gridley. After full discussion the following votes were passed:

"Voted, That no Bro. Present, shall for the future take any News Paper Printed by Thos. Fleet, or that said Fleet may be Concerned in.

Voted, That no Bro. Present shall give any encouragement to sd. Fleets Paper; or to him in his Business by Advertisements or Otherways.

Voted, That Brors. Oxnard, L. Colvil, Gridley, McDaniel, Brockwell, Rowe & Price, be a Committee, to wait upon the Lieut. Governour, & Council, to Complain against a Scandelous piece of Ribaldry in sd. Fleets Paper, and pray their Order for Prosecuting the Printer their of.

Voted, That the Treasr. of this Lodge do pay unto sd. Committe our proportion of whatever Expense may Acrue upon a Procecution of the aforesaid Fleet, or others, should such Prosecution Ensue."

The Grand Lodge on January 11, 1750/1, also invited Gridley's attendance and

Voted: "That Letters be sent to the Several Lodges abroad under Our Rt W: G. M. acquainting them of the scandilous piece of Ribaldry in T. Fleets paper, and Instructing them by all means to discourage sd paper &c., and it was desir'd of Bro. Gridley to form sd Letters which he propos'd to do."

Evidently the matter was again discussed in Grand Lodge on April 12, 1751, for Brother Gridley attended, though no formal action is recorded.

After his raising, Brother Gridley was attentive to his duties in the Masters Lodge, becoming Junior Warden December 1, 1752, and Senior Warden July 6, 1753. He was the active member of a Committee which revised its By-Laws according to a report presented and adopted December 7, 1753.

Brother Gridley retired from office in the Masters Lodge December 7, 1753, evidently in anticipation of his unanimous election as Master of the First Lodge, December 26, 1753. In passing, it is interesting to note his presence at the Masters Lodge on January 4, 1754, when his pupil, associate at the Bar, and opponent in the great case regarding the Writs of Assistance, James Otis, was raised.

October 11, 1754, at a Grand Lodge held by Henry Price after the death of Thomas Oxnard and attended by our Brother Benjamin Franklin of Philadelphia, a petition was adopted for Gridley's appointment as Grand Master. This petition is an historic document, and sets forth many facts of great interest well known to the Brethren at that time.

It reads as follows:

"To the Right Honourable and Right Worshipfull James Brydges Marquis of Carnarvan Grand Master of the Free and Accepted Masons of England.

The Petition of the Grand Committee of the Grand Lodge whose names are hereunto Subscribed in behalf of said Lodge

Humbly Sheweth

That last June it pleased Allmighty God to vacate Solomons Chair by the death of Our late Right Worshipfull Grand Master Thomas Oxnard Esqr upon which Our Right Worshipfull Brother Mr Henry Price formerly Grand Master Reasumed the Chair Pro tempore, and at the Grand Lodge or Quarterly Communication held at the Concert Hall in Boston October 11th 5754 it was voted that a Petition should be drawn up and Presented to your Lordship praying that all Future Grand Masters should be deputed for three years only, but With this Reservation that notwithstanding if the Lodge should see cause to Continue the same Grand Master longer in the Chair the said Deputation should continue and remain in full force the said Continued Term, and that he should remain Grand Master from the Expiration of the time of his First appointment or Continuance to the Instalment of another.

We therefore humbly sollicit your Lordships concurrence with the said Vote, and Request your deputation in favour of Our Right Worshipfull Bro^r Jeremy Gridley Esqr Councellour at Law our Grand Master Elect.

And Whereas Masonry Originated Here anno 5733, and in the year following Our then G. M. Price received orders from G. M. Craufurd to Establish Masonry in all North America in Pursuance of which the Several Lodges hereafter mentioned have rec^d Constitutions from us. We therefore Crave due Precedency, & that in order thereunto Our G. M. Elect, may in his deputation be stiled G M of all North America, and your Petitioners as in duty Bound shall ever Pray.

Hugh McDaniel
Benjamin Hallowell
Charles Brockwell
James Forbes
Robert Jenkins
William Coffin
Henry Leddell"

See Chapter VII, *supra*.

There was considerable delay in receiving a reply to this petition from the Grand Master in London, and on August 6, 1755, Henry Price wrote a letter supplementing this petition, as follows:

"Worthy and Dear Bro^r:—It was with the utmost pleasure I saw a Letter from you to the Honble Peter Leigh Esqr with his Deputation appointing him Grand Master of South Carolina the last year and whom I have had the pleasure of Seeing in our Lodges in Boston.

I would Inform you that as I Rec^d my Deputation from the Right Honble Lord Montague in April 1733 Signed by Thos Batson Esqr D.G.M. George Rook and James Moor Smith Esq^{rs} G. W., made out by Bro^r Reed late Grand Secretary for North America, which I held four Years and Constituted several Lodges, and was succeeded in the office by Br: Tomlinson, and after him Bro: Oxnard who Dying it Reverted back to me again according to the Constitutions. Now with my consent all the Brethren in North America have made Choice of our Bro^r Jeremy Gridley Esqr Councellor at Law to be Grand Master for Three Years, and then the Brethren to have power to Continue him or apply for a new Grand Master, and as our numbers of Gentlemn increase here and we are the oldest (or first Constituted) Regular Lodge in America We have made application to the Grand Master of England for our said Bro^r Gridley, which application and Three Guineas we sent per Capt John Phillips last Dec to our Revd Bro. Entick Minister at Stepney desiring him to forward the affair, but we are Surpriz'd that we have not yet Rec'd the Deputation, nor a Line from Bro Entick, whose Receipt we have for The Three Guineas p^d to him by the said Capt John Phillips who using the London Trade may be now found at the new England Coffee House at Change Time.

I Therefore beg the favour of you to make enquiry after the Money, and application Transmitted as aforesaid to Bro^r Entick and as much as in you lies forw^d the affair, which I shall acknowledge as a great favour and will be a Service to Masonry in These parts.

Masonry has had as great Success in America since my Settling here as in any part of the World (except England). Here is not less than Forty Lodges sprung from my First Lodge in Boston. Therefore we desire that our Deputation may be made out for all North America or over all North America. I shall be glad of a few Lines from you even though you should have made out and forwarded our Deputation before this Reaches you; as I shall have sundry things to Communicate to you from Time to Time and cannot do it but by Letter to you, most of my old acquaintance of Masons being either Dead or Remov'd from London. I have some remote thoughts of once more seeing London with all my Brethren in the Grand Lodge after Twenty Two years absence, In the

mean Time I am Sir! Your most affect^e and faithful Bro^r and Hum^ble Servt
Boston New England
  August 6, 1755

                              (Endorsed)
                          Copy of a Letter
                       Desiring J. Gridley's Dep.
                              1755"

The Deputation, however, was already on its way and arrived in Boston August 21, 1755, and was ordered to be recorded upon the minutes of the Grand Lodge where it may be found in full (1 Mass. 40). On August 25, 1755, a Special Committee of the Grand Lodge met to make plans for the "Instalment" and on September 22nd a Special Communication of the Grand Lodge was held to "chuse Stewards to Provide for the Feast at the Instalment of the Grand Master." These elaborate preparations for the Instalment came to fruition October 1, 1755. This was made an occasion of considerable ceremony. The official account in the Proceedings of the Grand Lodge reads as follows:

At a Grand Lodge Held at Concert Hall this day The Right Worshipful Jeremy Gridley Esqr, appointed Grand Master of Masons in North America, by the Right Worshipful the Marquis of Carnarvon Grand Master of Masons, was installed in that office (at Concert Hall). The three Lodges in this Town and the Master & Wardens of the Portsmouth Lodge in New Hampshire with a great number of Brothers were present Cloathed with White Aprons and Gloves, and after the Instalment, accompanied their Grand Master in Procession to Trinity Church in this order, First Walked the Sword Bearer, carrying a drawn Sword, in one hand and the Book of Constitutions in the other, Next came the Several Lodges according to their Juniority, closed with the Wardens and Master, cloathed with their Jewells, Four Stewards with white wands went before the Grand Treasurer and Secretary cloathed with their Jewels, who were followed by the Past Grand Officers, after these walked the Grand Wardens with their Jewels, and the Present and the late Grand Master cloathed with their Jewels and Badges, closed the Procession. At Church the Revd Mr. Hooper read Prayers, and the Revd. Mr. Brown Preached an excellent Sermon on the occasion to a Numerous and Polite Audience, after Service the Sword Bearer and Stewards walked before the Grand Master, and the Procession was made in a reversed order back to Concert Hall, where an Elegant Dinner was prepared, and the afternoon was Spent in Harmony and Mirth. The whole Ceremony and attendance was with the greatest Decency, and made a Genteel appearance.

This record is supplemented by a list of names of Brethren, sixty-seven in number, including the foremost men of Boston and vicinity in all trades and professions.

The original records of the Lodge at Portsmouth, N. H., for the meeting of October 16, 1755, set forth that

Last Lodge night being first night of the Quarter there was no Lodge held the Master & Wardens were at Boston being Summoned thither by the Right Worshipful Brother the Deputy Grand Master of North America to attend a Grand Procefsion of Masons there and to Install our Right Worshipful Brother Jeremy Gridley Esqr in the office of Grand Master of Masons in all North America, who Rec^d a Commifsion for that office from our Right Worshipful Brother Henry Bridges Marquis of Carnarvon Grand Master of Masons and the said Jeremy Gridley was accordingly installed in his said office at Boston on Wednesday the first day of October Currant.

Gridley appears to have appreciated the courteous loyalty of the Brethren of the Lodge in Portsmouth in thus suspending a meeting in order that their Master and Wardens might assist at his installation. The records of the Lodge under date of June 14, 1756, show that "Right Worshipful Bro. Jeremy Gridley, Grand Master of Masons in North America" was a visitor in the Lodge.

The Boston Marine Society is among the oldest existing Boston institutions. At first it was known as the Fellowship Club and on December 5, 1752, adopted a proposal to incorporate and a Bill for a Charter drawn by Gridley. As a result, the Marine Society was chartered February 21, 1754, and in grateful acknowledgment voted the Freedom of the Society for life to Gridley and (February 26, 1754) adopted its By-Laws as drafted by him.

Sometime prior to May 19, 1755, Gridley had moved from Boston to Brookline, for he was then chosen to represent Brookline in the General Court, succeeding himself in 1756 and 1757, and again in later years. In Boston, he was a communicant at Trinity Church. In Brookline, in 1756, he bought a "space or spot" in the meeting-house "on the Middle Side Next the Middle Alley" for five pounds six shillings and eight pence.

The Grand Lodge had a gala day on the Feast of Saint John the Evangelist which was celebrated on an unknown date between January 31, 1757, and April 8th of the same year. On January 31st a Special Communication of the Grand Lodge had been called at which Gridley as Grand Master proceeded to make Masons "at sight" of Captain Harry Charters, Captain Gilbert McAdams, Aid-de-Camp, Doctor Richard Huch, Mr. John Appy, Secre-

tary to the Earl of Loudoun, and Mr. John Melvill
(who came to town from Marblehead with Brother
Lowell on purpose to be made a Mason). The Grand
Master's elder brother, the celebrated Richard Gridley,
(of whom see page 303), conducted the ceremonies of the
Entered Apprentice and Fellow Craft Degrees. These
Brethren, with the largest number ever recorded in the
early history of the Grand Lodge, attended the celebration of the Feast of Saint John the Evangelist of which
I have spoken, at which were present His Excellency
John, Earl of Loudoun, late Grand Master of Masons
of England, and His Excellency Charles Lawrence, Esq.,
Governor of Halifax. The length of the list of Brethren
attending and the notable names occurring in the list
make it evident that this was one of the greatest festivals
of the early days of the Fraternity in America (1 Mass.
49).

March 5, 1759, he was for the third time chosen Moderator of the Town Meeting of Brookline, and continuously thereafter acted in that capacity, as for instance on
June 13, 1759, October 17, 1759, December 19, 1759,
December 24, 1759, and March (?), 1760, when he was
chosen Selectman and Assessor.

On January 14, 1760, he appointed Robert Jenkins
Deputy Grand Master of Masons in Rhode Island with
the full authority of a Provincial.

And now, at the height of his career, we come to the
most celebrated case in which he was counsel, that concerning the Writs of Assistance, first argued in February,
1761. (I shall not deal with this case in detail. The
student may find a good discussion in Quincy's Massachusetts Reports, particularly in the Appendix.) For
present purposes it is sufficient to state that these writs

were practically what is now known as search-warrants except that the place to be searched was not stated in the writ, but was left to that Customs Officer of the Royal Service to whom the writ was committed that he might seek anywhere for smuggled goods. They were undoubtedly lawful, and had been issued in the Mother Country itself in similar form and for identical purposes. Moreover, they were no more oppressive, *per se*, than certain provisions of the tax and revenue laws of to-day. But the Colonies had a much deeper underlying grievance against the Crown which took this occasion to burst forth. It is undoubted, also, that Otis knew of no precedent and believed them unlawful. But that was due to the paucity of law-books and the lack of sources of information. Indeed, after the first argument, the Court itself adjourned the case until the judges could communicate with England and get necessary information. Gridley appeared for the Crown and in favour of issuing the writs; Thatcher and Otis for the merchants and against such action.

It has been said that the cause for which Gridley appeared aroused distrust of him by his associates. Nothing could be farther from the truth. While the great mass of the people were violently opposed to the writs, yet they recognized his position as counsel, presenting to the best of his ability that position which he was retained to maintain. Throughout his life thereafter, as will be seen, he continued to appear on one side or the other of almost every case of moment reported from then until his death. He was revered by the Bar, by the Fraternity, and by the community at large. Bitterly as Otis opposed him in this celebrated cause, he nevertheless wrote a magnificent tribute to Gridley which will later appear.

May 18, 1761, he was again chosen Moderator of the Brookline Town Meeting; also July 3.

November 19, 1761, was the day of the great hearing —the second argument concerning the Writs of Assistance. An eye-witness (John Adams, later President of the United States) has given us a graphic word picture of this notable occasion from which has been painted the magnificent mural decoration in the State House in Boston.

"In this chamber near the fire," he says, "were seated five judges with Lieut. Governor Hutchinson at their head, as Chief Justice, all in their new fresh robes of scarlet cloth, in their broad bands and immense judicial wigs. In this chamber were seated at a long table all the Barristers of Boston, and its neighbouring County of Middlesex, in their gowns, bands and tye-wigs. They were not seated on ivory chairs, but their dress was more solemn and more pompous than that of the Roman Senate when the Gauls broke in upon them. In a corner of the room must be placed, wit, sense, imagination, genius, pathos, reason, prudence, eloquence, learning, science, and immense reading hung by the shoulders on two crutches covered with a cloth great coat, in the person of Mr. Pratt, who had been solicited on both sides, but would engage on neither being about to leave Boston forever, as chief justice of New York."

The Court who sat on this august occasion were Chief Justice Hutchinson, Benjamin Lynde, John Cushing, Peter Oliver, and Chambers Russell. The counsel engaged were again Gridley in favour, and Thatcher and Otis against the application, and in the words of President Adams, "Then and there was the first scene of the first act of opposition to the arbitrary claims of Great

Britain. Then and there the child Independence, was born."

The whole day and evening, we are told, was taken up by the hearing, although Gridley found time to preside as Moderator of the Brookline Town meeting some time that day. At the conclusion of the trial judgment was immediately given in favour of that for which Gridley contended, and a careful study of the case at this impartial distance satisfies the student that it was given correctly and as the court should have decided. The real quarrel of the people was with the policy of the home government and with the rules of law which it imposed, not with the interpretation of the law. The Court had no business to change the law. That was for the law makers. It was the business of the Court merely to enforce the law as it was made for them. That they did and did correctly. Gridley but pointed out the proper interpretation of the law as it stood. Otis's appeal was rather an eloquent voicing of the restive spirit of a people convinced that the law was being used as an instrument of oppression.

It was at this term of Court that judges and barristers were first appareled as in the Courts of England. Gridley was present with his associates in gown and band and tie-wig.

Instead of finding him thereafter estranged from his fellows, we find constant records of his presiding over the Grand Lodge and over the town meetings of Brookline, and on numerous occasions a public officer and upon important committees. Otis continued to be his warm friend.

On April 1, 1767, he dined at the home of James Otis with a company of ladies and eminent gentlemen, but it was his last social appearance and his health was breaking. On May 25, 1767, he was appointed King's Attorney General, in lieu of Edmund Trowbridge who had been appointed to the Bench. Jonathan Sewall, Esq., wanted to be Attorney General—indeed he was appointed Special Attorney General, but this being disagreeable to Gridley a new office was created for him which was called Solicitor General. The same day Gridley was again chosen Town Moderator of a meeting which was adjourned to June 12th. He, however, was in very poor health. He had not attended the Grand Lodge of April 27th, and on June 12th the town meeting was obliged to adjourn because of his indisposition until June 29th. He was too ill to appear at Grand Lodge on June 24th and John Rowe, his Deputy, presided. The Town Meeting on the 29th, indeed, was again adjourned because of his indisposition until July 13th. Struggling against the inevitable, he presided at the Town Meeting on July 13th and at one later meeting the date of which is not given, but he was unable to attend the Grand Lodge on July 24th and ordered that no meeting be held until October in consequence. A Special Communication had to be called, however, on September 1st which he was unable to attend, being then near dissolution, his death occurring on September 10, 1767.

At the time of his death he was Grand Master of Masons in North America, Attorney General for the Province of Massachusetts Bay, a member of the Great and General Court of said Province and a Justice throughout the same, Colonel of the First Regiment of Militia, President of the Marine Society, Selectman and Assessor of Brookline, and the leader of the Boston Bar.

Surely these honours belie the statement of those who
would have us believe that he had lost caste because of
his arguments on the Writs of Assistance.

A Special Grand Lodge on September 11, 1767, made
plans for Masonic participation in a most elaborate
funeral (1 Mass. 118-120) held in the Representatives'
Chamber on September 12. John Rowe writes interestingly of it in his diary (1 Mass. 420).

12th Sept Saturday 1767. Cool & Fair Wind, in the
Afternoon I attended the Funeral of our Right Worship-
ful Jerry Gridly Esqr. Grand Master, as Deputy Grand
Master, the Officers of his Regiment Marched in Order
First, then the Brethren of St Andrews Lodge, then the
Stewards of the Grand Lodge, then the Brethren Pro-
miscuously two & two, then the Wardens of the Second
Lodge, then the Wardens of the first Lodge, then the
Wardens of the Masters Lodge, then the three Masters
of the three Several Lodges—then the past Grand Of-
ficers & the Treasurer, then the Grand Wardens then
myself as Deputy Grand Master, then the Tyler with the
Grand Masters Jewell on a Black Velvet Cushion—the
Corpse—the Bearers were the Lieut Governour, Judge
Trowbridge, Justice Hubbard, John Erving Senr Esqr,
James Otis Esqr & Mr. Samuel Fitch. Then followed
the Relations—after them the Lawyers in their Robes—
then the Gentlemen of the Town & then a great many
Coaches, Chariots, & chaises. Such a multitude of Spec-
tators, I never Saw at any time before since I have been
in New England.—after his Body was Interr'd wee Return'd in Form to the Town house (from whence his
corps was taken from at the Beginning of the Procession,) in the Same Order as wee first walked.—I do not
much approve of Such parade & Show—but as it was his
& his Relations desire, I could not well Avoid giving my
Consent. I think the Number of the Brethren that At-

tended was 161.—upon the Whole it was as well Conducted & in As Good Order as the Nature of it would admit.

A full account of the services, order of procession, and names of the Brethren who attended is recorded in the original records of the Grand Lodge of Massachusetts (and printed in 1 Mass. 118 to 124 inclusive). It demonstrates his conspicuous position in public life and the affection as well as the veneration of his contemporaries; lawyers and laymen, men in official and private life alike, joining to do him honour. The bearers were the Lieutenant Governor and Chief Justice Hutchinson, Judge Trowbridge, Councillors Hubbard and Erving, and Barristers James Otis and Samuel Fitch.

The unique obituary printed in the Boston papers at the time of his death, on good evidence is believed to have been written by his friend and former pupil, sometimes his associate, at others his bitterest antagonist, James Otis. As printed in the *Boston Gazette* for Monday, September 14, 1767, it reads as follows:

On Thursday last died here, Jeremy Gridley Esqr. Attorney-General of the Province, and a Member of the General Court; His funeral was attended on Saturday with the Respect due to his Memory by the Members of the Council and the Judges of the Superior Court in Town, the Gentlemen of the Bar, the Brethren of the Society of Free Masons, of which he was Grand Master, the officers of the First Regiment, of which he was Colonel, the Members of the Marine Society, of which he was President and a great Number of the Gentlemen of the Town:—

"Strength of Understanding, Clearness of Apprehension, and Solidity of Judgment were cultivated in him by a liberal Education and close thinking:

"His extensive Acquaintance with Classical and almost every other part of Literature, gave him the first Rank among Men of Learning:

"His thorough knowledge of the Civil and Common Law, which he had studied as a Science, founded in the Principles of Government, and the Nature of Man, justly placed him at the Head of his Proffession:

"His tender Feelings relative to his natural and civil Ties; his exquisite Sensibility and generous Effusion of Soule for his Friends, were Proof that his Heart was as Good as his Head was sound, and well qualified him to preside over that antient Society, whose Benevolent Constitutions do Honour to Mankind:

"He sustained the painful Attacks of Death with a Philosophical Calmness and Fortitude, that resulted from the steady Principles of his Religion. He died in the 62nd year of his age."

(It should read 66th year of his age.)

(A reproduction of the official letter of October 2, 1767, to Henry Price, recalling him to the chair upon Gridley's death is herewith inserted. See 1 Mass. 125.)

When Jeremy Gridley came to the Bar of the Province it was unworthy to be called a learned profession. Indeed next to none of the practitioners at the Bar were educated men. And even the Bench had held few lawyers. The first judge who had even been a lawyer was Judge Lynde, elevated in 1712. The clergy had held and continued to exercise for many years a control over all civil government and especially over the judicial department. The Court which had condemned to death those poor unfortunates accused of witchcraft, for instance, consisted of seven Judges. The Chief Justice was the clergyman Stoughton. With him sat Sewall, a business man, but educated for the church; Winthrop and Gedney, physicians; and Richards, Curwin, and Seargeant, merchants. No lawyer had anything to do with this notorious Court. Even Checkley, the Attorney General, was a merchant and a military man. In these modern days when considerations are urged for subjecting the Courts to popular will, would it not be wise to remember the sad results of this popular tribunal which allowed itself to be swayed by the loud outcries of the populace?

In such an incipient state of the development of the legal profession, Gridley with an all around education stood forth conspicuous as an able and learned man. His reading and study were extensive and his mind logical and accurate. He was an easy and graceful writer, being imbued with the spirit of classical literature. As a speaker he was "rough and ungraceful, hesitating in his utterance but energetic in his manner, and impressive by his peculiarly emphatic use of language. Even to the court his manner is said to have been magisterial when expressing any opinion in their presence."

A good illustration is reported in the case of Banister v. Henderson (Quincy's Mass. Reports, 141).

It had been held that there might be cross-remainders between two devisees. Gridley was contending that there might be among three. Messrs. Otis and Auchmuty were opposing him. A part of the reported dialogue follows:

Mr. Gridley. It is the bufinefs of the Law to explain the Pregnancy of Expreffion, and when this Pregnancy is drawn out, this is the mighty Confufion, this is the terrible Bugbear. The Lawyers who talk of the Abhorrence of the Law, the Confufion, the Awkwardnefs, and I don't know what all, of Crofs Remainders were afleep, I believe, and had their Heads muffled up in Napkins.

Boston October 2: 5767.

Right Worshipful Brother.

It having pleased Almighty God to take from this Transitory Life to a better, that great Ornament of Learning of the Law, and of Masonry, Our Right Worshipful Brother Jeremy Gridley Esqr. Grand Master of Masons in North America to the great Loss of this Country in General, and of Masonry in Particular. And as Masonry from its first Establishment in America, has always been under the Government of a Grand Master, and a Grand Lodge, duly Constituted by the Grand Master of England: The Said Grand Lodge on Account of the above Bereavement came to a Resolution last Evening to Elect a New Grand Master, in the Room of the former at some convenient Time hence: In the mean Time the Constitutions point out to us that the Vacancy be filled by the past Grand Master, to govern Masonry till a new one is Elected here, and Constituted from England: Therefore the Grand Lodge & me to write to you (in their Name,) on whom the Office Constitutionally Reverts; that You would be pleased to attend at the next Grand Lodge, or Quarterly Communication, to be held at the Bunch of Grapes Tavern in Boston on the fourth Friday in October, Instant, in Order for your Resuming said Office, as the Practice in the like Cases has hitherto been. I am,

Right Worshipful Brother, with great Truth
Your Affectionate Brother, and
Very humble Servant.

Abrm. Savage Gr. Sec.

To the Right Worshipful Henry Price Esqr.
Past Grand Master of Masons in North America

FACSIMILIE OF LETTER RECALLING PRICE TO THE CHAIR IN 1767

Mr. Auchmuty. I don't underſtand ſuch Reflections.

Mr. Gridley. I meant no Reflection on you, sir.

Mr. Otis. Mr. Auchmuty, I did not take Mr. Gridley intended to reflect upon us, but on all the Judges of England.

Mr. Gridley. What mighty Difficulty to former People I can't tell: 'tis very plain now. Croſs Remainders may be among 2; why not 3?

Gridley's commanding ability, far and away superior to his predecessors in his chosen profession, led to his being rightly called the "Father of the Boston Bar." His office was the principal school for students of the law. The most distinguished lawyers who became his contemporaries and successors, such as James Otis, Oxenbridge Thatcher, John Adams, William Cushing, and Chief Justice Pratt, received their professional education in his office and under his instruction. Of Otis and Adams he remarked that he had reared two young eagles who were one day to peck out his eyes. Of Gridley more than any other it may be said that he elevated the Boston Bar from comparative chaos and ignorance to the dignity of a learned profession.

Remuneration in these days was not excessive. For an important argument and trial eight dollars was the fee. Five dollars was the limit for a jury argument and two dollars for a continuance. No wonder there were only ten lawyers in Boston at the time, and no wonder that Gridley himself died insolvent. Practically the whole of his estate was his library, a complete inventory of which is among the probate records (Suffolk County, Mass.) and which was, for those days, extensive and magnificent. (In the inventory of his estate filed in the Probate Court in Boston on March 18, 1768, it was appraised at £209 3s 4d. This was probably what the library had brought at auction, for it was thus sold on February 2, 1768.)

He was succeeded as Attorney General by Jonathan Sewall, who was appointed to the office November 18, 1767.

Jeremy Gridley was buried in Tomb No. 9 of the Granary Burying Ground in Boston, erected by his father-in-law, Hon. Ezekiel Lewis. Until May 11, 1916, it remained unmarked, though his name and fame have remained as one of the foremost men of the day.

Though they never will find a place in classic literature, yet typical of the times and of the man, the lines printed with his obituary as written *ex tempore* (probably also by Brother James Otis) must be quoted.

Jeremiah Gridley Barrister-At-Law.

"Of Parts and Learning, Wit and Worth possess'd,
Gridley shone forth conspicuous o'er the rest:
In native Powers robust, and smit with Fame,
The Genius brighten'd and the Spark took Flame;
Nature and Science wove the laurel Crown,
Ambitious, each alike, conferr'd Renown.
High in the Dignity and Strength of Thought,
The Maze of Knowledge sedulous he sought,
With Mind Superior Studied and retain'd.
And Life and Property by Law sustain'd.
Generous and free, his lib'ral Hand he spread,
Th' Oppress'd relieved, and for the Needy Plead;
Awake to Friendship, with the ties of Blood
His Heart expanded and his Soul o'erflow'd.
Social in Converse, in the Senate brave.
Gay e'en in Dignity, with Wisdom grave;
Long to his country and to Courts endear'd,
The Judges honour'd and the Bar rever'd.

Rest! Peaceful Shade! innoxious as they Walk
May slander babble and may censure talk,
Ne'er on thy Mem'ry cast a Blot—
But human Frailties in thy Worth forgot."

1916 Mass. 84-124 *et cit.*

1748, May 25,   Boston.
   Meeting of the First Lodge.
        O.R.; A.B.

1748, June 3,   Boston.
   Meeting of the Masters Lodge.
        O.R.; A.B.

1748, June 8,   Boston.
   Meeting of the First Lodge.
        O.R.; A.B.

1748, June 22,   Boston.
   Meeting of the First Lodge. Sidney George and Capt.
John James made.
        O.R.; P.L.; A.B.

1748, July 1,   Boston.
   Meeting of the Masters Lodge. Election.
        O.R.; A.B.

1748, July 13,   Boston.
   Meeting of the First Lodge. Brothers Nicholas Fer-
ritor and Thomas Vavasour admitted.
        O.R.; P.L.; A.B.

1748, July 27,   Boston.

Meeting of the First Lodge. Capt. Michael Buttler made.

       O.R.; P.L.; A.B.

1748, August 5,   Boston.

  Meeting of the Masters Lodge.
       O.R.; A.B.

1748, August 10,   Boston.

  Meeting of the First Lodge.
       O.R.; A.B.

1748, August 24,   Boston.

  Meeting of the First Lodge.
       O.R.; A.B.

1748, August 31,

       Portsmouth, New Hampshire.

Meeting of the Lodge. "Admitted Masons to the Fellow Craft, Viz:

  Cap. Brother Henry Barnsley

  Brother Smith

  Brother Michael Henry Pascal

  Brother Gardner

  Brother Wallis

  Brother Jenness"

       O.R.

1748, September 2,   Boston.

  Meeting of the Masters Lodge.
       O.R.; A.B

1748, September 14,   Boston.
Meeting of the First Lodge.
O.R.; A.B.

1748, September 28,   Boston.
Meeting of the First Lodge.
O.R.; A.B.

1748, September 29,
          Portsmouth, New Hampshire.
Meeting of the Lodge.   Messrs. Campble and Richard
Ion (I'on) made.
O.R.

1748, October 7,   Boston.
Meeting of the Masters Lodge.
O.R.; A.B.

1748, October 12,   Boston.
Meeting of the First Lodge.   Brother William Dalton
admitted.
O.R.; P.L.; A.B.

1748, October 20,
          Portsmouth, New Hampshire.
Meeting of the Lodge.   Election.
O.R.

1748, October 25,   Boston.
Meeting of the First Lodge.   Jonathan Fuller made,
Brothers William Ellery admitted, Andrew Ramsey
(Ramsay) admitted and passed.
O.R.; P.L.; A.B.

1748, November 3,
          Portsmouth, New Hampshire.
   Meeting of the Lodge. Nathaniel Wheelwright made
and passed.
          O.R.

1748, November 4,   Boston.
   Meeting of the Masters Lodge.
          O.R.; A.B.

1748, November 9,   Boston.
   Meeting of the First Lodge.
          O.R.; A.B.

1748, November 17,   Boston.
   Meeting of the First Lodge. Bar'w (Bartho.) Svere,
Fran's Baulos, and William Ross made.
          O.R.; P.L.; A.B.

1748, November 23,   Boston.
   Meeting of the First Lodge. Brother David Littlejohn
admitted.
          O.R.; P.L.; A.B.

1748, December 2,   Boston.
   Meeting of the Masters Lodge.
          O.R.; A.B.

1748, December 14,   Boston.
   Meeting of the First Lodge. Election.
          O.R.; A.B.
          1 Mass. 9.

1748, December 15,
>   Portsmouth, New Hampshire.
Meeting of the Lodge. Election.
>   O.R.

1748, December 27,   Boston.
Celebration of the Festival by the Grand Lodge.
>   O.R. of First Lodge.

1748, December 28,   Boston.
Meeting of the First Lodge.
>   O.R.; A.B.

1748/9, January 6,   Boston.
Meeting of the Masters Lodge. Election. Brothers
Andrew Ramsey (Ramsay), Belthar Bayard, Aenneas
McKay, William Day, and Jona. Dwight raised.
>   O.R.; P.L.; A.B.

1748/9, January 11,   Boston.
Meeting of the First Lodge.
>   O.R.; A.B.

1748/9, January 19,
>   Portsmouth, New Hampshire.
Meeting of the Lodge.
>   O.R.

1748/9, January 25,   Boston.
Meeting of the First Lodge.
>   O.R.; A.B.

1748/9, February 3,   Boston.
  Meeting of the Masters Lodge.
        O.R.; A.B.

[1748/9, February 8,   Boston.
  Meeting of the First Lodge.   Capt. Benjamin Stoddard, Peter McTaggart, and Elias D'Larue made.
        O.R.; P.L.; A.B

1748/9, February 16,
              Portsmouth, New Hampshire.
  Meeting of the Lodge.
        O.R.

1748/9, February 22,   Boston.
  Meeting of the First Lodge.
        O.R.; A.B.
        1883 Mass. 164.

1748/9, March 3,   Boston.
  Meeting of the Masters Lodge.
        O.R.; A.B.

1748/9, March 8,   Boston.
  Meeting of the First Lodge.
        O.R.; A.B.

1748/9, March 22,   Boston.
  Meeting of the First Lodge
        O.R.; A.B.

1748, circa.   San Domingo.
  Lodge organized at Cap, which worked for 35 years
thereafter.
        1920 Mass. 112.

Chapter XXIII

1749

1749, April 5,   Boston.
   Meeting of Auditing Committee of the Masters Lodge.
      A.B.

1749, April 7,   Boston.
   Meeting of the Masters Lodge. Brother Thomas
Pearson raised.
      O.R.; P.L.; A.B.

1749, April 12,   Boston.
   Meeting of the First Lodge. Brother Hugh McKay
admitted.
      O.R.; P.L.; A.B.

1749, April 26,   Boston.
   Meeting of the First Lodge.
      O.R.; A.B.

1749, May 5,   Boston.
   Meeting of the Masters Lodge.
      O.R.; A.B.

1749, May 10,   Boston.
   Meeting of the First Lodge. Capt. James H. Ewing
(Euing) made. Brother Robert Gardner admitted.
      O.R.; P.L.; A.B.

1749, May 24,   Boston.
  Meeting of the First Lodge.
          O.R.; A.B.

1749, June 2,   Boston.
  "Being Masters Lodge night; Adjourned on Account of the House being taken up by the General Court."
          O.R.

1749, June 14,   Boston.
  Meeting of the First Lodge.   Election.
          O.R.; A.B.

1749, June 24,   Boston.
  Celebration of the Festival.   There is no record of this celebration, but the First Lodge appointed Stewards therefor at its meeting on June 14, and there is in the archives of the Grand Lodge of Massachusetts an original letter in the handwriting of Charles Pelham, Secretary, signed by him and by the Master and Wardens of the First Lodge recommending Brother Robert Jenkins to the Master, Wardens and Brethren of any Lodge in London, and which is dated "From the Lodge in Boston N. Engld. held June 24th A.D. 1749."
          1 Mass. 395.

1749, June 28,   Boston.
  Meeting of the First Lodge.
          O.R.; A.B.

                    Philadelphia.
  Meeting of Tun Tavern Lodge.   With this meeting the known records of this Lodge begin.   It is evident,

At a Lodge held on Monday the 29.th Aug.t 1749
at the Tun Tavern in Water Street Phila.

Present Bro.r Griffin M.r
                    Vidal S:W
                    Swan J:W

Murray Sec.

Members present   Visiting Brothers
Bro.r Mullan   Bro.r Corffe   Bro.r Flanegan
    Davis   Ord   Parker
    Wright   Woddale

Proceeded to Business

M.r Parker being Balloted for the Preceeding Lodge was
accordingly this Night made in due Form

Bro.r Mullan mov'd that a Petition be sent to M.r Benj.
Franklin, Provincial Grand Master of Pensilvania
to grant us a Deputation under his Sanction
the Master appointed Bro.r Vidal, Corffe, & Mullan
to draw up the same, and to present it

                Ten o'Clock Lodge Clos'd

At a Lodge held on Wednesday the 6.th Sep.r 1749
at the Tun Tavern in Water Street Phila.

Present Bro.r Griffin M.r
                    Swan   S:W
                    Wright J:W

Murray Sec.
                Visiting Bro.r Cummins
No Business done; Ten o'Clock Lodge Clos'd

PAGE OF RECORD BOOK OF TUN TAVERN LODGE

however, that it was not its first meeting. The record book is now owned by the Historical Society of Pennsylvania.

O.R.

Freemasonry in Pennsylvania seems now to be reviving, though official authority for this Lodge is unknown.

See 1749, Aug. 29, *infra.*

In a volume written by Brother Sachse, the Librarian of the Grand Lodge of Pennsylvania, and compiled at the request of the Grand Master (1906), the claim is made that this record book of Tun Tavern Lodge is "the oldest American Masonic minute book known."

Benjamin Franklin as a Free Mason, 85.

It has, however, been common knowledge for many years that the original minute books of the Masters Lodge in Boston, beginning December 22, 1738; of the First Lodge in Boston, beginning December 27, 1738, and of the First Lodge in Portsmouth, N. H., beginning October 31, 1739, all of which have been personally examined by the author during the preparation of this book, are in their proper custody and available for inspection. Quotations and facsimiles from some of these were published in the proceedings of the Grand Lodge of Massachusetts as early as 1871. Copies of these proceedings were in Brother Sachse's possession during his entire service as librarian and the writer has personal knowledge that he had seen them before 1906. From this and other similar instances, at least one of which has been referred to above, it is evident that statements made by Brother Sachse must be verified before being accepted as correct.

See 1914 Mass. 277.

1749, July 3,   Philadelphia.
Meeting of Tun Tavern Lodge.
    O.R.

1749, July 5,   Philadelphia.
Meeting of Tun Tavern Lodge. John Ord and John Slydorn (Schleydhorn) made, Brother Hugh Wright passed, and Brother John Eve raised and admitted.
    O.R.

1749, July 7,   Boston.
Meeting of the Masters Lodge. Election. Brother Jonathan Fuller raised.
    O.R.; A.B.

1749, July 10,   Boston—Pennsylvania.
Provincial Grand Master Oxnard of North America appointed Benjamin Franklin Provincial Grand Master for Pennsylvania.
    The Picture of Philadelphia, (1811) 289.
    1888 Mass. 155.
    1906 Mass. 90.
    See also 1734/5, February 21; 1738, June 24;
        1741, June 24, *supra*.

1749, July 12,   Boston.
Meeting of the First Lodge.
    O.R.; A.B.

              Philadelphia.
Meeting of Tun Tavern Lodge. Brothers Phillips and Stephen Vidal admitted.
    O.R.

1749, July 26,   Boston.

Meeting of the First Lodge. Samuel Massey, Paul Douxsaint, and Lewis Peach made.

   O.R.; P.L.; A.B.

1749, August 2,   Philadelphia.

Meeting of Tun Tavern Lodge. John Fisher made, Brothers Foster and Thomas Blake passed, and Hugh Wright raised.

   O.R.

1749, August 4,   Boston.

Meeting of the Masters Lodge. Brothers John Rae and Samuel Levens raised.

   O.R.; P.L.; A.B.

1749, August 5,   Philadelphia.

Meeting of Tun Tavern Lodge. Three Brethren discharged from membership.

   O.R.

1749, August 9,   Boston.

Meeting of the First Lodge.

   O.R.; A.B.

     Philadelphia.

Meeting of Tun Tavern Lodge. Election. Brothers John Ord and Thomas Blake admitted.

   O.R.

1749, August 16,   Philadelphia.

Meeting of Tun Tavern Lodge. Edward Hemlin and Flanegan made. Brother Walter Murray passed.

   O.R.

1749, August 23, Boston.

Meeting of the First Lodge. Brother Robert Anderson passed.

O.R.; P.L.; A.B.

Philadelphia.

Meeting of Tun Tavern Lodge.

O.R.

1749, August 29, Philadelphia.

Meeting of Tun Tavern Lodge at which it was voted that a petition be sent to Benjamin Franklin, Pro. G. M. of Pennsylvania by appointment of Pro. G. M. Oxnard of North America, to grant the Lodge a Deputation under his sanction.

Dr. William Parker made.

O.R.

1749, September 1, Boston.

Meeting of the Masters Lodge.

O.R.; A.B.

1749, September 5, Philadelphia.

First meeting of the Provincial Grand Lodge under the Deputation granted Franklin by Oxnard, and a revival of the earlier St. John's Lodge under that Deputation.

The Picture of Philadelphia, (1811) 289.

IV Gould 239.

On the records of the Grand Lodge at Boston for April 10, 1752, we find:

"For the Lodge att Philadelphia Bro^r McDaniel appeared and paid for their Constitution   31 „ 10 „ 0"

1 Mass. 20.

1749, September 11, Philadelphia.

Brothers Murray, Phillips, Edward Hemlin, Dr. William Parker, William Mason, and John Ord passed. Brothers John Slydorn and Flanegan passed and admitted.

O.R.

1749, September 13,   Boston.
Meeting of the First Lodge.
O.R.; A.B.
1883 Mass. 163.

1749, September 27,   Boston.
Meeting of the First Lodge.
O.R.; A.B.

Philadelphia.
Meeting of Tun Tavern Lodge. John Simes made. Brother Capt. Richard Savage passed.
O.R.

1749, October 4,   Philadelphia.
Meeting of Tun Tavern Lodge. Capt. James Whyte made. Brother John Simes Passed and Brothers Thomas Blake and Wasdale raised.
O.R.

1749, October 6,   Boston.
Meeting of the Masters Lodge.
O.R.; A.B.

1749, October 11,   Boston.
Meeting of the First Lodge. Henry Leddell, Saml.

Calef, Benj. Badger, and Capts. John Bennett and Benj. Clifford made. Brothers John Leverett and William Epps passed, Edmund Quincy and Henry Bowers admitted.

> **O.R.; P.L.; A.B.**

In the original records of the Lodge this is the first time that the word "Passed" has been used in connection with the Fellow Craft Degree. In all previous incidents, although the Pelham List (written later) has used the word "Passed," the original record has used the phrases "Raised Fellow Craft," or "made Fellow Craft."

1749, October 12,   Philadelphia.

Meeting of Tun Tavern Lodge. Brother Capt. Vina Leacroft passed. Brother Capt. James **Whyte** passed and raised.

> **O.R.**

1749, October 25,   Boston.

Meeting of the First Lodge.

> **O.R.; A.B.**

1749, October 26,

         Portsmouth, New Hampshire.

Meeting of the Lodge on board the British Frigate America of fifty-four guns, then building at Portsmouth. Mr. Farr made and passed. Mr. Kipling made.

> **O.R.**

1749, November 1,   Philadelphia.

Meeting of Tun Tavern Lodge. Enas Batter, John Boude, and John Bruliet made. Brothers John Ord and William Mason raised.

> **O.R.**

1749, November 3,   Boston.
  Meeting of the Masters Lodge.
        O.R.; A.B.

1749, November 8,   Boston.
  Meeting of the First Lodge.   James Thompson and
Capt. James Bruce made.   Brothers Peter Oliver and
John Indigot admitted.
        O.R.; P.L.

        Philadelphia.
  Meeting of Tun Tavern Lodge.   Brother Enas Batter
passed.   Brother Foster, Flanegan, and Capt. Michael
James passed and raised.   Brother Capt. James Whyte
admitted.
        O.R.

1749, November 22,   Boston.
  Meeting of the First Lodge.   Brother John Huston
admitted.
        O.R.; P.L.; A.B.

        Philadelphia.
  Meeting of Tun Tavern Lodge.   Brother John Bruliet
passed.   One member was fined two shillings for "swearing two Oaths."   Another, one shilling sixpence for im-
properly addressing the Master.
        O.R.

1749, November 29, Philadelphia.
  Meeting of Tun Tavern Lodge.   Mr. Flanegan made
and passed.   Brother John Boude passed.   Brother
Michael James admitted.
        O.R.

1749, December 1,   Boston.

Meeting of the Masters Lodge.   Brothers Alexander Ross, William Epps, and John Bennett raised.
> O.R.; P.L.; A.B.

1749, December 4,

> Portsmouth, New Hampshire.

Another meeting of the Lodge on the Frigate America. Brothers Smith, Pascal, Wallace, Jenness, and Campble raised.
> **O.R.**

1749, December 6,   Philadelphia.

Meeting of Tun Tavern Lodge.   Brothers Walter Murray, Enas Batter, and John Bruliet raised.
> **O.R.**

1749, December 11,

> Portsmouth, New Hampshire.

Another meeting of the Lodge on board the Frigate America.
> **O.R.**

1749, December 13,   Boston.

Meeting of the First Lodge.   Election.
> **O.R.; A.B.**

> Philadelphia.

Meeting of Tun Tavern Lodge. William Shute, Franklin Manny, and Capt. Thomas Glentworth made. Capt. Richard Harris made and passed.   Brother Falkner (Falckner) admitted.
> **O.R.**

1749, December 22,   Boston.

Meeting of the First Lodge.   Jacob Tuthill, Martin Beker, Roscow Sweeny, and Capt. Gilbert Faulkner made.   Samuel Wells "raised F.C."

> O.R.; P.L.; A.B.

1749, December 23,   Philadelphia.

Meeting of Tun Tavern Lodge.   Capts. Jenkins and Tege made.

> O.R.

1749, December 24, Boston—Newport.

Pro. G.M. Oxnard granted a Constitution for a Lodge to be held at Newport, R.I.

> L.M.R. 482.
>
> 1749, December 27, *infra.*

1749, December 27,   Boston.

The Grand Lodge celebrated the Festival by attending Christ Church where a sermon was preached by Rev. Brother Charles Brockwell, after which they repaired in procession to the Royal Exchange Tavern "Where was an elegant Dinner provided, at which were several Gentlemen of Note, besides the Fraternity."

> 1 Mass. 9.
>
> *Boston Evening Post* for January 1, 1749/50, P-t.
>
> *Boston Post Boy* for January 1, 1749/50, P-t.
>
> O.R. of First Lodge.
>
> 1883 Mass. 165.

Rev. Brother Brockwell's sermon entitled "Brotherly Love Recommended" was printed and published in Boston immediately by John Draper in Newbury Street. An original copy thereof is in the archives of the Grand Lodge of Massachusetts containing the vote of thanks to the preacher passed by the Grand Lodge. A burlesque in doggerel of the procession of the Grand Lodge on this day was printed and circulated in 1750 and reprinted in 1795. One of each edition is in the archives of the Grand Lodge of Massachusetts. It is reprinted in 1 Mass. 473.

In the evening there was also a meeting of the First Lodge.

O.R.; A.B.
19 M.F.M. 51.

The *Boston Weekly News Letter* for January 1, 1749/50 contains Draper's advertisement of Brockwell's sermon.

P-t.

On January 9, 1749/50, the First Lodge paid 50 Pounds for the printing of the sermon.

A.B.

Newport, Rhode Island.

The First Lodge at Newport held its first meeting as is shown by the following paragraph which appeared in the *Boston Weekly News Letter* for January 1, 1749/50:

"On the 27th ult. being the Festival of St. John the Evangelist the first regular Lodge of free and accepted Masons was congregated and held at Newport on Rhode Island; by Virtue of a Warrant given them by the Grand Master of North-America."

P-t.

And the *Boston Post Boy* for January 15, 1749/50, contained the same item.

P.-t.

Philadelphia.

Meeting of Tun Tavern Lodge.   Election.

O.R.

1749/50, January 3, Philadelphia.

Meeting of Tun Tavern Lodge.   Brother Tege passed and Brother Richard Harris raised.

O.R.

1749/50, January 5,   Boston.

Meeting of the Masters Lodge.   Election.

O.R.; A.B.

1749/50, January 9, Philadelphia.

Meeting of Tun Tavern Lodge.   Brother Jenkins passed and raised.

O.R.

Boston.

Meeting of Auditing Committee of the First Lodge.

A.B.

1749/50, January 10,   Boston.

Meeting of First Lodge.   Joseph Gorham and John Brown made.

O.R.; P.L.; A.B.

1749/50, January 24,   Boston.

Meeting of the First Lodge.

O.R.; A.B.

Philadelphia.

Meeting of Tun Tavern Lodge. Capt. John Austin made and passed. Brothers William Shute and Thomas Glentworth passed. Brother Tege raised.

O.R.

1749/50, January 26, Boston.

Meeting of Auditing Committee of the Masters Lodge.

A.B.

1749/50, February 2, Boston.

Meeting of the Masters Lodge. Brothers Edmd. Quincy, Benja. Clifford, Henry Bowers, John Leverett, Robt. Jenkins, John Brown, and Benj. Stoddard raised.

O.R.; P.L.; A.B.

1749/50, February 8, Philadelphia.

Meeting of Tun Tavern Lodge. Brothers John Slydorn and John Boude raised.

O.R.

1749/50, February 12, Boston.

The *Boston Evening Post* contains an advertisement of the Constitutions of the Freemasons to be sold by the publishers of the paper.

P.-t.

1749/50, February 14, Boston.

Meeting of the First Lodge. James Steward (Stewart), William Tyler, and Nathaniel Gilman made.

O.R.; P.L.; A.B.

1749/50, February 15, Boston.

Meeting of the Grand Lodge for the Constitution of the Second Lodge in Boston, to be held at the Royal Exchange Tavern on the third Thursday in every month.

1 Mass. 9.

On the O. L. this Lodge was first numbered 141.

L.M.R. 91.

Philadelphia.

Meeting of Tun Tavern Lodge.

O.R.

1749/50, February 28, Boston.

Meeting of the First Lodge.

O.R.; A.B.

1749/50, March 1, Philadelphia.

Meeting of Tun Tavern Lodge.

O.R.

1749/50, March 2,   Boston.

Meeting of the Masters Lodge.

O.R.; A.B.

1749/50, March 5, Philadelphia.

Meeting of Tun Tavern Lodge. Anthony Duchee made. Brothers Franklin Manny passed and Thomas Glentworth and William Shute raised. Brother John Boude admitted.

O.R.

1749/50, March 7,   Boston.

Meeting of the Grand Lodge for the Constitution of

To the Rt. Honble & Rt. Worshipful The Grand Master of England: The Humble Remonstrance of The Rt. Worshipful The First Lodge of Free and Accepted Masons, and the other Lodges, hereunto Subscribing

Sheweth,

That from the Accot. of the Transactions from the inchoation of Masonry in No. America 5733 to the present Year We have had Successively Three Grand Masters Deputed from the Grand Lodge who have each in their respective Commissions been Distinguish'd under the Title of Provincial Grand Masters of North America, Which Distinction if it implies Chief signifies that there may Divers Grand Masters in different Provinces who are still subordinate to him as Chief, and therefore from him and him only or his Deputy should solicit or Receive their Deputations which some Lodges have not Observ'd; Or vice versa; if by Provincial Grand Master is imply'd a Power vested in the Grand Master over that Province only wherein he Resides or to which he is appointed then our Grand Masters have Exceeded in Granting Deputations to Distant Provinces as Philadelphia, Carolina, Antigua in the West Indies &c, which has promoted so Considerably ye Interest of Masonry in North America; and which power if limited to that Restrain'd must have prov'd detrimental to the whole Craft, as must evidently appear from the present flourishing situation in those Lodges who have Receiv'd their Original from this Lodge.

We therefore beg leave to observe to the Rt. Honble and Rt. Worshl. Grand Master that We have always look'd upon our Grand Masters in the most General Obvious and uncircumscribed sence of the Words, and if his sentiments shou'd agree with ours Our Prayer is as Masonry in British America has wholly Originated from us, and has made and still continues to make such an unexampled Progress.

That the Rt. Honble and Rt. Worshipful Grand Master would please to take our Prayer into Consideration and Grant to Our Rt. Worshipful Brother Thomas Oxnard Esqr. our present Grand Master or his successors for ever for the time being, a Full and Plenary Commission to act as Grand Master in and over all the Lodges in the Provinces of Massachusetts Bay, New Hampshire, Connecticut, Rhode Island and Providence, New York, New Jerseys, Pensilvania, Maryland, Virginia, North and South Carolina, Georgia, Newfound Land, and Nova Scotia, all which Provinces are Generally Distinguish'd under the Name of North America; And that all future Deputations or Constitutions be from him or his Deputy only, and that all Lodges in the District aforesaid do Communicate and Correspond with the Grand Lodge in North America thus Constituted, that from thence an Account of their several Proceedings may be Transmitted Annually to the Grand Lodge in England, as is now done by us, and to which we Referr you.

Chas. Brockwell M.
John Leverett S.W. } Of the First Lodge
Daniel Gookin J.W.

John Rowe M.
[illegible] S.W. } Of the Masters Lodge
Thos. Allen J.W.

Colville M.
Jas. Forbes S.W. } Of the second Lodge
Thos. Aston J.W.

Chas. Pelham M.
Thos. Newman S.W. } Of the Third Lodge
John Indicott J.W.

Dated at Boston N. England Octor. 7. A.D. 1751. and of Masonry 5751.

Chas. Pelham G. S.

FACSIMILE OF THE "HUMBLE REMONSTRANCE" OF OCTOBER 7, 1751

the Third Lodge in Boston, to be held at the White Horse Tavern on the first and third Wednesday in every month.

> 1 Mass 9.

> Philadelphia.

Meeting of Tun Tavern Lodge. Brothers William Shute and Thomas Glentworth admitted.

> O.R.

1749/50, March 13, Philadelphia.

William Allen exhibited a patent signed by Lord Byron, the Grand Master of England, appointing him Provincial Grand Master for Pennsylvania.

> The Picture of Philadelphia, (1811) 290.

> See page 68.

This being from the fountain head and from an authority superior even to Oxnard's, was at once recognized by Franklin and his associates of the then existing Provincial Grand Lodge. Franklin became Deputy Grand Master. Those who were his officers under Oxnard's Deputation all remained in line but like himself demoted one station. Word of this and some similar matters having come to Boston the Brethren there, after long and careful consideration, prepared a remonstrance on October 7, 1751 to the Grand Master of England.

> 1 Mass. 396.

> Facsimile presented herewith. See page 235.

The four Lodges in Boston very properly pointed out that Oxnard's Commission granted by Lord Ward, Grand Master of England, September 23, 1743, q.v., made him "Provincial Grand Master of North America." (1 Mass. 8.) and that, therefore, Deputations for the Provinces here should issue from him in the future as they had in the past. When Franklin visited the Grand Lodge at London on November 17, 1760, he was recognized as "Provincial Grand Master of Philadelphia" which is at least a recognition of Oxnard's Commission to him.

O.R. of English Grand Lodge.

Perhaps even more to the point is the recognition of the loyalty of Pennsylvania to Oxnard when on April 10, 1752, Bro. McDaniel appeared for the Lodge at Philadelphia and paid for its constitution thirty-one pounds and ten shillings.

1 Mass. 20.

1749/50, March 14,   Boston.
Meeting of the First Lodge. Capt. Hugh Purdie made. Rev. Brother Samuel Quincy passed.

O.R.; P.L.

Philadelphia.
Meeting of Tun Tavern Lodge. Brother John Reily admitted.

O.R.

1749,   Nova Scotia.
During this year a Lodge was Constituted at Halifax, Nova Scotia, by the Grand Lodge of England.

L.M.R. 92.

Note.

This completes the chronological record of every Masonic event which concerns the Western Hemisphere prior to the close of the legal year 1749 of which the author has been able to learn.

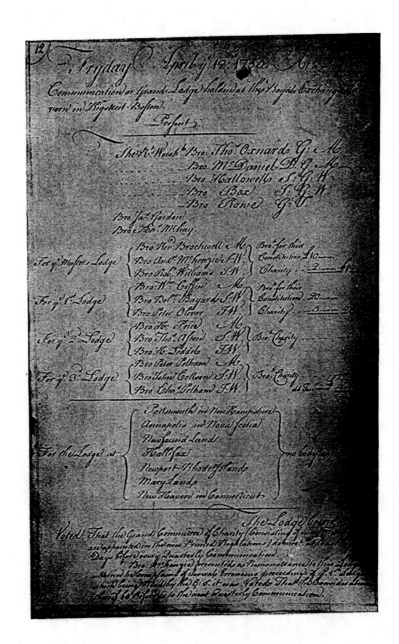

FACSIMILE OF PART OF RECORD OF MEETING OF GRAND LODGE
IN BOSTON, APRIL 13, 1750

That the record may be brought down to the beginning of the first bound volume of contemporaneous (i.e., written at the time of the events recorded) records of the earliest American Grand Lodge records extant, viz: those of the Grand Lodge at Boston, the following five days are added.

1750, March 28,   Boston.

Meeting of the First Lodge.   Brother Walter Logan admitted.

      O.R.; P.L.; A.B.

Philadelphia.

Meeting of Tun Tavern Lodge.   One member was excluded from the Lodge "for aiding and assisting in making two Brothers Irregular." Brother Hampton admitted.

      O.R.

1750, April 4,   Philadelphia.

Meeting of Tun Tavern Lodge.   Brother William Gamble passed and raised.   Brother Franklin Manny raised and admitted.

      O.R.

1750, April 7,   Boston.

Meeting of the Masters Lodge.   Brothers Gilbert Faulkner and Rev. Samuel Quincy raised.

      O.R.; P.L.; A.B.

1750, April 11,   Boston.

Meeting of the First Lodge.

      O.R.; A.B.

      1883 Mass. 164.

Philadelphia.

Meeting of Tun Tavern Lodge.   Peter Hudson made. Brother Archdall admitted.

O.R.

1750, April 13,   Boston.

With the meeting of the Provincial Grand Lodge this day, its continuous contemporaneous record commences in the handwriting of Charles Pelham who was Secretary of the First Lodge as well as Grand Secretary.

O.R.

1 Mass. 10.

1900 Mass. 127.

Massachusetts has now in the Masonic Temple in Boston official Grand Lodge records, made contemporaneously with the events recorded, from April 13, 1750, to the present day, except for a short hiatus during the Revolutionary War while its Grand Secretary, a Tory, was in Nova Scotia.

Chapter XXIV

ARCANA OF THE PERIOD

There are radical differences between the degree system of this period and the present time. Because of the secrecy surrounding the ritual it is impossible to know the whole story or to write it even if we did know it.

Let us first collate what little there is to guide us and draw our conclusions afterwards.

As early as June 24, 1731, we have the record of an "entrance" fee.

On July 30, 1733, certain Brethren signed a petition in which it was recited that some of them were "made here." The words "entered" and "made" have a technical reference to the first degree, which is now familiar by constant use.

The word "admitted" appears first on October 24, 1733, meaning then as now "admitted to membership in a Lodge," but having no reference to any degree.

The earliest American By-Laws or Regulations of a Lodge were adopted October 24, 1733, but there is no reference therein to any degrees. We find that Masons were "made" and a certain limited number of them were "admitted." Nothing more until February 9, 1736/7, when the degree of Fellow-Craft is mentioned for the first time. The language of the vote quoted under that date, above, shows that the second degree had theretofore been worked. It is more than three years and a half later, however, before we have any written record of the working of this degree. Then, in Portsmouth,

373

New Hampshire, "Capt. Andrew Tombes was made a Mason and *raised* to a Fellow-Craft." (The italics are mine.) From then on there is confusion in terminology. Sometimes Brethren are recorded as "made Fellow Craft," more often "raised Fellow Craft." On July 22, 1747, Brother McKenzie was "Rais'd Fellow Craft in due Form" and yet when Brother Pelham made up his list (1751) he says that Brother McKenzie was "pass'd Fellow Craft." From and after October 11, 1749, the record of the First Lodge in Boston usually uses the word "passed" when referring to the second degree, although as late as December 22, 1749, we still find "raised Fellow Craft."

The records which we have of Tun Tavern Lodge, Philadelphia, beginning June 28, 1749, use the words "entered," "passed" and "raised" as we use them now.

Those who are familiar with the history of the ritual and its development in England, Ireland and Scotland, will at once, I think, conclude rightly that the first degree, in these early days in America, contained what has now been expanded into the first and second; also that the second degree corresponds to what is now the third. But few Brethren advanced beyond Entered Apprentices, upon which degree all general business was transacted.

But what shall we say when we find a Masters Lodge constituted December 22, 1738? Before then the only references to Masters were to the Masters of Lodges. The Masters, who were then in Boston, gathered together to form "The Masters Lodge." It is practically certain that the founders of this Lodge had not all been actual presiding Masters of Lodges. All then in Boston who are known to have been such are recorded as present at the first regular meeting, January 2, 1738/9, but there were others. At the next monthly meeting, with ten present and Henry Price in the Chair, George Monerieff was "raised a Master." Under the By-Laws of the Lodge, the candidate had to pass an examination in open Lodge on the two previous degrees before he could be advanced. He must, accordingly, prove that he had previously been "raised a Fellow Craft." What then was the Masters' degree? Again we must appeal to the ritualistic history of Freemasonry in the British Isles. I believe the answer to be that the degree worked by the Masters Lodge was what is sometimes known as the "Chair Degree" or installation of a Master, absorbed nowadays in the United States by the Royal Arch Chapter and transformed into the degree of "Past Master."

Until nearly the end of the eighteenth century the Masters' degree was conferred in Boston by this Masters Lodge, which was the child of the "Moderns" and by another Masters Lodge which met under the charter of the Lodge of St. Andrew, which was the child of the Grand Lodge of Scotland which in the second half of the eighteenth century had affiliations with the "Antients" and used a similar ritual. Even to-day the degree of "Past Master" is conferred by authority of the Grand Lodge of Pennsylvania upon Brethren who never have been elected to preside over a Lodge.

Here I begin to tread upon dangerous ground, for if I write anything plainly enough for the initiated to understand, it must not be said in a way whereby it may become legible or intelligible to the profane. Let me attempt it by saying that there were many clauses in the Fellow-craft degree of the middle of the eighteenth century which are only to be found in the present third degree.   If the Master Mason of to-day could transport himself back to that period and see the second degree worked, he would, for instance, hear distinct allusions to five points of *fellowship*.   And why, indeed, should not these things which appertain to fellowship be imparted to a Fellow of the Craft?   Likewise, he would have found in the making, not in the crafting, the inculcation of charity toward a worthy brother.   Many other clauses of our present second would have been found in the then first, many of the third in the then second.   These things we learn from across the sea.   The actual ritual of the early days in America is an unfathomable mystery, except what we learn by applying our present knowledge gained through generations of instructive tongues, attentive ears and not too accurate memories to the few known American facts hereinbefore mentioned, and to the results of studies of the situation in London at the time of the emigration from there of the founders of Masonry here.

Those who brought Freemasonry from England to New England, to Pennsylvania, to South Carolina, to Georgia, to New York, and to its other earliest homes in what is now the United States, came here before the drastic changes in ritual made by the English Grand Lodge about the end of the fourth decade of the eighteenth century.

Due largely to some alleged exposés and to the unwillingness of certain Lodges located within its jurisdiction to yield allegiance and submission, the Grand Lodge of England, between 1730 and 1740, but principally in 1739,

(1) Abolished the installation ceremony of the Worshipful Master;

(2) Handed some of the secrets of the office of Installed Master over to the third degree;

(3) Remodelled the third degree;

(4) Exchanged certain vital secrets between the first and second degrees;

(5) Essentially changed the symbolism of preparation;

(6) Materially condensed the lectures;

(7) Omitted and cut down parts of the ceremonies; and

(8) Made some minor additions.

These ritualistic changes and some structural alterations in Grand Lodge gave occasion for a Masonic war. A rival Grand Lodge sprang up in 1751, called themselves the "Antients," dubbed the older body the "Moderns," and grew in number and power. They propagated the art both in England and America, and even gained international alliances alienating other grand bodies from the "Moderns."

The changes made by the "Moderns" and the strength of the "Antients" both had their influence in America. The effect was felt more especially later than the period with which this book deals. The changes of 1739 doubtless found their way across the sea more or less during the following decade. Visits were constantly being exchanged, new deputations were being issued covering various parts of the new world, and new Lodges were being constituted.

Doubtless the Masters Lodge was one of the results of this period of transition. But what happened here has never been put in writing, full records were not kept, and what few books of record were made are mostly lost. There is little more which probably can ever be said on the subject, for the radical changes were abandoned when, on April 12, 1809, the Grand Lodge (Moderns) voted: "That this Grand Lodge do agree in opinion with the Committee of Charity that it is not necessary any longer to continue in force those measures which were resorted to in or about the year 1739 respecting irregular Masons, and do therefore enjoin the several lodges to revert to the Antient Landmarks of the Society." Reconciliation, amalgamation, unity and harmony did not come, in England, until 1813, although in the United States it soon followed the close of the Revolutionary War.

The facts stated in this chapter are demonstrable. The conclusions are my own inferences from the few, the very few, known facts, and are offered merely for what they are worth.

NOTE: See discussion by Ball in 5 Q.C.A. 136; "The difference between English and Irish Rituals treated Historically," by J. H. Lepper, published by Irish Lodge of Research, 200, in 1920; "The Causes of Divergence in Ritual," by Roscoe Pound, 1915 Mass. 143, reprinted in *The Builder* for November, 1917.

Chapter XXV

CONCLUSION

For the statements of fact hereinbefore contained the original sources of information have been examined. References by way of citation have been included which will lead the reader to those original sources of information if he desires to pursue his inquiries further and verify the facts for himself.

Little probative value has been given to the text of any author later than Preston (1772), except only where he has actually quoted the language of the authority upon which the statement has been made. I have assumed the correctness of the actual quotations in Mackey's "History of Freemasonry in South Carolina"; and in McClenachan's and Lang's Histories of Freemasonry in New York; in Sachse's "Benjamin Franklin as a Freemason" and "Old Masonic Lodges of Pennsylvania"; and in some other works cited.

A brief summary of some of the principal events in the introduction of Freemasonry into the western hemisphere may be made as follows:

1. Freemasonry was introduced into the Colonies of North America at an unascertained period in the early part of the 18th century.

2. These earliest Lodges were "occasional," meeting "according to the Old Customs." They had no charters or warrants, but met as other Lodges had met prior to the organization of the Grand Lodge system.

3. The first Freemason definitely known to be in the western hemisphere was Governor Jonathan Belcher of Massachusetts Bay Colony, in 1705.

4. The earliest use in America in writing or in print of the word "Freemason" (so far as now known) was in the *Boston News Letter* for January 5, 1718/9.

5. The first Lodge meeting in the western hemisphere, the knowledge of which is supported by something more than pure tradition, was probably held in King's Chapel, Boston, in 1720.

6. The first known American newspaper account relating to Freemasonry was published in Boston, May 25, 1727.

7. The first deputation for a Provincial Grand Master in the western hemisphere was that issued June 5, 1730, by the Duke of Norfolk to Daniel Coxe, appointing him Provincial Grand Master for New York, New Jersey and Pennsylvania for two years. There is no evidence that this deputation was ever exercised.

8. The first American newspaper item concerning a Lodge meeting in the western hemisphere (so far as now known) was published in the *Philadelphia Gazette* for December 8, 1730.

9. The oldest American Lodge account-book known is "Libr B," beginning with June 24, 1731, belonging to a Lodge meeting "according to the Old Customs"—that is to say, without charter or warrant, in Philadelphia.

10. The first known Warrant, Deputation, Commission, or other authority, issuing from the Grand Lodge of England or its Grand Master (or from any other Masonic organization or officer, for that matter) to be exercised in America was that (April 13, 1733) by vir-

tue of which Henry Price founded a Provincial Grand Lodge in Boston, July 30, 1733.

11. The first regular and duly constituted Lodge in America was the First Lodge in Boston, July 30, 1733.

12. The first Lodge in America to be registered by the Grand Lodge of England in the official list of Lodges was the First Lodge at Boston.

13. The first Masonic officer in the Western World to have jurisdiction over the whole of North America was Henry Price, whose authority was extended thus broadly in August, 1734.

14. The first Masonic book published in America was Franklin's Reprint (Philadelphia, 1734) of Anderson's Constitutions.

15. The first exercise by any Masonic authority in America of the right to grant provincial Masonic powers was the appointment of Benjamin Franklin as "Provincial Grand Master of the Province of Pennsylvania," February 21, 1734/5, by Henry Price, "Grand Master of His Majesty's Dominions in North America."

16. Regular authority was granted for the establishment of duly constituted Freemasonry in New England in 1733; in all North America in 1734; in Pennsylvania in 1734; in South America in 1735; in South Carolina, Georgia and New Hampshire in 1735 or 1736; in the West Indies and New York in 1737; in Antigua and Nova Scotia in 1737/8; in Jamaica and St. Christopher in 1739; in the Barbados in 1739/40; in Bermuda, 1742; in Newfoundland, 1746; in San Domingo, 1748; and in Rhode Island, 1749.

17. By the close of the first half of the century not less than forty Lodges had sprung from the Provincial

Grand Lodge in Boston. Others had been warranted direct from London.

18. The first anti-Masonic movement known upon this side of the Atlantic was successfully directed against the Fraternity in Pennsylvania, beginning in 1737.

19. The earliest record book still preserved of any Lodge in the Western Hemisphere is that of the Masters Lodge in Boston, beginning December 22, 1738.

20. The existing records of the First Lodge in Boston begin on December 27, 1738.

21. The known records of St. John's Lodge of Portsmouth, N.H., begin October 31, 1739.

22. The known records of Tun Tavern Lodge at Philadelphia begin June 28, 1748.

23. The contemporaneous records of the Provincial Grand Lodge at Boston begin April 15, 1750, and Massachusetts has Grand Lodge records continuously from that date to this, being the oldest Grand Lodge records known in the western hemisphere.

24. The first procession of a Masonic Lodge in public in America, now known, was that of the Lodge at Charleston, South Carolina, on May 26, 1737.

25. The first public procession in America definitely known to be in regalia was that in Boston, June 24, 1737.

26. The first time that a Lodge in America is known to have attended church in due form was at the Barbados, June 24, 1740.

27. The first record of the construction of a Masonic hall in the western hemisphere is dated April 4, 1744, and concerns the Lodge room of "The Great Lodge at St. John's in Antigua."

28. The earliest copy now extant of a sermon deliv-

ered to the Fraternity is that of the Rev. Bro. Brockwell at Christ Church, Boston, preached at the festival of St. John the Evangelist in 1749.

29. The Freemasonry in America of the period dealt with is that emanating from the Grand Lodge of England, organized in 1717, known as "Moderns." Just as this period closes, the Grand Lodge known as the "Antients" began to exercise its influence in America.

30. The leading men of the Colonies in mercantile, military and civil life were in these early days members of the Fraternity. Illustrations of this have appeared in the various sketches of some of the principal officers which will be found in this volume.

31. The ritual was in a more or less fluid condition during all of this period. See Chapter 24.

32. Henry Price was, as he said himself, the "Founder of Duly Constituted Freemasonry in America."

33. The Grand Lodge founded by Henry Price, July 30, 1733, has maintained a continuous existence from that day to this. The same is true of the First Lodge in Boston, now St. John's Lodge. These two bodies, over one hundred and ninety years old at the present writing, have successfully weathered all storms of war and persecution. The Grand Lodge of Massachusetts and its eldest child are, therefore, entitled to precedence as the two oldest existing organizations of Freemasons in the western hemisphere. I am not aware of any Masonic body in America existing at any time during the first half of the eighteenth century which is able, by unassailable evidence, conclusively to demonstrate unbroken continuity from its establishment until to-day except the Grand Lodge of Massachusetts. In

all other cases there are still broken links in the chain of proof. It is my fervent hope that future research will weld many broken links.

As an encouragement to other workers in similar fields, let me say that at one time it was believed that the Grand Lodge founded by Henry Price suspended operations from 1775 until 1787.

16 M.F.M. 195.

By constant delving into the secrets of the past, the error of that belief was shown by 1914.

1914 Mass. 273.

And in the ten years since then I have found more facts as yet unpublished. They are what lawyers call cumulative evidence,—interesting but not essential to the proof.

We have now learned how the seeds were sown in America for the birth and growth of Freemasonry. Its influence upon the establishment and development of the institutions of the United States does not so powerfully appear during the period treated by this book as it will when the Masonic history of the last half of the 18th century is adequately presented. A study of the tremendous influence which Freemasonry had in the pre-Revolutionary days, in the years of that war, and throughout the formative period of American institutions, will demonstrate that Freemasonry has exercised a greater influence upon the establishment and development of American civilization and the fundamentals of this Government than any other single institution.

Neither general historians nor the members of the Fraternity since the days of the first Constitutional Conventions have ever realized how much the United States of America owes to Freemasonry, and how great a part it played in the birth of the nation and the establishment of the Landmarks of that civilization which has given to the citizens of this great land the liberty which they enjoy, and by indirection has guided the development of all civilization of the world in those countries where the accomplishments of war are not the *ultima thule* of human endeavour.

We cannot fail profoundly to be interested to learn more of this institution during the eighteenth century, in order that the real facts may be presented to the world. When they are, Freemasonry in the United States will not only be prouder of its past than it is to-day, but—what is more vital—will be thoroughly impressed with its duty energetically to protect and preserve the free institutions of America which it was the privilege of our Masonic forebears to establish.

INDEX